A Practitioner's Guide to Supporting Graduate and Professional Students

This guide helps faculty and student affairs practitioners better serve graduate and professional school students as they navigate what can be an isolating, taxing, and unfamiliar context.

Providing actionable strategies, as well as a common language for practitioners to advocate for themselves and for their students, this book is a quick start manual that defines current issues around graduate and professional student development. Drawing together current resources and research around post-baccalaureate student outcomes, this book explores the diverse student needs of graduate and professional students and provides a clear understanding of their social, personal, and psychological development and how to support their success.

Case studies showcase specific examples of practice including a holistic development model for graduate training; integrating academic, personal, professional, and career development needs; promising practices for engagement; a diversity, equity, and inclusion approach to access and outcomes; how graduate schools can be important partners to student affairs professionals; and examples of assessment in action.

This book provides tools, resources, communication strategies, and actionable theory-to-practice connections for practitioners, professionals, and faculty at all levels who work to support post-baccalaureate student thriving.

Appendix available for download online at www.routledge.com/9780367639884 on the tab that is entitled "Support Material."

Valerie A. Shepard has worked as a student affairs practitioner for over a decade and has held leadership positions in the NASPA Administrators in Graduate and Professional Student Services (AGAPSS) Knowledge Community. She is a Senior Writer at UCLA Recreation, USA.

April L. Perry has more than 15 years of experience across student affairs and academic units in higher education. She is currently Associate Professor of Higher Education and Student Affairs at Western Carolina University, USA.

A Practitioner's Guide to Supporting Graduate and Professional Students

Edited by
Valerie A. Shepard and
April L. Perry

Routledge
Taylor & Francis Group

NEW YORK AND LONDON

Cover image: © Getty Images

First published 2022
by Routledge
605 Third Avenue, New York, NY 10158

and by Routledge
4 Park Square, Milton Park, Abingdon, Oxon, OX14 4RN

Routledge is an imprint of the Taylor & Francis Group, an informa business

Library of Congress Cataloging-in-Publication Data
Names: Shepard, Valerie A., 1980– editor. | Perry, April L.,
1983– editor.
Title: A practitioner's guide to supporting graduate and professional
students / edited by Valerie A. Shepard and April L. Perry.
Description: New York, NY: Routledge, 2022. |
Includes bibliographical references and index.
Identifiers: LCCN 2021040696 (print) | LCCN 2021040697 (ebook) |
ISBN 9780367620349 (hardback) | ISBN 9780367639884 (paperback) |
ISBN 9781003121671 (ebook)
Subjects: LCSH: Graduate students—Services for—United States. |
Graduate students—Counseling of—United States. | Student affairs
services—United States.
Classification: LCC LB2371.4 .P73 2022 (print) |
LCC LB2371.4 (ebook) | DDC 378.1/794—dc23
LC record available at https://lccn.loc.gov/2021040696
LC ebook record available at https://lccn.loc.gov/2021040697

ISBN: 978-0-367-62034-9 (hbk)
ISBN: 978-0-367-63988-4 (pbk)
ISBN: 978-1-003-12167-1 (ebk)

DOI: 10.4324/9781003121671

Typeset in Perpetua
by codeMantra

Access the Support Material: www.routledge.com/9780367639884

Contents

CONTENTS

CONTENTS

Preface

At present, research and guidance for student affairs practitioners who work with graduate and professional (G&P) students is limited. There are some histories, resources, and promising practices available, but what already exists is neither curated for student affairs professionals nor is it easily accessible. This book is an effort to gather resources in a way that will be readily available to practitioners at all levels, as well as to work toward creating a common language that contributes to improving communication among professionals and faculty who work to support post-baccalaureate student thriving. We recognize that professionals who support G&P students include those who serve in a range of roles, from a recent graduate of a student affairs graduate program who is working with G&P students for the first time, to a professional with no background in the study of higher education who may have been hired because they have a particular terminal degree, to an academic dean who may have some or no background in the study of higher education. Even practitioners who have graduated from a student affairs or higher education doctoral program may not have any experience with graduate or professional students outside of their own discipline. This book is intended to provide tools, resources, communication strategies, and actionable theory-to-practice connections for anyone who serves within that vast range of professional roles.

A secondary audience for this book is both faculty and students in higher education graduate preparation programs who are willing to learn about graduate students and who wish to do their own research to add to the knowledge base. As we have seen in our professional experience, currently in many higher education preparation programs, curriculum that addresses post-baccalaureate student development and experience is not available. Many of those who work with graduate and professional students who have graduated from higher education preparation programs have a background in the study of higher education, but from an undergraduate student-focused lens. To address this gap in training, in 2016, the NASPA Administrators in Graduate and Professional Student Services

(AGAPSS) Knowledge Community initiated a curriculum project designed to build modules that could be implemented in already-existing higher education preparation program courses. Chapter 10 discusses this ongoing project and provides results from a pilot study conducted in 2020, both before and after the COVID-19 pandemic campus closures.

As *A Practitioner's Guide* is meant to be a general handbook for professionals, it necessarily will not include all topics; we intend it to be a catalyst for further research, conversations, and community-building among all stakeholders in the higher education community who support G&P students thriving. As such, professionals may read the book from start to finish or may select a chapter on a particular topic. The case studies in Chapters 4–9 can also stand alone and provide immediately actionable, practical examples that professionals can adapt to their own campuses.

DESCRIPTION OF CONTENTS

Part I begins with an overview of the G&P education landscape and context for graduate and professional school enrollment. Chapter 2 pairs discipline-specific data from a variety of reporting agencies and associations with literature examining the graduate student experience to help provide professionals with an initial road map for understanding the diversity of graduate and professional program types and how it applies to their professional practice related to student engagement and support. Chapter 3 then uses Maslow's Hierarchy of Needs as a framework to examine the diverse student needs of G&P students and the ways in which they are distinct from those of their undergraduate counterparts. As post-baccalaureate needs are diverse, complex, and interconnected, the authors present a holistic approach in which professionals can then form a foundation for developing thoughtful, comprehensive, and ongoing programs of assessment to identify and address the particular needs of students on their specific campus.

Part II of the book, Chapters 4–9, is a collection of research and successful strategies based on specific aspects of the G&P student life cycle, starting with onboarding (Chapter 4) and ending with assessment (Chapter 9). Each of the chapters contains multiple case studies for specific examples of practice. Chapter 4 specifically addresses G&P orientation models as a stage-based process, beginning with first-year onboarding and expanding to models that offer G&P students tiered training and stage-based information (sometimes called reorientation). Chapter 5 centers around a holistic development model for graduate training, integrating academic, personal, professional, and career development needs. It follows this model through the unique challenges and opportunities in each area, including advising and mentoring, highlighting theory, support services, and promising practices for professionals to consider as they work to improve the overall student experience.

Chapter 6 highlights a variety of promising practices designed to support graduate students' engagement and holistic development, as well as the importance of partnerships among Student Affairs, Academic Affairs, and other units to develop better communication and overall systems of student support. Fostering student advocacy is also emphasized as a promising practice to improve graduate student engagement and activity in campus life. Chapter 7 discusses how structures that have been built to support graduate and professional student success often overlook the intersectional identities that are as present for graduate-level students as they are for undergraduates. This one-size-fits-all approach may result in the exclusion of many students who need these resources and programs, thereby creating a gap in access and opportunity. Chapter 7 outlines how this gap can be bridged by creating a different scaffolding system that takes into consideration the needs and identities of diverse graduate student populations (race/ethnicity, first-generation, military-affiliated, low- and middle-income, LGBTQIA+, parents/caregivers, disabled, international) culminating in community, and identifies data-driven strategies to build a community by supporting the individual needs of these diverse student populations. The authors outline successful programs and resources that have been implemented at graduate and professional schools that improve students' sense of belonging and success.

Chapter 8, written from the perspective of a graduate school dean and assistant dean, discusses how graduate schools are best positioned to create inclusive, affirming interdisciplinary environments for graduate and professional education: a space and place where graduate students may thrive. Chapter 8 provides practical lessons learned that give an understanding of graduate student life and how graduate schools can be important partners to student affairs professionals to ensure that traditional student affairs services are properly tailored for, visible, and accessible to G&P students. As stated in earlier chapters, such graduate school support, along with partnerships with student affairs professionals, must be intentional, preferably centralized in some form, and reflected in organizational structure. Chapter 8 also underlines the need for the leadership of the graduate dean, who may be best positioned to champion the cause, and the engagement of graduate school personnel in partnering on this crucial effort to provide holistic G&P student support. Finally, Chapter 9 illuminates a variety of ways in which professionals can assess G&P student experience and overall program effectiveness. Chapter 9 provides a deep dive into what assessment is, its role in institutional effectiveness at the program and department level and at the university level, and provides strategies for how professionals can incorporate assessment into their specific practice. It includes examples of assessment in action, including how to develop and use logic models to design evidence-based practice and how professionals can use assessment data to strengthen arguments for resources and collaborations specific to the G&P populations they support.

Part III looks to the future of G&P student services. Chapter 10 shares the story of the "curriculum project"; as mentioned above, it is an ongoing project that the NASPA AGAPSS Knowledge Community initiated in 2016. The curriculum project works to create and provide curriculum about graduate and professional students that faculty may add to student affairs preparation programs. Faculty can either add these modules to an existing course or use them to create an additional class or assignment. The curriculum project addresses the lack of expertise that these programs have about working with graduate and professional students. Chapter 11 concludes the book by identifying current gaps in research and discussing possibilities for future efforts to improve graduate and professional student services. Following Chapter 11 is a Resource Appendix that lists books, reports, associations, and tools for learning more about G&P education and student services.

Acknowledgments and Dedication

Valerie A. Shepard: Thank you to all of the contributors; I would like to acknowledge in particular volunteers, past and present, within the NASPA Administrators in Graduate and Professional Student Services Knowledge Community (AGAPSS) who contributed to the development of this book. It was a collective effort that would not have happened without work from many members throughout the past several years. Thank you as well to members of the Graduate Career Consortium who provided insight. I would also like to acknowledge and thank all those who support graduate and professional students in the higher education community.

Thank you to all of the graduate and professional students I have met and worked alongside; this book is informed by you and dedicated to you, and I am deeply grateful for the opportunity to learn from the wisdom of such a talented group of leaders. Thank you to my coeditor, April Perry; it has been so good to work together with you throughout this project, and I appreciate our friendship and collaboration. Thank you to my colleagues at UCLA, in particular my colleagues at UCLA Recreation. Finally, thank you especially to Dave and Lena for your love, incredible patience, and unfailing support. I'm dedicating this work to you, too.

April L. Perry: I'd like to thank and acknowledge every author and contributor of this work for being a part of making this book a reality! I'd like to acknowledge my coeditor and friend, Val Shepard, who was so wonderful to collaborate with at each step in this process. Also, I'd like to recognize the members of AGAPSS and everyone who works with G&P students—thank you for caring so deeply and passionately about graduate and professional students and being committed to advancing this line of research and practice.

I'd like to dedicate this book first to my family—Lane, Prescott, and Pennon—who so graciously support me in everything I pursue (my first book in this case!), but more importantly love me unconditionally. Additionally, I'd like to dedicate this work to every WCU HESA graduate student who has helped me learn and grow into a stronger educator, scholar, and practitioner. Thank you for allowing me to live out my life calling (educating and mentoring) while also challenging me to continue (and never stop!) honing my practice.

PART I

GRADUATE STUDENTS BY THE NUMBERS

What We Know; What We Still Don't Know

Chapter 1

Introduction

Context, Research, and Applications

Katherine Hall-Hertel, Lisa C. O. Brandes, and Valerie A. Shepard

Graduate and professional (G&P) students are some of the most valuable constituencies of the higher education enterprise in the United States and around the world. For the past 200 years, scholars and writers have argued that graduate education makes a college a university, produces national and international leaders, and creates new knowledge and technology for societies (Berelson, 1960; Newman, 1852; Pelikan, 1992). According to the National Center for Educational Statistics, "In fall 2019, some 3.1 million students were enrolled in post-baccalaureate degree programs in the United States" (Institute of Education Sciences, National Center for Education Statistics [NCES-a], n.d.). Post-baccalaureate degree programs include master's and doctoral programs, as well as professional doctoral programs such as law, medicine, and dentistry. Since first being established in the United States in the mid-1800s, graduate education has expanded at an increasing rate: in 2018–2019, postsecondary institutions within the United States conferred about one million graduate degrees, an increase of 20% since 2009–2010. These included 833,700 master's degrees and 187,600 doctoral degrees (doctoral degrees include, e.g., PhD, EdD, MD, DDS, and JD) (NCES-b, n.d.). Chapter 2 of this book will expand on these statistics, but given that adults aged 25–34 with a master's degree or higher who worked full time reported a median salary that was 26% higher than adults with a bachelor's degree in the United States, and from 2010 to 2019, higher educational attainment was associated with higher earnings, there is reason to expect these enrollment trends to continue or even accelerate (NCES-c, n.d.).

While these data help illustrate how the graduate population differs from that of the traditionally aged 18–24-year-old undergraduates, graduate students are not just older versions of undergraduates. Many of these graduate students are returning for their degree after a break in their education, and age often corresponds to institution type and part-time or full-time student status. In fall 2019, for example, about 75% of full-time post-baccalaureate students at public

DOI: 10.4324/9781003121671-2

and private institutions were under the age of 30; however, among part-time graduate students, a majority in private for-profit, private nonprofit, and public institutions were over 30 years old (NCES-d, n.d.).

Awareness that G&P students need support for their holistic ability to thrive in their educational pursuits is growing within the higher education community. Building inclusive campus programs and services that are attuned to respecting G&P students' intersectionality and centering the needs of those who hold marginalized identities should be the goal as a higher education community. Additionally, G&P students are experiencing increasing levels of stress and anxiety that affect students from marginalized and underserved populations disproportionately in comparison with those in the majority (Council of Graduate Schools, 2021). Existing inequities accelerated by the COVID-19 pandemic, including structural racism in the United States, also negatively affect G&P students' mental health and well-being, student experience, and academic success. Despite the need, research on G&P student experience in general and on the experiences of specific communities in particular is sparse. Indeed, currently available research largely focuses on doctoral students, obscuring the experience of master's students, who represent the majority of the student population in U.S. graduate programs. Providing relevant, effective, coordinated G&P student-focused services remains a challenge on most campuses. While many deans have committed to such action (Council of Graduate Schools-a, n.d.), those who work in student affairs roles need actionable strategies to support G&P students' success. Meeting that challenge with promising practices and practical examples from a student affairs lens is the focus of this book.

A Practitioner's Guide is a collection of resources and practical guidance for holistically serving G&P students. The impetus for the writing of this book is not recent: it grew out of advocacy in Student Affairs for recognizing the unique needs of G&P students that began in the 1990s. *A Practitioner's Guide* is based in research, but is not a research text; rather, it is a practical handbook for professionals—including Student Affairs professionals, as well as faculty who may serve in student services roles—that support G&P students. Our intention is that professionals will use the information in this guide as a starting point for their daily work at their institutions. We also aim to connect professionals to their own community of support and provide pathways for engaging in ongoing efforts to share promising practices, ideas, knowledge from lived experience, and research to support G&P student success. This introductory chapter aims to provide a brief context for the current state of the field by presenting available research, responses thus far, and the gaps *A Practitioner's Guide* aims to fill.

CURRENT STATE OF THE FIELD

Terminology

Within the field of Student Affairs, literature on G&P students continues to be sparse. As is reflected throughout the chapters of this book, even referring to this large, diverse population of students continues to be a challenge, and there are currently no agreed-upon terms available. Throughout *A Practitioner's Guide*, contributors use "post-baccalaureate," "G&P," "Graduate and Professional Students (GAPS)" and "graduate students" interchangeably to describe this population as a whole, though occasionally contributors use "graduate" to describe students in graduate degree programs only rather than in professional degree programs. Some contributors use "post-baccalaureate" as a catchall term to describe all students who have already completed a bachelor's degree and are pursuing additional education; others do not use the term "post-baccalaureate" to describe G&P students, instead preferring to refer only to students who are engaged in programs that end in a degree rather than post-baccalaureate studies that provide additional education but are not in themselves degree-granting.

G&P-focused student affairs professionals have learned that there is a need to unpack the term *students* to clearly define what is open to whom, and even seek to add modifiers on websites, brochures, event titles, and materials. With this broader focus, we invite the higher education community to embrace that graduate students are students, too, and that they need and deserve relevant services and a community that includes them and supports their ability to thrive.

Research on G&P Students

Graduate student development (where "graduate" refers to degree-seeking G&P students) has been viewed as a *new* issue suitable for the well-known New Directions for Student Services (NDSS) monograph series. A 1995 NDSS volume on graduate students focused on *Student Services for the Changing Graduate Student Population* (Pruitt-Logan & Isaac, 1995). The audience for this first volume was student affairs professionals unfamiliar with graduate students' experiences; the text begins with an illustrative diary of a day in the life of a typical doctoral student. Chapters cover the basic problems of graduate education and the doctoral advisors' view, functional G&P issues like housing and career services, and needs of diverse graduate populations. This 1995 volume notes that, until recently, graduate schools and programs depended largely on faculty to provide support for students, if at all. Student life activities designed for graduate students had been virtually nonexistent due to a fundamental misunderstanding—that G&P students already possessed college or university experience as undergraduates

5

and were presumed not to need such services. A 2006 NDSS volume, *Supporting Graduate & Professional Students: The Role of Student Affairs*, revisits these issues from within student affairs, with chapters and illustrative examples from G&P student affairs professionals recently appointed and working in this growing functional area (Guentzel & Nesheim, 2006). Some research on the link between G&P orientation and retention also exists (Cusworth, 2001), with most recommendations focusing on mentoring as a key component (Pfund et al., 2014).

Conversely, a comparative study of doctoral student attrition (Lovitts, 2001), which can be as high as 50% nationally in the United States, demonstrates the divergence in faculty perceptions of why graduate students leave or do not finish their programs and the barriers to persistence that students themselves report that they face. While faculty stated that they understand graduate student attrition to be due largely to poor academic performance on the part of students, graduate students cite lack of mentoring, finances, inclusion, and family concerns as barriers to persistence and completion. Golde and Dore's (2001) *At Cross Purposes*, a study of graduate student career expectations, similarly demonstrates the divide in what faculty and graduate program leaders think of as successful career outcomes for doctoral students, namely research faculty positions, and the aspirations of the students themselves, who seek to pursue a variety of teaching, service, industry, and government jobs after graduation. A focus on academics alone, often from the faculty or institutional perspective, misses much in graduate students' lived experiences that can contribute to or hinder their success.

The Council of Graduate Schools (CGS), which primarily involves graduate school or program deans and provides academic statistics on graduate education, publishes recommendations for *best practices* for academic administration, and in some cases, to support graduate student success (Council of Graduate Schools-b, n.d.). Most graduate deans come from the faculty and many have some administrative experience, but minimal understanding of student affairs, thereby often reinforcing the academic affairs-student affairs divide. CGS offers supplemental training for new deans, as well as helpful guidance for recruitment, retention, and academic and administrative processes, but actionable recommendations for graduate student development, graduate student life, and graduate student support are less available.

Most recently, CGS began its own study of graduate student mental health in partnership with the JED Foundation, a nonprofit organization that works to prevent suicide (Council of Graduate Schools, 2021), with pilot programs at several graduate schools. Other recent CGS efforts include a report detailing Hispanic-Serving Institutions' role in expanding the graduate pipeline and a review of professional development for science, technology, engineering, and mathematics (STEM) graduate students (Council of Graduate Schools-b, n.d.).

While these are valuable contributions to graduate student services, they focus largely on *academic or administrative* issues rather than typical *student affairs* services within student life and student development. CGS reports offer a wealth of information and do a credible job identifying issues that negatively affect graduate student experiences, persistence, and completion. However, providing answers and strategies that are actionable for those who work in student affairs roles, predictably, is more difficult and will take collaboration and engagement. At many institutions, graduate students are not included in (undergraduate-focused) student life services offered on campus, so the graduate school may increasingly be called upon to try to organize everything for its own students, or not. Partnerships and engagement with student affairs professionals are necessary to create and sustain such programs.

In *The New PhD*, Cassuto and Weisbuch (2021) argue for a genuine reform of the doctoral education process, again from an academic lens, focused on primarily an academic audience of faculty program directors and deans. As its name says, this new book is focused mainly on doctoral education, with some applications for master's degree programs. The authors call for an overhaul of graduate education, including using a student-centered lens to provide services to support students holistically, to best prepare them for jobs they want and can get. They also include a list of current and previous reform efforts and resulting publications. A spate of newer publications argues for an overhaul of doctoral education in particular, but focuses primarily on the curriculum, high cost, and low completion rates in these programs rather than practical applications for student affairs professionals who work primarily with G&P students.

Shifting from an Economy-Centered to a Student-Centered Lens

Graduate education has been studied at the macro or national level, particularly from the point of view of filling national workforce needs in academic, research, industry, and professional fields (see the appendix of this book for a list of historical documents and resources). G&P education is often seen as a production cycle with students, especially those who complete PhD or JD degrees, understood to be apprentices, economic, or educational outputs (future faculty, professionals), failed outputs (attrition, non-completion, unsuccessful job searches), or even victims of economic downturn and labor market instability in recent decades. Some studies have included graduate students as part of the *unfaculty*, with little value on their own and seen mainly in support of the faculty research enterprise (Graham & Diamond, 1997; Kerr, 1963). Predictions about the U.S. academic job market are notoriously unreliable and attempts to modify graduate education to accommodate the markets are doomed to fail (Millar et al., 1998). Multiple cycles of academic job boom and bust, and *Quit Lit* from the 1970s–1980s through the mid-2000s to today give testament to the pain and disappointed hopes of generations of underemployed doctoral degree recipients (Shreve, 2018). While positive job outcomes are a vital component of the graduate education enterprise, it should not be the primary one. Looking at the student experience specifically—their needs, aspirations, and interests—has been gaining traction as another lens for understanding and action in graduate education.

In more recent decades, higher education, scientific, and student affairs professionals have begun turning the top-down market supply-and-demand or labor placement-centric view on its head. Some studies see graduate education as serving the needs of the graduate students first. For example, at a 1998 U.S. National Science Foundation (NSF)-sponsored Forum, Jules Lapidus (then head of the CGS) argued that "…the apprenticeship model of graduate education needs to be replaced with a model that is driven by the educational needs of the student rather than the research needs of the faculty" (Millar et al., 1998, p. 17). At the same Forum, Eamon Kelly (then Chair of the U.S. National Science Board) also noted problems with the faculty-centered apprentice model: "…the suspicion that time to degree for some graduate and postdoctoral students is prolonged not to benefit their education, but rather to provide a source of cheap labor…" (p. 13). These were revolutionary words in many of the halls of academe, which usually view graduate students as adults without development needs, apprentices to be molded, research workers, or mere outputs from degree programs to follow in their mentors' paths.

Shifting from an Undergraduate Student to Graduate Student Lens

Student affairs professionals can often respond more easily to these calls for changing perspectives, which sound familiar to practitioners attuned to student development theory and student needs. Yet, as noted earlier, a focus on *graduate* students as students was new in the 1990s, even for student affairs professionals. It was not until 2004 that the National Association of Student Personnel Administrators (NASPA) and the American College Personnel Association (ACPA) published *Learning Reconsidered*, which discussed "the diversification of students and a growing emphasis on the unique needs of returning adult learners and of *graduate and professional students*" (p. 7, italics added).

Given the recent demands for (1) more and specialized resources both to serve G&P student needs and (2) addressing challenges to student access, equity, and thriving within and subsequent to G&P education, it is not surprising that from the 1990s through the early 2000s, there was a subsequent growth in new programs, services, and positions for designated G&P-focused student affairs professionals. It would be natural to assume that current student affairs practitioners and Higher Education-Student Affairs graduate programs are working systematically within themselves, between one another, and in their professional environments to address these critical issues for graduate students. However, at present, this is still not the case. Too often, implicitly or explicitly in practice, the standard definition of a *student* for the purposes of providing student services and support continues to be an undergraduate student, with the specific needs and concerns of G&P students often tacked on as an afterthought, if they are considered at all. G&P students often attempt to access a generically titled campus resource or program only to be told it is not designed for or open to them as G&P students, but are really undergraduate-focused programs or designed from a lens that does not support the specific needs of G&P students. Campuses that are primarily G&P student-serving often have programs and services that avoid this distinction by default, as their population does not include undergraduate students, and can offer models of promising practices for changing this focus.

Previous guides to good practice (Guentzel & Nelsheim, 2006; Pontius & Harper, 2006) have addressed this particular mindset within student affairs practice, and suggest some useful guiding questions for inquiry for professionals to start to address G&P specific needs:

- How does this particular campus service or program apply to G&P students?
- Could we adapt this event in specific ways to appeal to post-baccalaureate students?
- Does it make programmatic sense to plan an event designed to serve both traditionally aged undergraduates and G&P students, who may vary widely in age and interests and may include both undergraduate students and post-baccalaureate students who may teach or supervise them?
- From our position on campus, who else can we partner with to inform and serve our particular populations of G&P students without reinventing the wheel and creating entirely new programs and services?
- And in general, always: What About Graduate Students (WAGS)?

Contemporary student affairs work is also centrally concerned with inclusion, especially for students from underserved communities and groups, such as first-generation degree holders, racially minoritized students, sexual and gender minoritized students, international students, students with lower socioeconomic status, students with disabilities, student parents, student veterans, and undocumented students. As theory and research demonstrate, events and services that are *open to all students* may not actually serve all students and will not serve the particular needs of students from particular populations or degree programs. Chapter 2 will discuss the diverse degree programs of graduate education in more detail, and Chapter 3 gives an overview of G&P student needs and how they are distinct from those of undergraduate students.

The Need for More Research

Very few comprehensive works address the holistic needs of graduate students. Even when there is student-centered theory or research available, it is not clear if or how it works for G&P students, as these were generally developed on and for undergraduate students. Theories of adult learning may apply to some G&P students, illustrating how individuals repeat development in loops and return to specific developmental tasks each time they take on a new role (Taylor & Hamdy, 2013), and certainly concepts of self-directed learning apply to graduate students (Merriam et al., 2001). While adult learning theories do not apply to every graduate student, such concepts support the idea that graduate students do have specific developmental needs.

In 2012, the book *Black Graduate Education at Historically Black Colleges and Universities: Trends, Experiences, and Outcomes* presented an in-depth study of "the historical nature of graduate education at HBCUs and the programs' impact on society" (Palmer et al., 2012, p. 3). Although this book is a research text primarily aimed toward a faculty audience rather than student affairs practitioners, it addresses graduate student experience, success, engagement, socialization, student development, and alumni giving, and mentions that research on graduate education at historically black colleges and universities (HBCUs) before this work was "basically nonexistent" (p. 2) despite numerous studies of undergraduate students at HBCUs. The editors theorize that higher education researchers thought existing research on undergraduate education at HBCUs could apply to the graduate student experience, which "cannot be further from the truth," because "graduate students have different needs, obligations, experiences, and expectations than undergraduate students" (p. 2). The book also calls for further research, and recommends increasing comprehensive graduate programs at HBCUs "and other minority-serving institutions" (Taylor, 2012, p. 250). One of the more recent books on student success in G&P education is *Supporting Graduate Students in the 21st Century: Implications for Policy and Practice* (Felder & St. John, 2014). In their conclusion, the editors underline that research on graduate education continues to be in its infancy:

> Part of the problem [in graduate and professional student services] is that it has taken decades to adapt the theories, concepts, and methods used to

study admissions, retention, and other key structures that support student experience [from those that apply to undergraduate students to the graduate and professional student experience]. In addition, as with scholarship on undergraduates, the dominant theories have reinforced the marginalization of underrepresented groups.

(p. 243)

While leading organizations such as CGS, recent publications, and G&P students themselves have noted the importance of services that are traditionally within the purview of student life areas in Student Affairs to support students' persistence and thriving, the literature that is available for the most part does not have practical applications for student affairs professionals who work with G&P students.

ACCREDITATION AND STANDARDS IN G&P EDUCATION

Why and how we study, measure, and perhaps even serve graduate students may be attributable, in part, to the requirements established by accrediting bodies, as well as the metrics for success established by governing systems in each state, or the lack thereof. For example, the Southern Association of Colleges and Schools (SACSCOC) is the regional accrediting body for higher education in 11 states. While SACSCOC provides detailed requirements for undergraduate education, it offers broad *guidance* for most graduate educational standards (www.sacscoc.org). Colleges may risk their accreditation if they fail to meet the clearly defined standards for undergraduate education. Significant resources, therefore, including time and money, are spent maintaining compliance at the undergraduate level. Some professional school accrediting bodies establish specific expectations for their programs in law, medicine, or business, and licensing board requirements often guide schools of nursing and social work, for instance. Far fewer external agencies apply standards of operations and achievement to graduate education, especially in the arts and sciences.

Where standards exist, they can be useful to leaders in graduate education. As a model of such advocacy, in 2008–2009, a group of graduate student affairs professionals convinced the Council for the Advancement of Standards in Higher Education (CAS) to work collaboratively in developing a new standard for G&P student programs and services (cas.edu/standards). The standards are considered guidelines or *best practices* that inform institutional practice as well as assessment, and can be a general guide for institutions interested in getting started in serving graduate students. These new CAS standards create a basic set of expectations for student affairs services for graduate students, including having professional staff devoted to graduate or professional students within schools or centrally within student affairs, and relevant policies, spaces, and services to meet graduate student needs across the range of campus services.

As mentioned above, professional school programs (i.e., medical, dental, pharmacy, law, etc.) differ significantly from arts and science graduate programs, especially doctoral ones. Whereas graduate student experiences can vary widely by discipline, professional school students move through the curriculum in a cohort or in fairly predictable ways, with expected graduation years. A professional program is, in essence, a single discipline with highly focused graduate students pursuing advanced professional training, licensure, or credentials. These programs tend to be strongly regulated by outside accrediting agencies that address most aspects of professional school, including the faculty and curriculum, physical space, library resources, and student engagement offered at a given school. Because of these associations, the student services provided in a professional school may bear little resemblance to the holistic student development promulgated by Student Affairs or Higher Education preparation programs. Simply put, few if any of these professionals have training in student affairs, so their recommendations for student services tend to reflect their particular profession's standards.

At the same time, highly regulated professional programs tend to have more outcome data available, because they are tuition- and market-dependent *self-supporting* schools and they depend upon measuring good completion and career outcomes. While professional school graduation rates are much higher in law or medicine than in academic doctoral programs, research that analyzes the reasons behind successful outcomes or disparities in time to degree or attrition still remain elusive. For example, the Association of American Medical Colleges (AAMC) has found that student attrition rates for all medical degree programs over a recent 20-year period (1995–1996 to 2014–2015) is quite low, at an average of 3.3% for all programs; yet, student attrition rates and time-to-degree varied by degree type and program, with more students leaving for nonacademic than academic reasons (AAMC, 2020). Certainly, the high tuition in professional programs plays a role in completion rates, where students cannot afford to leave the program without a degree. Gathering information about completion rates for different programs together could help to identify gaps in current research into student outcomes and student success in professional programs as well as identify best practices that could inform practitioners who work with students in G&P degree programs with much higher attrition rates than others. As for career outcomes, recently the Graduate Career Consortium's (GCC's) Career Outcomes Committee has created a database of member institutions' master's-level, other graduate-level, and postdoctoral-level career outcomes. As of September 2020, they have found that 63% of GCC member institutions report their graduate alumni career outcomes publicly (Collins et al., 2020).

While increasing access to graduate programs is necessary to ensure equitable opportunity and a more diverse workforce, these inclusion efforts have generally not been coordinated. If these are critical national priorities, then focused resources and strategies are needed to address them. Professional associations and accrediting bodies could be a mechanism of change, provided these external forces can effectively make the case for equitable graduate student access and for student services that support persistence and retention. Knowledge of accrediting and funding bodies and different completion rates can be useful for student affairs professionals seeking to learn national trends and apply them to localized advocacy for G&P student support services on their own campuses.

COMMUNITIES OF PRACTICE FOR G&P PROFESSIONALS

As we have seen, in the 1990s campuses, publications and the higher education community increased their focus on student services for G&P students. We cannot claim to know whether the national reports, attrition, and job market challenges spurred universities to begin to create new graduate student services and add staff, if changes were locally initiated or were caused by something else entirely (i.e., local budget cuts or graduate student activism), but there was a growth in G&P-focused professionals, centers, and career and student life programs. With this increase came a need for a network of G&P practitioners to share ideas and to support one another. As was the case and continues to be the case for student affairs professionals who are focused on serving G&P students, they may be an office of one. They either have no particular training in student affairs (i.e., they may have been hired for their position because they have a similar terminal degree to the students they are serving) or their student affairs training and experience was mostly undergraduate-focused. At the 1998 annual meetings of the two leading U.S. student affairs associations, NASPA and ACPA, scholar-practitioners persuaded the organizers to allow them to hold initial informal meetups of members working with G&P students. These first roundtables at the NASPA annual conference in Philadelphia and at the ACPA convention in St. Louis launched discussions about including G&P students in the associations' focuses. In 1999, this informal group became recognized as an official NASPA Network for Graduate and Professional Student Services (GAPSS), later called the Administrators in Graduate and Professional Student Services (AGAPSS) Knowledge Community. The ACPA Commission on Graduate and Professional Student Affairs (CGPSA) followed in 2003, with similar activities for its members, including some ACPA-NASPA membership crossover.

13

These networks have become a community of practitioners and an avenue for involvement and leadership within NASPA and ACPA for those working with post-baccalaureate students. As a Knowledge Community, AGAPSS began to prioritize outreach to student affairs professionals and creating its own knowledge to support G&P student affairs practice through conferences, webinars, publications, peer networking, and external review teams. Common practices that campuses have implemented include dissertation boot camps, comprehensive orientations, G&P-specific career services, diversity initiatives, support for students with children, health, mental health, and dental services, and graduate student life programs and centers. It has now been over ten years since a guide to graduate orientations was published (Tokuno, 2008) and 15 years since the last major student affairs book on G&P students (Guentzel & Nesheim, 2006). This new book, *A Practitioner's Guide*, is designed to build community among the growing number of professionals who support G&P students and provide information about the current state of the field, promising practices, and actionable theory-to-practice examples that professionals can apply to their current work.

The contributing authors in this book believe in building a community that supports G&P student success. We want G&P students to thrive in their personal and professional lives. Well-informed, thriving student affairs professionals are needed to support these students within the higher education community. These G&P student affairs professionals need to feel supported and energized within their own community as they create initiatives, enhance existing services, and share knowledge about programmatic successes. We recognize that this book does not and cannot address all aspects of every program and population; each of the topics discussed in the case studies and chapters could be book-length topics themselves. Our goal is that readers will use this book as a practical guide and apply the content as a starting point to meet the specific needs of the students on their campus and in their local program environments. As we know, there is no one-size-fits-all in G&P education. The authors intend that this book will serve as a go-to resource for all those working to advance G&P student services, whether you are a new professional, a seasoned professional, a student, a faculty member or a dean, or a graduate student council looking for service models for your campus. Welcome.

REFERENCES

American College Personnel Association (ACPA), & National Association of Student Personnel Administrators (NASPA). (2004). *Learning reconsidered: A campus-wide focus on the student experience*. NASPA/ACPA. https://www.naspa.org/book/learning-reconsidered-a-campus-wide-focus-on-the-student-experience

Association of American Medical Colleges (AAMC). (2020, October). *Data snapshot: Graduation rates and attrition rates of U.S. medical students.* Retrieved July 22, 2021 from https://www.aamc.org/media/48526/download

Berelson, B. (1960). *Graduate education in the United States.* McGraw-Hill.

Cassuto, L., & Weisbuch, R. (2021). *The new PhD: How to build a better graduate education.* Johns Hopkins University Press.

Collins, T. R. L., Layton, R. L., MacDonald, J. E., Ramadoss, D., Tessel, M. A., & Wheeler, R. (2020). *Institutional graduate career outcomes database 2020* [Database of publicly available graduate alumni career outcomes of member institutions compiled by the Career Outcomes Committee, last updated December 12, 2020]. Graduate Career Consortium. Retrieved July 24, 2021, from https://doi.org/10.17605/OSF.IO/28DN6

Council for the Advancement of Standards in Higher Education. (2019). *Standards for graduate and professional student programs and services [Revised 2017]. CAS professional standards for higher education* (10th ed.). Author. www.cas.edu

Council of Graduate Schools. (2021). *Supporting graduate student mental health and well-being: Evidence-informed recommendations for the Graduate Community.* Retrieved July 22, 2021 from https://cgsnet.org/ckfinder/userfiles/files/CGS_JED_Grad%20Student%20Mental%20Health%20Report.pdf

Council of Graduate Schools(a). (n.d.). *Supporting mental health and well-being for graduate students: A statement of principles and commitments of graduate deans.* Retrieved June 14, 2021, from https://cgsnet.org/ckfinder/userfiles/files/CGS%20Mental%20Health%20Statement%20and%20Signatories_050521.pdf

Council of Graduate Schools(b). (n.d.). *Best practices.* Retrieved July 22, 2021, from https://cgsnet.org/best-practices

Cusworth, S. (2001). *Orientation and retention of counseling PhD students: A qualitative study* (ED458513). ERIC. https://eric.ed.gov/?id=ED458513

Felder, P. P., & St. John, E. P. (Eds.) (2014). *Supporting graduate students in the 21st century: Implications for policy and practice.* AMS press.

Golde, C., & Dore, T. M. (2001, January). *At cross purposes: What the experiences of today's doctoral students reveal about doctoral education.* [Report.] The Pew Charitable Trusts.

Graham, H. D., & Diamond, N. (1997). *The rise of American research universities: Elites and challengers in the postwar era.* Johns Hopkins University Press.

Guentzel, M. J., & Nesheim, B. E. (Eds.) (2006, Fall). Supporting graduate & professional students: The role of student affairs. *New Directions in Student Services.* Jossey-Bass. http://www.phd-survey.org

Kerr, C. (1963). *The uses of the university.* Harvard University Press.

Lovitts, B. E. (2001). *Leaving the ivory tower: The causes and consequences of departure from doctoral study.* Rowman & Littlefield.

Merriam, S. B., Caffarella, R. S., Cranton, P., & Wlodkowski, R. J. (2002). *Adult learning: Theories, principles and applications.* John Wiley & Sons, Incorporated.

Millar, T. S., Mason, S. A., Gunter, R. L., & Millar, S. B. (1998, June). *Synthesis of the science, mathematics, engineering and technology graduate education forum (Arlington, Virginia, June 29–30, 1998)* (ED472039). ERIC. https://files.eric.ed.gov/fulltext/ED472039.pdf

National Center for Education Statistics [NCES-a]. (n.d.). *Postbaccalaureate enrollment.* U.S. Department of Education, Institute of Education Sciences. Retrieved July 14, 2021, from https://nces.ed.gov/programs/coe/indicator/chb

National Center for Education Statistics [NCES-b]. (n.d.). *Graduate degree fields*. U.S. Department of Education, Institute of Education Sciences. Retrieved July 14, 2021, from https://nces.ed.gov/programs/coe/indicator/ctb

National Center for Education Statistics. [NCES-c]. (n.d.). *Annual earnings by educational attainment*. U.S. Department of Education, Institute of Education Sciences. Retrieved July 22, 2021, from https://nces.ed.gov/programs/coe/indicator/cba

National Center for Education Statistics. [NCES-d]. (n.d.). *Characteristics of postsecondary students*. U.S. Department of Education, Institute of Education Sciences. Retrieved July 14, 2021, from https://nces.ed.gov/programs/coe/indicator/csb

Newman, J. H. (1852). *The idea of a university defined and illustrated*. Oxford. https://www.newmanreader.org/works/idea/

Palmer, R. T., Hilton, A. A., & Fountaine, T. P. (Eds.) (2012). *Black graduate education at Historically Black Colleges and Universities: Trends, experiences, and outcomes*. Information Age Publishing.

Pelikan, J. (1992). *The idea of the university: A reexamination*. Yale University Press.

Pfund, C., Branchaw, J., & Handelsman, J. (2014). *Entering mentoring*. W.H. Freeman & Co.

Pontius, J., & Harper, S. R. (2006, Fall). Principles for good practice in graduate and professional student engagement. In M. J. Guentzel & B. E. Nesheim (Eds.), *Supporting graduate & professional Students: The role of student affairs* (pp. 47–58). *New Directions in Student Services*. Jossey-Bass.

Pruitt-Logan, A. S., & Isaac, P. D. (Eds.) (1995, Winter). Student services for the changing graduate student population. *New Directions for Student Services, 42*. Jossey-Bass.

Shreve, G. (2018, April 4). Quit Lit then and now. *Inside Higher Education*. https://www.insidehighered.com/views/2018/04/04/comparison-quit-lit-1970s-and-today-opinion

Taylor, D. C. M., & Hamdy, H. (2013). Adult learning theories: Implications for learning and teaching in medical education: AMEE Guide No. 83. *Medical Teacher, 35*(11), e1561–e1572. https://doi.org/10.3109/0142159X.2013.828153

Taylor, M. C. (2012). On a wing and a prayer: The future of graduate education at HBCUs. In R. T. Palmer, A. A. Hilton, & T. P. Fountaine (Eds.), *Black graduate education at Historically Black Colleges and Universities: Trends, experiences, and outcomes* (pp. 223–252). Information Age Publishing.

Tokuno, K. A. (Ed). (2008). *Graduate students in transition: Assisting students through the first year*. National Center for the First-Year Experience and Students in Transition. University of South Carolina.

Chapter 2

Brief History, Background, and Definitions

Matthew W. Imboden and Marlaina Kloepfer

It is an exciting time to be a higher education professional working in support of graduate student and degree program success. The institutional and industry-wide significance of post-baccalaureate student recruitment, retention, engagement, and success continues to increase, and yet there remains much to be studied and shared about this student population and the work of the student services professionals who support them. In this chapter, we provide an overview of the current state of U.S. graduate student populations and academic programs. Admittedly, a comprehensive and appropriately nuanced description of *who graduate students are today* is a near impossibility in a work of this length. Our ambition is to highlight important and consequential elements of the contemporary graduate education landscape and its students, who are as multifaceted and deserving of independent engagement as undergraduate populations that often spend comparatively more time in the spotlight. In this way, we hope to provide an initial roadmap to this world that also inspires interested readers to go further.

At the time of this writing, graduate students represented more than 15% of total U.S. higher education enrollments and over 25% of all awarded degrees (National Center for Education Statistics [NCES], 2020). Overall graduate student enrollments also continue to steadily increase as they have for decades on a trajectory that has notably outpaced undergraduate program growth over the same period (Gardner & Barker, 2015). Particularly rapid growth is observable in some specific disciplines and evolving program formats, including postsecondary non-degree programs such as graduate certificates where the number of credentials awarded increased by 19.6% between 2018 and 2019 alone (Okahana et al., 2020). In ways that will go on to be explored in this chapter, this kind of dynamism in programs and enrollments is further enriched by the remarkable diversity of student identities, backgrounds, and career motivations within graduate populations themselves, though necessary progress

DOI: 10.4324/9781003121671-3

toward equity certainly remains among historically underrepresented students in some fields.

As these graduate populations have continued to grow and develop in recent years, so has the community of professionals who engage and support them. Because graduate student services offices and roles will likely be called upon to play a more significant part in their organizations in future years, it is important for practitioners to be equipped with a sense of the historical and contemporary contexts for their work. Therefore, we hope to contextualize this overview of the graduate enrollment landscape in a way that empowers student services professionals to find a clearer voice for articulating their own significance and standing within the wider field of student affairs practice. Motivated by the needs of this dynamic student population, graduate student services professionals are serving at the leading edges of professional innovation and higher education administration during a very consequential time for the industry.

HISTORY OF GRADUATE EDUCATION

Evolving dynamics in the areas of funding, governance, politics, and the interests of the general population not only help us understand the current state of graduate education, but these variables have also influenced the overall history of our field. Geiger's (2016) *Ten Generations of American Higher Education* (e.g., Reformation Beginnings, Colonial Colleges, Republican Education, The Passing of Republican Education, The Classical Denomination Colleges, New Departures, Growth and Standardization, Mass Higher Education and Differentiation Between Wars, The Academic Revolution, and Privatization and the Current Era) describes each era as it relates to what was happening in both the United States and the higher education industry. It was during Geiger's *Generation Six (1850–1890): New Departures* where graduate education was established. Along with the emergence of graduate education, 40 women's colleges were chartered, Lincoln University and Wilberforce University provided free college education to African Americans, and the Morrill Land Grant Act was established (Geiger, 2016). Another important shift in the mission within Higher Education was occurring during this same time, which also influenced the development of graduate education: institutions additionally focused on research rather than strictly learning (Goldin & Katz, 1999). Graduate education's foundation, connected to academic elitism and serving a predominantly white, male, and upper class, still influences biases present in systems of today (St. John & Felder, 2014).

Similar to previous generations (and those after), the educational philosophy was evolving to meet the needs of the changing economy and professionalization of the industry; however, some of the same struggles (e.g., funding, public support, and international competition and comparison) have also remained unanswered since the first PhD program was offered at Yale in 1860 (Storr, 1953). The curriculum of that first PhD program included two years of study culminating with a final examination. If a student did not have a background in a classical language, they would need special permission to complete the program (Storr, 1953). The first PhD in education was granted in 1893 from the Teacher's College, but the first EdD would be granted in 1920 from the Harvard Graduate School (Perry, 2012). Even in the 1800s the leaders of the institutions were trying to identify the purpose of graduate education. They were trying to determine if the purpose tied to scholarly activity and exploration, or if it was a professional education (Storr, 1953). Daniel C. Gilman, the second President of Yale who led during the creation of the first graduate degree, was concerned that lack of a clear vision for curriculum and a lack of leadership in the development of these new academic programs could result in graduate education becoming the "step child" of the institution (Storr, 1953, p. 132). There was continued growth yet a differentiation in numbers of graduates as more programs emerged. From 1898 to 1910, the University of Chicago, Columbia, Harvard, Pennsylvania University, Yale, Johns Hopkins, and Cornell all conferred 200 or more PhD degrees, compared to Illinois, Stanford, Minnesota, Princeton, California, and Michigan, which conferred fewer than 100 degrees each during the same time period (Thelin, 2004).

As more graduate programs were developed in both the liberal arts and sciences, the programs offered through independent professional institutions declined (Goldin & Katz, 1999). Instead, professional programs within universities increased (Goldin & Katz, 1999). Graduate programs in education were also being influenced by the distinction between learning and research and what that meant for curriculum design, pedagogy, and overall mission of the program. Thomas Hill, President of Harvard in 1865, both acknowledged and attempted to define the difference between academic and professional programs when he wrote, "the general perfection and improvement of the pupil" and "culture and instruction which fits...for some chosen walk of life" in referring to liberal arts education and professional education (Clifford & Guthrie, 1988, p. 3, as cited in Perry, 2012, p. 6). Questions about the purpose and identity of the different types of graduate programs, especially those in education, are still being refined today. For example, Table 2.1 illustrates the guiding principles and the design concepts that The Carnegie Project on the Education Doctorate (CPED) uses to "test, refine, and validate principles for the professional doctorate in education" (The Carnegie Project on the Education Doctorate, n.d., para. 5). Other disciplines (e.g., nursing, engineering,

TABLE 2.1 The Carnegie Project on the Education Doctorate's Guiding Principles and Design Concepts

Guiding Principles	Design Concepts to Build Programs
Is framed around questions of equity, ethics, and social justice to bring about solutions to complex problems of practice.	*Scholarly Practitioners*: They blend practical wisdom with professional skills and knowledge to name, frame, and solve problems of practice.
Prepares leaders who can construct and apply knowledge to make a positive difference in the lives of individuals, families, organizations, and communities.	*Signature Pedagogy*: This is the pervasive set of practices used to prepare scholarly practitioners for all aspects of their professional work.
Provides opportunities for candidates to develop and demonstrate collaboration and communication skills to work with diverse communities and to build partnerships.	*Inquiry as Practice*: This is the process of posing significant questions that focus on complex problems of practice. By using various research, theories, and professional wisdom, scholarly practitioners design innovative solutions to address the problems of practice.
Provides field-based opportunities to analyze problems of practice and use multiple frames to develop meaningful solutions.	*Laboratories of Practices*: These are settings where theory and practice inform and enrich each other.
Is grounded in and develops a professional knowledge base that integrates both practical and research knowledge and that links theory with systemic and systematic inquiry.	*Dissertation in Practice*: This is a scholarly endeavor that impacts a complex problem of practice.
Emphasizes the generation, transformation, and use of professional knowledge and practice.	*Problem of Practice*: This is a persistent, contextualized, and specific issue embedded in the work of a professional practitioner, the addressing of which has the potential to result in improved understanding, experience, and outcomes.
	Mentoring and Advising: These should be guided by equity and justice, mutual respect, dynamic learning, flexibility, intellectual space, supportive learning environments, cohort and individualized attention, rigorous practices, and integration.

Source: Carnegie Project on the Education Doctorate (n.d.), as printed in *The CPED Framework*. Retrieved from https://www.cpedinitiative.org/the-framework.

and business) are thinking through similar distinctions in program and curriculum design to distinguish the research and scholarship-based programs from the professional practice-based programs.

This continued push for professionalization within an academic institution guided by the needs of professions has increased the number of practice-based graduate degrees offered across disciplines. Some professional fields that have had a long history within graduate education such as medicine, law, and preparation for the clergy are now becoming a smaller portion of the student population as increases in programs like business, education, and health sciences occur (Okahana et al., 2020). The Academic Programs and Enrollments section later in this chapter will provide additional insight into the current interest and enrollments of these types of programs.

DEFINITIONS

Previous studies of graduate education have defined graduate students by their academic discipline, profession, years in their profession, age, gender, and race (Pifer & Baker, 2014). These subcategories are helpful in describing and then understanding this diverse student population, but do not provide us with holistic insight into the complexities of the multiple identities (e.g., professional, relational, and personal) of our graduate students (Pifer & Baker, 2014). Student affairs professionals working with the graduate student population and within the academic disciplines are active members of the community (faculty members, advisors, and administrators) and should be in the constant practice of refining our processes within the socialization context (Weidman et al., 2001). This community or team becomes even larger when working within professional or clinical programs, as field preceptors and other clinical supervisors join the team in delivering academic experiences to students. With each new disciplinary area or student type that emerges in graduate education, we need to be mindful of not being stagnant and using a one-size-fits-all mentality or cookie-cutter practices for orientation or service delivery (Weidman et al., 2001). We, as student affairs professionals, are important for the reciprocal and nonlinear models of socialization that focus more on knowledge acquisition than on cognitive outcomes (Weidman et al., 2001).

Institution Types

Understanding and categorizing graduate education goes beyond the simplistic view of private vs. public institutions. Although these two classifications do provide insight into funding and governance structures, which highlight and define differences across other categories, they do not provide a sufficiently comprehensive view of characteristics that are important for understanding graduate programs and students. The Carnegie Classification (Table 2.2), which many institutions use to differentiate themselves and reporting agencies use to describe institutions, consists of two larger categories to define graduate schools based on the programs they offer: post-baccalaureate degree-granting institutions and research/scholarship doctoral degrees. Carnegie further distinguishes institutions that offer medical education degrees from the research/scholarship degrees. How an institution fits into one of the two larger categories relies on the type of programs in which they confer degrees. Both classifications use academic disciplines and prevalence of degrees as a measure to refine and organize institutions. The National Center for Education Statistics (NCES) also noted the increase of the diversity among doctoral degree programs when they differentiated two of their award-level descriptions. In the 2010–2011 NCES data collection process, institutions had three additional award levels to code their post-baccalaureate programs, which included Doctor's Degree-Research/Scholarship, Doctor's Degree-Professional Practice, and Doctor's Degree-Other. This addition of doctoral degree types is important to us as practitioners because each program type includes different pedagogical practices and influences, culminating projects, and career trajectories. Thinking about the CPED's framework mentioned earlier in this chapter helps us to understand why distinguishing the differences between doctoral programs is a valuable lens for us to use when understanding program type.

Academic Programs and Enrollments

In the previous decade, graduate education has been an area of dynamic potential for many institutions and academic programs, with steady growth in enrollment and revenue. We, as practitioners and researchers, sometimes use graduate education in a broad way to describe and define a multitude of program types and outcomes; however, graduate education can also be appraised with more nuances through an understanding of many of its historically defining degree programs and formats. There are many points of data available through a variety of organizations that report on enrollment data within academic programs. These sources include governmental agencies, professional accrediting bodies, and testing agencies. Understanding data sources and the scope of the organization presenting the data is a valuable skill set for the student affairs professional, as it provides another layer of detail in understanding our home programs and student population, as well as identifying gaps or biases in the data presented. The following subsections provide examples of organizations where a student

TABLE 2.2 Graduate Instructional Program Classification

Post-baccalaureate	Degrees Awarded
Single program—(Education or Business)	1. Master's or professional practice/other doctoral degrees in education as their only post-baccalaureate program. 2. Master's or professional practice/other doctoral degrees in business as their only post-baccalaureate program.
Single program—Other	Master's or professional practice/other doctoral degrees in a single field other than education or business as their only post-baccalaureate program.
Comprehensive programs	At least one master's degree or professional practice/other doctoral degrees in each of the humanities, social sciences, and Science, Technology, Engineering, and Mathematics (STEM*) fields, as well as such graduate degrees in one or more professional fields.
Arts and sciences-dominant	Master's or professional practice/other doctoral degrees in some arts and sciences fields may also award master's or non-research doctoral degrees in other fields, but in lesser numbers.
Education-dominant with arts and sciences	Master's or professional practice/other doctoral degrees in both arts and sciences and professional fields, and the field with the largest number of such graduate degrees was education.
Business-dominant with arts and sciences	Master's or professional practice/other doctoral degrees in both arts and sciences and professional fields, and the field with the largest number of such graduate degrees was business.
Other-dominant with arts and sciences	Master's or professional practice/other doctoral degrees in both arts and sciences and professional fields, and the field with the largest number of such graduate degrees was a professional field other than business or education.
Education-dominant with other professional programs	Master's or professional practice/other doctoral degrees in professional fields only, and the field with the largest number of such graduate degrees was education.
Business-dominant with other professional programs	Master's or professional practice/other doctoral degrees in professional fields only, and the field with the largest number of such graduate degrees was business.
Other-dominant with other professional programs	Master's or professional practice/other doctoral degrees in professional fields only, and the field with the largest number of such graduate degrees was a field other than business or education.

continued...

23

TABLE 2.2 continued...

Post-baccalaureate	Degrees Awarded
Research Doctoral	
Single program—Education	Research doctoral degrees in education but not in other fields (they may have more extensive offerings at the master's or professional practice/other doctoral level).
Single program—Other	Research doctoral degrees in a single field other than education (they may have more extensive offerings at the master's or professional practice/other doctoral level).
Comprehensive programs with medical/veterinary school	Research doctoral degrees in the humanities, social sciences, and STEM* fields, as well as in medicine, dentistry, and/or veterinary medicine, may also offer master's and professional practice/other doctoral degrees in other fields.
Comprehensive programs, no medical/ veterinary school	Research doctoral degrees in the humanities, social sciences, and STEM* fields may also offer master's or professional practice/other degrees in fields other than medicine, dentistry, or veterinary medicine.
Humanities/social sciences-dominant	Research doctoral degrees in a range of fields, with the largest number of research doctorates in the humanities or social sciences.
STEM-dominant	Research doctoral degrees in a range of fields, with the largest number of research doctorates in the STEM* fields.
Professional-dominant	Research doctoral degrees in a range of fields, and the largest number of research doctorates were in professions other than engineering (such as education, health professions, law, public policy, or social work).

Source: Carnegie Classification of Institutions of Higher Education (n.d.). *About Carnegie Classification*. Retrieved from http://carnegieclassifications.iu.edu/.

affairs professional can find data for understanding graduate enrollment statistics by program type.

National Center for Education Statistics

The NCES within the Department of Education fulfills the "congressional mandate to collect, collate, analyze, and report complete statistics on the condition of American education" (NCES About Us, n.d., para. 1). NCES provides definitions for doctoral degree, master's degree, and post-baccalaureate certificate used within their reporting. In *The Condition of Education 2020* glossary of terms, NCES divides the doctoral degree into three categories: Research/Scholarship,

Professional Practice, and Other. A research/scholarship Doctoral Degree requires "the preparation and defense of a dissertation based on original research, or the planning and execution of an original project demonstrating substantial artistic or scholarly achievement" (NCES, n.d., https://nces.ed.gov/programs/coe/glossary.asp#doctors). Doctoral degrees in this category include: PhD, EdD (education), DMA (music), DBA (business), and others. A professional practice doctoral degree "is conferred upon completion of a program providing the knowledge and skills for the recognition, credential, or license required for professional practice" (NCES, n.d., https://nces.ed.gov/programs/coe/glossary.asp#doctors). Professional practice doctoral degrees include: PharmD (pharmacy), DVM (veterinary medicine), JD (law), and others. The third category of other degrees includes those that do not match the descriptions or requirements of either the research/scholarship or professional practice categories.

The research vs. professional practice distinction also helps define the two types of master's degrees according to NCES. Examples of master's degrees that represent scholarship and research-focused curriculum include MA (master of arts) and MS (master of science) programs (NCES). Professionally based Master's Degrees include: MBA (business), MEd (education), MEng (engineering), and others (NCES). According to the Carnegie Classifications Update in 2018, doctoral universities represent the largest percentage of enrollment with 36% of the overall enrollment, but just 10% when looking at the data by number of institutions. Master's colleges and universities represented 20% of the total enrollment (Indiana University Center for Postsecondary Research, 2021).

In their 2020 *Condition of Education*, NCES found that there were 184,000 doctoral degrees conferred in 2017–2018. Health professions and legal programs represented 62% of those degrees, followed by education (7%), engineering (6%), and biological studies (4%). In 2017–2018, 820,000 master's degrees were conferred (NCES). Half of the master's degrees were in three disciplines: business (23%), education (18%), and health professions (15%) (NCES, n.d.).

CGS/GRE Annual Survey of Graduate Enrollment

Since 1986, the *CGS/GRE Survey of Graduate Enrollment* (Okahana et al., 2020) has attempted to collect data from graduate programs to provide insight into both the current landscape of Graduate Education, as well as a longitudinal view of the data compared to ten years prior. In 2019, the survey collected data from 561 institutions from all regions of the United States (Okahana et al., 2020). However, as we enter the second decade of the millennium, the survey noted some trends which may be both illustrative and predictive of changes in Graduate Education.

TABLE 2.3 First-time Graduate Enrollment by Broad Field, Gender, and Attendance Status, Fall 2019

Broad Field	Total	Men		Women		Full Time		Part Time	
Total	518,721	207,494	40.7%	302,204	59.3%	343,778	66.3%	174,821	33.7%
Arts and humanities	24,174	10,067	41.7%	14,096	58.3%	19,434	80.4%	4,740	19.6%
Biological and agricultural sciences	23,482	9,514	40.5%	13,968	59.5%	19,743	84.1%	3,739	15.9%
Business	85,220	43,618	52.9%	38,840	47.1%	54,972	64.5%	30,248	35.5%
Education	77,292	17,658	23.9%	56,151	76.1%	34,453	44.6%	42,747	55.4%
Engineering	43,443	30,939	71.2%	12,504	28.8%	34,942	80.4%	8,501	19.6%
Health sciences	67,352	14,290	21.2%	53,036	78.8%	45,398	67.4%	21,954	32.6%
Mathematics and computer sciences	37,595	24,413	65.4%	12,917	34.6%	27,191	72.3%	10,404	27.7%
Physical and earth sciences	11,536	6,747	58.5%	4,789	41.5%	10,265	89.0%	1,271	11.0%
Public administration and services	27,272	5,658	20.9%	21,474	79.1%	18,846	69.1%	8,426	30.9%
Social and behavioral sciences	39,903	13,094	34.6%	24,793	65.4%	29,593	74.2%	10,310	25.8%
Other fields	36,258	13,567	37.6%	22,482	62.4%	23,106	63.7%	13,152	36.3%

Note: Because not all institutions responded to all items, details may not sum to totals. Percentages are based on total of known gender or attendance status.

Source: CGS/GRE Survey of Graduate Enrollment and Degrees as printed in Okahana et al. (2020).

Similar to previous years, graduate programs in education, business, and the health sciences continue to be the largest student populations in 2019 (Okahana et al., 2020). Overall, the number of applications to graduate programs flattened in 2019, due to an increase in applications to doctoral programs paired with a slight decrease in applications to masters programs. According to the *CGS/GRE Survey* (Okahana et al., 2020), applications to "Very High Research Doctoral Universities" and "High Research Doctoral Universities" increased slightly between 2018 and 2019 compared to a decrease (−2.8%) in applications to "Masters Colleges and Universities" and "Doctoral Professional Universities" (−9.9%). Graduate Certificates increased by 19.6%, with education, business, and health sciences representing the disciplines with the most interest. Applications have increased over the past ten years in all disciplines except for the Arts and Humanities.

Although the survey completed by the Council of Graduate Schools/Graduate Record Examinations (CGS/GRE) is helpful in understanding larger trends by application numbers and enrollment, it does not include data representing first professional programs, such as doctoral programs in veterinary medicine, medicine, pharmacy, law, and other disciplines, which may represent additional trends or areas of growth similar to or different than those covered in the CGS/GRE annual survey. For example, in 2019 enrollment in law (JD) programs was down by 23.5% (Law School Transparency, n.d.). The inclusion of a dissertation or research focus in the curriculum, as well as professional licensure at the completion of a doctoral program, are some of the distinguishing factors between the professional programs and the other doctoral programs included in the *CGS/GRE Survey* (Indiana University Center for Postsecondary Research, 2021).

National Student Clearinghouse Research Center

The National Student Clearinghouse Research Center collects data from institutions that enroll many of the students who are currently seeking postsecondary education in the United States. As part of their fall 2020 update, 76% of Title IV degree granting institutions participated and provided insight into enrollment trends in the first fall semester influenced by the COVID-19 pandemic. Despite a 3.3% decrease in undergraduate enrollment in the fall of 2020, graduate enrollment had an increase of 2.9% (National Student Clearinghouse Research Center, 2020). For-profit institutions had the largest increase in graduate enrollment in the fall 2020 semester with a 7.4% increase. Public institutions had an increase of 3.6%, and private institutions had the smallest increase with 1.4% when compared to the fall of 2019. When comparing growth by credential type, graduate certificates had the largest increase in enrollment. While enrollment growth in doctoral programs remained similar from the fall of 2019–2020 (2.9%) and the fall of 2018–2019 (2.4%), enrollment in masters-level programs increased in the fall of 2020 by 3.4% compared to 1.3% in the fall of 2019.

Other Resources by Discipline/Profession

Because the diverse landscape of graduate education can be heavily influenced by specific academic disciplines, professional organizations that represent the field of study are also an important stakeholder in reporting enrollments and can help to highlight the nuances of their respective fields. These very same organizations also influence accreditation processes and the professionalization of students in the graduate programs themselves. Reporting from these organizations can help describe the differences in trends as they occur. For example, in the fall of 2020 when enrollment to undergraduate programs was on a decline and there were only modest increases in graduate enrollment, specific academic areas within graduate education were seeing greater increases. In November 2020, while still in the middle of their application cycle, the American Association for Osteopathic Medicine (AACOM) was reporting an 18.2% increase in the number of applications compared to the very same time in the cycle the previous year (American Association of Colleges of Osteopathic Medicine [AACOM], 2020). The Law Schools Admission Council reported a 32% increase in applications during the fall 2020 as compared to the previous year and the Association of American Medical Colleges reported an increase of 18% in applications compared to the previous year (Jaschik, 2020).

Other examples of such discipline or profession-specific entities that manage and report on elements of graduate enrollment data abound. For example, additional Law resources include the American Bar Association's required and publicly available data disclosures (http://www.abarequireddisclosures. org/Disclosure509.aspx); for graduate education in theology, the Association of Theological Schools' enrollment data and trend reports (https://www.ats. edu/resources/research-and-data) holds a wealth of information, and insights into graduate business education are available via the Association to Advance Collegiate Schools of Business (AACSB) centralized data reports on enrollments and institutional operations (https://www.aacsb.edu/data/data-reports/survey-reports), or even reports from testing agency or student recruitment players such as the Graduate Management Admission Council (https://www.gmac. com/market-intelligence-and-research/assessment-data). These resources are valuable for not only learning about student numbers and demographics but for tracing the emergence of new degree categories throughout graduate education, such as the specialized master's degrees in graduate business education which now far outpace the traditional MBA, or graduate credentials specifically aimed at creating and equipping mid-level practitioners to address key staffing needs in dynamic industries like healthcare.

While such area-specific insights into degree program enrollments are informative, there are many emerging categories of continuing and graduate education that likely escape these reporting systems. In a true reminder of the diverse and dynamic nature of our graduate student populations, we can potentially see graduate student services work also extending into unique non-degree program formats and experiences that carry so-called alternative credentials or next generation credentials (e.g., micro-credentials, digital badging, passports, certificates, certifications, etc.). Such education and training options, which are appearing both inside and outside of traditional higher education institutional settings, sometimes in partnership with or completely operated by corporate entities, are helping to shape the future of the lifelong learning conversation nationally. Graduate student services administrators need only look at the many contemporary news headlines to see this element of the education environment changing around them by the day. How the needs of these students are identified and supported may be an important part of the long-term future of the graduate student services discourse.

GRADUATE STUDENTS

Demographics such as gender, race, and socioeconomic status have an influence on the graduate student experience, especially as these variables relate to admissions, retention, and success in the different institution types. In his 2013 manifesto, Soares identified that institutions were failing the post-traditional learner because of their institution-centric view when using categories such as adult learners, non-traditional, and part-time learners to describe their student population. Instead, Soares urged us to think about our students as Post-Traditional Learners who are "wage earners for themselves and their families, combine work and learning at the same time or move between them frequently, and seek academic/career advising to navigate their complex path to a degree" (2013, p. 2). Acknowledging this shift in who students are outside of their graduate programs helps us to understand how other milestones we measure within academic programs may also be affected. This section will present the changing graduate student profile and a discussion of how the student experience can be influenced by one's identity.

The median time to degree completion in a doctoral program has decreased over the last decade; however, the median time is not equal across student populations or academic disciplines (National Science Foundation [NSF], 2019). The median time for completion of a doctoral degree (after starting the program) was 5.8 years across all academic disciplines in 2017 (National Center for Science and Engineering Statistics [NCSES], 2020). Humanities and the Arts had the longest median with 7.1 years to completion, followed by Education with 6.3 years to completion (NCSES, 2020). In their 2019 *Survey of Earned Doctorates*, NCES found that the median time to completion of a doctoral degree did not vary much between men (5.7 years) and women (5.8 years) across all disciplines. This same survey found that range in median time to completion was larger across race and ethnicities when examining the data across all disciplines: 5.9 years for Hispanic or Latino Students, 6.5 years for American Indian or Alaska Native Students, 5.8 years for Asian Students, 5.9 years for Black or African American Students, and 5.8 years for White Students (NCSES, 2020).

Funding Graduate Education

Changes in the economy and enrollment can also affect the funding that is available to graduate students. For institutions where the budget is enrollment driven, there may be fewer scholarships and assistantships that would otherwise make attending graduate school more accessible. Educational benefits available through employers which help adult learners attend graduate school may also be affected by the challenges of an uncertain economic climate. This lack of funding sources could result in more graduate students seeking loans (and increasing their debt) to help finance their education. Although the percentage of graduate students who were former recipients of federal Pell grants has been increasing (from 32.5% in 2007/2008 to 45.8% in 2015/2016), there is a concern that the absence of a Pell grant program for graduate education can continue to create inequality in debt among students (Okahana, 2018). There is already a gap in debt between former Pell grant recipients and those who did not receive Pell grants upon graduate program completion. First year students in professional practice programs had the smallest difference ($39,106 and $35,000) between former Pell grant recipients and those who did not (Okahana, 2018). This inequity in debt amount after pursuing a graduate degree is extended by the continuing inequity in pay once in the workforce. Although those who hold a master's degree or higher have median earnings greater than their counterparts in other educational attainments, there is still a difference in earnings by gender (NCES, 2020). There was a difference of $20,100 between the median earnings of males and females (ages 25–34) with a master's degree or higher in 2018 with males out-earning females (NCES). In their *2020 Condition of Education*, NCES also found that there was a difference in median earnings amongst races for those who have a master's degree or higher. Those who identified as Asians earned $80,100 compared to their White ($63,000), Hispanic ($59,900), and Black ($53,800) colleagues.

International Graduate Students

First-time enrollment of international students in graduate programs increased in the fall of 2019 to 20% (Okahana et al., 2020). This increase followed six years of decline in first time enrollment of international students in graduate programs (Okahana et al., 2020). International students had the highest first-time enrollments in mathematics and computer sciences (54%) and the lowest first-time enrollment in public administration and services, education, and health sciences (Okahana et al., 2020). Despite representing some of the largest enrollment numbers for international students, international applications to graduate programs in business and engineering decreased between 2018 and 2019 (Zhou et al., 2020). In alignment with the increase in graduate applications presented earlier in this chapter by Okahana et al. (2020), the masters- and certificate-level programs had the largest increase in interest from international students (Zhou et al., 2020). Prior to the fall of 2020 and its challenges (e.g., travel restrictions and student visas restrictions related to online learning), trends in international enrollment had remained consistent with certain countries consistently representing a majority of international applications and enrollment. Between the fall of 2018 and 2019, the largest increase in applications (11%) and first-time enrollments (22%) were from students in the sub-Saharan African countries (Zhou et al., 2020). Applications (4%) and first-time enrollments (11%) also increased during that same year from Mexico (Zhou et al., 2020). Information from the Council of Graduate Schools, International Graduate Applications and Enrollment, fall 2019 (Figure 2.1) provides additional data on application and first-time enrollment of international students between fall 2018 and fall 2019.

International student enrollment trends, especially those of new students, were influenced by the COVID-19 global pandemic. It was during the fall of 2020 that these changes in application, student visa approvals, and enrollment differed from the trends of the previous years. When compared to the fall of 2019, there was a 72% decrease in new international student enrollment (U.S. Immigration and Customs Enforcement [ICE], 2021). During the time of this writing, many U.S. Embassies and Consulates were still not regularly processing student visas, which could also be contributing to both the decrease in fall 2020, but also the future of fall 2021 (Redden, 2021). All regions in the United States had decreases in international student records during the 2019–2020 year, but the northeast region experienced the largest decrease (−19.4%) during this time

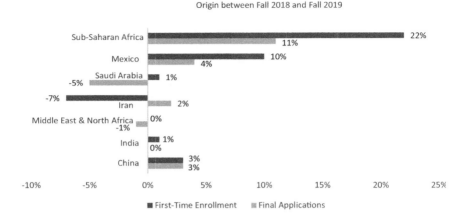

One-year Change in International Graduate Applications &
First-time Enrollment by Selected Country & Region of
Origin between Fall 2018 and Fall 2019

FIGURE 2.1 One-year Change in International Graduate Applications and First-time Enrollment by Selected Country and Region of Origin between Fall 2018 and Fall 2019.

Source: As printed in Zhou, E., Mitic, R. R., West, C. P. L., & Okahana, H. (2020). *International graduate applications and enrollment: Fall 2019.* Washington, DC: Council of Graduate Schools.

(ICE, 2021). California continued to be the state that hosted the largest percentage of international students during this challenging year (ICE, 2021).

Online, Working, and Commuting Students

In ways that hardly require acknowledgment for graduate student services practitioners, any discussion of graduate students and programs includes important considerations for program delivery modes and the life activities of these student populations. Earlier in this chapter, we invoked the work of Louis Soares and the call to reframe our fundamental expectations of students as *post-traditional learners* whose needs have evolved from the typologies more commonly seen as historically normative (Soares, 2013). While that call for renewed vision should rightly extend throughout all of postsecondary education, it is crucial to recognize the ways in which considerations for adult, parenting, working, and/or commuting students have already been fundamental to graduate student services for many years. Indeed, for many graduate students, their educational pursuits are frequently only one of the many activities in which they are involved, with additional commitments ranging from their professional work to caregiving for children, spouses, relatives, or friends, as well as their other community leadership or volunteer responsibilities (Fairchild, 2003).

This reality has shaped the program design and delivery of graduate education not only in curricular and classroom approaches that focus on ensuring value and relevance for students typically funding their own education, but also in the timing and format of program experiences themselves. In this way, graduate learning experiences in part-time, evening, weekend, and/or online degree program formats are relatively common contexts where graduate student services professionals enact customized procedures and ongoing support for their students. In recent years, as online education strategies have matured at many institutions, this work can include student services delivered directly to students or in partnership with contracted service providers and outsourced online program management firms. Such emerging considerations are yet another reminder of the inherent diversity of student identities, needs, and developmental contexts present in graduate student populations today. In ways we will go on to explore below, these graduate student services contexts are increasingly becoming laboratories for innovation across the profession.

Impacts on the Student Experience

In ways that this chapter has highlighted throughout, the graduate student landscape is complex and dynamic, but there are ways in which student services professionals can access and analyze helpful data at student, program, and disciplinary levels. Such awareness is important for our practice of supporting the student experience. Being able to translate data points into the narrative of the lived student experience within our academic programs helps us to create systems that support student success in a mindful and holistic way. The *one-size-fits-all* or *the way it has always been done* approach is not inclusive and often creates challenges that hinder the success of our students and our programs. For example, the academic culture of a humanities graduate program (the pedagogy, networks of support, measures of success, and career outcomes) does not necessarily translate to the academic culture of an engineering program. Attempting to translate practices from a research-based doctoral program to a clinical or professional-based doctoral program also creates a similar mismatch. The differences between academic cultures of on-ground and online experiences are even greater. Student type and additional identity characteristics outside of gender, race, and ethnicity (e.g., first-generation, online, part-time) can also influence the student experience (Gardner & Gopaul, 2012; Gardner & Holley, 2011). To approach all programs and students the same is a great disservice and ignores opportunities to create student-centered support services. As higher education

33

professionals working to support graduate students across program type and discipline, it is valuable to recognize that the lived student experience within our programs vary depending on student type.

Since the development of graduate education and its systems were influenced by the European model, many of the Eurocentric practices create and protect a system that celebrates exclusivity instead of the inclusion of the experiences of underrepresented and racially minoritized (URM) students (Omotola McGee, 2020). Traditional socialization models by design can perpetuate outdated practices while expecting students to "adopt these norms and rules outright, which can undermine their self-efficacy and potentially exclude them from participating in other normal practices of the academy" (Gildersleeve et al., 2011, p. 109). Graduate education is a smaller microcosm of the higher education industry and therefore shares the same challenges of systemic racism. In their 2016 study of racism experienced by students of color in graduate programs, Truong et al. found that students of color experience racism in both direct and indirect (secondhand or vicarious) ways. Because of vicarious racism (specifically, trickledown racism), mentoring and advisory relationships were negatively affected with faculty members of color as they too were "investing energy in navigating the racism within their department" (Truong et al., 2016, p. 236). Examining the culture and the socialization process within the academic programs (e.g., recruitment strategies, onboarding practices, and creating mentoring networks supporting students and faculty) is an important and actionable way for student affairs professionals to become more engaged with practices that hinder or contribute to the student experience, while still recognizing the importance of informal networks for enacting support systems for students of color (Gildersleeve et al., 2011).

Initial Impacts of the COVID-19 Pandemic

2020 and the ensuing academic year brought many new challenges and unknowns, as is illustrated in the National Student Clearinghouse data presented earlier in this chapter. Trends and areas of growth from previous years may be influenced moving forward as institutions shifted delivery methods and general practices because of COVID-19. We have already highlighted initial influences of the COVID-19 global health emergency on international student enrollments, but the impact certainly extended to almost all elements of student and institutional life. Undergraduate enrollment at both private and public institutions decreased between the fall of 2019 and fall of 2020 (National Student Clearinghouse, 2020). Enrollment at Public Two-Year Institutions (Community Colleges) experienced a decrease of 9.5% in their enrollment between fall 2019 and fall 2020 (National Student Clearinghouse). Historically, in times of recession, learners return to higher education (mainly at the community college and graduate level) for some retooling. During the recession of 2016, however, enrollment in graduate programs did decrease overall. The unique economic uncertainty of COVID-19 has led to some unknowns in projecting enrollment at both the undergraduate and graduate level.

Moreover, the rise of COVID-19 across the United States during the spring of 2020 certainly forced many institutions and academic programs to move to online delivery or advance previously piecemeal online program strategies. Remote and hybrid learning became the norm, which continued through the spring and summer of 2021, and higher education professionals had to create support systems in an online environment that continued to acknowledge all three identities of a student (e.g., professional, relational, and personal) who was now experiencing the known challenges of graduate education while in a pandemic (Pifer & Baker, 2014). This move to new modes of support created an interesting paradigm shift for many institutions and academic programs as they had to transition their curriculum (e.g., lectures, labs, and exams) and support services in an online format quickly. For many, this was the first time they were teaching completely online in both a synchronous and asynchronous manner. In 2018, 65.9% of students at public institutions and 69.6% of students at private institutions did not have any distance education courses (NCES, 2019). During the same year, 62.5% of students at private for-profit (proprietary) institutions were exclusively in distance education courses (NCES, 2019). From the graduate student perspective, 30.7% of post-baccalaureate students were in exclusively distance education courses in 2018 (NCES, 2019). Because of COVID-19, the choice to be online for both the institution and the student was limited.

IMPLICATIONS FOR PRACTITIONERS AND PROFESSIONAL IDENTITY

It has now been 15 years since Pontius and Harper (2006) sounded a persuasive call to reexamine misconceptions in the student affairs community about the needs of the graduate populations we highlight in this chapter, and appropriately extend purposeful practices for engagement and support into graduate populations. Indeed, much progress has been made in recent decades to expand the scope and prevalence of effective professionalized student affairs work in graduate degree programs and communities, but we have only scratched the surface of the important work that remains. Given the diverse and varied landscape of graduate students and communities we have summarized here, there is no doubt that these students need and deserve professionals equipped with the requisite knowledge, skills, and abilities to meet their unique needs (see Chapter 3 for more on student needs). Admittedly, meeting these needs will require continued advocacy and formalization of graduate student affairs roles within many campus administrations. Such continued development on a national scale is key if graduate student affairs work is to continue growing beyond historically basic academic support approaches and into more integrative models rooted in holistic graduate student success that acknowledge our diversity of learners.

While many specific student development topics will be treated in much more detail later in this volume, it should be noted here that the current state of graduate education (with its evolving and expanding enrollments, program types, and delivery formats) provides an important lens through which graduate student services must be appraised and understood. Going back to the emergence of the student affairs profession itself in the early part of the 20th century, through the student population expansions of the GI Bill and the crucial diversification of the 1960s through today, our profession has always grown and evolved alongside and in response to the needs of students. As graduate student populations and their associated program formats continue to develop in the ways we have highlighted here, so must graduate student affairs work itself. Moreover, graduate student affairs professionals are positioned to make crucial contributions to the learning, development, and professional socialization of their students. While it may be true that the profession still has room to grow in terms of how student services are systematically enacted for graduate students on a broad scale, we wish to conclude this chapter by highlighting two ways in which contemporary graduate student services work is *already* strongly positioned for the future: the first comes as a result of some of its more pragmatic efficiencies, and the second is tied to the dynamic context of graduate education itself.

First, while graduate student affairs positions, teams, or units are arguably smaller or underfunded in comparison to the correlated undergraduate-serving offices, this small size often results in a necessary sense of focus, efficiency, and boundary-spanning seamlessness in graduate-serving student affairs roles. Graduate student services administrators often wear multiple hats and can collapse and integrate processes and procedures for the benefit of their students. Rarely could any graduate student services operation be accused of so-called *administrative bloat* in this way. Interactions that otherwise may have involved multiple exchanges with offices across academic and student affairs boundaries are often more holistically addressed in the context of a student's advisory relationship with an administrator. Graduate student services roles are also likely to be part of, or at least interact more often with, other aspects of university life rather than housed within large teams of other student affairs professionals who share a functional identity. This larger network can help to check assumptions or test ideas that might otherwise go unchallenged within group-think cultural dynamics. Furthermore, the innate focus at the graduate level on specific program outcomes (often specific research goals, professional career outcomes, or discipline-specific objectives) can provide student services professionals with a powerful tool for both individual motivation/development and community-building initiatives. This sense of purpose also helps to keep academic priorities central to the student experience, and often gives clear academic purpose and significance to the orientations, activities, involvement systems, coaching, and conduct systems that graduate student services professionals enact. In this way, a comparatively leaner and less expansive graduate student affairs function can actually find itself on the strong side of many of the financial and staffing dilemmas facing institutions today. It can be an aspect of our work to be proud of and held up as a model of organizational purpose, efficiency, and student-centricity where it is working well.

A second special and specific element of graduate student services work comes as a direct result of the multitude of academic program formats, disciplinary identities, and delivery modes we have highlighted in this chapter. Indeed, the evolving and innovative character of contemporary graduate education itself almost demands that graduate student affairs professionals continually experiment with new ideas, approaches, and assessments in an effort to meet the needs of their students. Consider, for example, the challenges and opportunities brought on by a reality like the rapid growth of short-term graduate-level certificate programs or one-year specialized/accelerated master's degree programs, where enrollments were recently observed to have doubled in the past decade (Ghee, 2017). These student settings often require administrators to reimagine many of the more traditional process assumptions and even the theoretical underpinnings of traditional student affairs practices. The increasing prevalence of online, part-time, commuting, and working graduate program students can certainly initiate similar considerations where graduate student services professionals provide key solutions to their campuses. In this way, instead of graduate student services professional practice existing on the margins of mainstream student affairs work, it can rightly claim a significant place in conversations about the future of the field itself—a claim most powerfully rooted in the diverse enrollment and innovative program development context summarized here.

As this chapter has discussed, the U.S. graduate education landscape continues to grow and evolve with complexity, all the while promising to become an ever-more important element of U.S. higher education. Graduate students enrolling in these academic experiences deserve student affairs administrators and advocates who are as innovative and ambitious as this graduate education industry itself. In answering this call, student affairs professionals who work with these graduate and professional students must continually seek opportunities to clarify and articulate their unique contributions to the broader student affairs discourse—and in doing so, advocate for the needs of the students we spotlight to be met. We hope that this initial roadmap of the landscape both informs a greater awareness of graduate education today and the indispensable work of graduate student services professionals who support graduate student success.

REFERENCES

American Association of Colleges of Osteopathic Medicine. (2020, November 16). *Applications to Osteopathic Medicine Schools hit all time high*. Retrieved from https://www.aacom.org/news-and-events/news-detail/2020/11/16/applications-to-osteopathic-medical-schools-hit-all-time-high

American Bar Association, Section of Legal Education and Admissions to the Bar. (2021). *Standard 509 disclosure*. Retrieved from http://www.abarequireddisclosures.org/Disclosure509.aspx

Association to Advance Collegiate Schools of Business. (2021). *Survey reports*. Retrieved from https://www.aacsb.edu/data/data-reports/survey-reports

Association of Theological Schools, The Commission on Accrediting. (2021). *Research and data*. Retrieved from https://www.ats.edu/resources/research-and-data

Carnegie Project on the Education Doctorate (n.d.). *The CPED framework*. Retrieved from https://www.cpedinitiative.org/the-framework

Fairchild, E. E. (2003). Multiple roles of adult learners. In D. Kilgore & P. J. Rice (Eds.), *New directions for student services: Meeting the special needs of adult learners* (Vol. 102, pp. 11–16). Josey-Bass. https://doi.org/10.1002/ss.84.

Gardner, S., & Barker, M. (2015). Engaging graduate and professional students. In S. J. Quaye & S. R. Harper (Eds.), *Student engagement in higher education* (pp. 339–354). Routledge.

Gardner, S. K., & Gopaul, B. (2012). The part-time doctoral student experience. *International Journal of Doctoral Studies, 7*, 63–78. http://ijds.org/Volume7/IJDSv7p063078Gardner352.pdf

Gardner, S. K., & Holley, K. A. (2011). Those invisible barriers are real: The progression of first-generation students through doctoral education. *Equity & Excellence in Education, 44*(1), 77–92. https://doi.org/10.1080/10665684.2011.529791

Geiger, R. L. (2016). The ten generations of American higher education. In M. N. Bastedo, P. G. Altbach, & P. J. Gumport (Eds.), *American higher education in the twenty-first century: Social, political, and economic challenges* (4th ed., pp. 3–34). Johns Hopkins University Press.

Ghee, K. (2017, May 31). You're getting a master's in what? *Wall Street Journal.* Retrieved from https://www.wsj.com/articles/youre-getting-a-masters-in-what-1496235600.

Gildersleeve, R. E., Croom, N. N., & Vasquez, P. L. (2011). Am I going crazy?!: A critical race analysis of doctoral education. *Equity & Excellence in Education, 44*(1), 93–114. https://doi.org/10.1080/10665684.2011.539472

Goldin, C., & Katz, L. F. (1999). The shaping of higher education: The formative years in the United States, 1890–1940. *Journal of Economic Perspectives, 13*(1), 37–62. https://scholar.harvard.edu/goldin/files/the_shaping_of_higher_education_the_formative_years_in_the_united_states_1890-1940.pdf

Graduate Management Admission Council. (2021). *Assessment data*. Retrieved from https://www.gmac.com/market-intelligence-and-research/assessment-data

Indiana University Center for Postsecondary Research. (2021, March 19). *2018 update facts & figures*. The Carnegie Classification of Institutions of Higher Education. https://carnegieclassifications.iu.edu/downloads/CCIHE2018-FactsFigures.pdf

Jaschik, S. (2020, November 30). Applications jump to law and medical school. *Inside Higher Ed*. Retrieved from https://www.insidehighered.com/admissions/article/2020/11/30/applications-jump-law-and-medical-school

Law School Transparency Data Dashboard. (n.d.). *Law school enrollment*. Retrieved from https://data.lawschooltransparency.com/enrollment/all/

National Center for Education Statistics. (n.d.). *NCES fast facts tool*. https://nces.ed.gov/fastfacts/display.asp?id=372#College_enrollment

National Center for Science and Engineering Statistics. (2020). *Doctorate recipients from U.S. universities: 2019*. NSF 21–308. National Science Foundation. https://ncses.nsf.gov/pubs/nsf21308/.

National Science Board, National Science Foundation. (2019). Higher education in science and engineering. *Science and Engineering Indicators 2020*. NSB-2019-7. https://ncses.nsf.gov/pubs/nsb20197/.

National Student Clearinghouse Research Center. (2020, November 12). *COVID-19: Stay informed with the latest enrollment information*. National Student Clearinghouse Research Center's Monthly Update on Higher Education Enrollment. National Student Clearinghouse. https://nscresearchcenter.org/stay-informed/

Okahana, H. (2018). *Data sources: Increasing numbers of graduate and professional students are former Pell recipients*. Council of Graduate Schools. https://cgsnet.org/data-sources-increasing-number-graduate-and-professional-students-are-former-pell-recipients-0

Okahana, H., Zhou, E., & Gao, J. (2020). *Graduate enrollment and degrees: 2009 to 2019*. Council of Graduate Schools. https://cgsnet.org/ckfinder/userfiles/files/CGS_GED19_Report_final2.pdf

Omotola McGee, E. (2020). Interrogating structural racism in STEM higher education. *Educational Researcher, 49*(9), 633–644. https://doi.org/10.3102/0013189X20972718

Perry, J. A. (2012). What history reveals about the education doctorate. In M. Macintyre Latte & S. Wunder (Eds.), *Placing practitioner knowledge at the center of teacher education: Rethinking the policy and practice of the education doctorate* (pp. 51–75). Information Age Publishing.

Pifer, M. J., & Baker, V. L. (2014). "It could be just because I'm different": Otherness and its outcomes in doctoral education. *Journal of Diversity in Higher Education, 7*(1), 14–30. https://doi.org/10.1037/a0035858

Pontius, J., & Harper, S. (2006). Principles for good practice in graduate and professional student engagement. In M. J. Gunetzel & B. E. Nesheim (Eds.), *New directions for student services*, No. 115 (pp. 47–58). Jossey-Bass.

Redden, E. (2021, March 30). Another uncertain admissions cycle for International Students. *Inside Higher Ed*. Retrieved from https://www.insidehighered.com/news/2021/03/30/prospective-international-students-face-logistical-hurdles-related-visas-and-travel

Soares, L. (2013). *Post-traditional learners and the transformation of postsecondary education: A manifesto for college leaders*. American Council on Education. http://www.acenet.edu/newsroom/Documents/Post-traditional-Learners.pdf

St. John, E., & Felder, P. (2014). Moving forward: Developing ongoing strategies for supporting graduate students. In P. P. Felder & E. P. St. John (Eds.), *Readings on equal education: Supporting* graduate students in the 21st century: Implications for policy and practice (Vol. 27, pp. 242–252). AMS Press Inc.

Storr, R. J. (1953). *The beginnings of graduate education in America.* The University of Chicago Press.

The Carnegie Classification of Institutions of Higher Education. (n.d.). *About Carnegie classification.* Retrieved from http://carnegieclassifications.iu.edu/.

Thelin, J. R. (2004). *A history of American Higher Education.* The Johns Hopkins University Press.

Truong, K. A., Museus, S. D., & McGuire, K. M. (2016). Vicarious racism: A qualitative analysis of experiences with secondhand racism in graduate education. *International Journal of Qualitative Studies in Education, 29*(2), 224–247. https://doi.org/10.1080/09518398.2015.1023234

U.S. Department of Education. Institute of Education Sciences, National Center for Education Statistics. (n.d.). *The condition of education 2020.* https://nces.ed.gov/programs/coe/

U.S. Department of Education, Institute of Education Sciences, National Center for Education Statistics. (n.d.). *Digest of Education Statistics 2019,* Table 311.15. https://nces.ed.gov/fastfacts/display.asp?id=80

U.S. Immigration and Customs Enforcement. (2021). *SEVIS by the numbers: Annual report on International Student trends.* U.S. Department of Homeland Security. https://www.ice.gov/doclib/sevis/pdf/sevisBTN2020.pdf

Weidman, J. C., Twale, D. J., & Stein, E. L. (2001). *Socialization of graduate and professional students in higher education: A perilous passage?* Prepared and published by Jossey-Bass in cooperation with ERIC Clearinghouse on Higher Education, Association for the Study of Higher Education, Graduate School of Education and Human Development, the George Washington University.

Zhou, E., Mitic, R. R., West, C. P. L., & Okahana, H. (2020). *International graduate applications and enrollment: Fall 2019.* Council of Graduate Schools. Retrieved from https://cgsnet.org/sites/default/files/civicrm/persist/contribute/files/CGS%20Fall%202019%20International%20Report.pdf?v=1

Chapter 3

Overview of Post-baccalaureate Student Needs

Brandon S. McLeod and George S. McClellan

Any meaningful discussion of the needs of post-baccalaureate students ought to begin with an important truth. Graduate students, while having many things in common with undergraduate students and each other, are both distinct from their undergraduate counterparts and incredibly diverse. Commenting on the relative lack of attention in the literature relative to that given to their undergraduate counterparts, Pontius and Harper (2006) state, "Graduate students have specific needs and face developmental challenges that may differ from, but are as important as, those experienced by undergraduates" (p. 48). Guentzel and Nesheim (2006) note with regard to the diversity within the broad construct of graduate students that they "in general are a heterogeneous group, more different than alike across programmatic types, disciplinary affiliations, and individual characteristics and experiences" (p. 2). Failing to recognize these important distinctions and discussing the graduate student experience or graduate students' needs monolithically is, as Guentzel and Nesheim wryly observe, "much like studying elephants, polar bears, and lemurs as members of the animal kingdom to identify their common needs" (p. 2). Weidman et al. also observe, "Graduate student clienteles have changed more than have the programs that attract them" (2001, p. 94). Indeed, graduate and professional students are far more diverse than the institutions that educate them, a circumstance which can make the already challenging task of completion even more difficult.

This chapter makes use of Maslow's Hierarchy of Needs (Maslow, 1987; McLeod, 2020) as a framework for presenting prominent needs of post-baccalaureate students. Specifically, we address some of the more salient physiological, safety, belongingness, esteem, cognitive, aesthetic, self-actualization, and transcendence needs of graduate students. The needs of the student are multifaceted and interconnected and may not fit explicitly into a single Maslowian category. In making use of Maslow's work in this way, we are mindful of the thoughtful critique of that work (see, e.g., Enright, 2018).

DOI: 10.4324/9781003121671-4

We are also mindful that our treatment of the needs of graduate students is by no means comprehensive. Rather, our intention is to provide a substantive introduction to literature, resources, and implications for practitioners. One final note on nomenclature before we move to the heart of our conversation. We make use of the term *graduate students* to include students in masters, doctoral, and terminal professional degree programs throughout for the sake of simplicity of language. We will use group specific language where appropriate.

PHYSIOLOGICAL

Maslow posits that "A person who is lacking food, safety, love, and esteem would probably hunger for food more strongly than for anything else" (1943, p. 373). Physiological needs include those things that are "biological requirements for human survival" (McLeod, 2020). With that in mind, we will explore two issues related to physiological needs: food insecurity and housing insecurity.

Food Insecurity

One review of the literature shows estimates of the rate of food insecurity on college campuses ranging between 35% and 42% (Bruening et al., 2017). Mallinson (2020), in a pilot study focused specifically on graduate students, finds that nearly one in four experienced food insecurity in the past month. Food insecure graduate students report poorer health (Farahbakhsh et al., 2015, 2017; Gallegos et al., 2014; Hughes et al., 2011; Patton-López et al., 2014), difficulty in concentration (Farahbakhsh et al., 2015, 2017; Gallegos et al., 2014; Munro et al., 2013), needing to drop a course (Silva et al., 2017), and lower grade point averages (GPA) (Haskett, Majumder et al., 2020; Patton-López et al., 2014). Food insecurity more frequently affects those students who reported being low socioeconomic status (Gallegos et al., 2014) and those whose primary income was loans or assistantships (Farahbakhsh et al., 2015, 2017), both conditions which describe the experience of many graduate students. Illustrating the need, while graduate students comprise about 20% of the total enrollment at the University of Alberta in Edmonton, 50% of the students who use the campus food bank are graduate students, 46.6% international students, and 24.1% caregivers of children (Farahbakhsh et al., 2015, 2017).

Housing Insecurity

Recent studies of undergraduate and graduate students observe that nearly 10% were homeless at some point in the last year (Haskett, Kotter-Grühn, et al., 2020; Haskett, Majumder, et al., 2020) and 36% were housing insecure within the last year (Goldrick-Rab et al., 2018). Where the rate of food security amongst graduate students may be alarmingly high, it is lower than that for undergraduates. The reverse is true for rates of housing insecurity (Goldrick-Rab et al., 2019). Graduate and professional student housing on campus is much more scarce than undergraduate housing.

There is a broader dimension of housing that must be recognized: housing in the form of legal residence in the United States. Adequately discussing the physiological and other needs of undocumented graduate and professional students is beyond the limitations of this chapter. Readers interested in a detailed discussion of this important topic are encouraged to consult *Navigating Graduate School: Resource Guide for Undocumented Students* (Cook & Gaylord, 2018).

SAFETY

Maslowian safety refers to stability, order, and freedom from fear. We will discuss debt, stress and mental health, sexual harassment, and unionization as issues representative of graduate student safety needs.

Debt

It is understandable, given enrollment demographics, that discussion of college debt often centers on undergraduate students, but graduate students, on average, borrow double the amount of the average undergraduate, approximately $40,000 (Belasco et al., 2014). Belasco et al. note that in the 2011–2012 academic year, graduate students borrowed more than double what was taken out in federal and private loans in 2001–2002 (2014, pp. 469–470). Such dramatic figures often belie the variation of debt across various post-baccalaureate degree categories, with professional students averaging over $100,000 and doctoral students averaging nearly $80,000 in graduate student debt (Webber & Burns, 2020). Professional students take on the highest amount of debt (Delisle et al., 2014), but the biggest increases between 2000 and 2008 were for professional doctorates outside of medicine "in fields such as education (EdD), psychology (PsyD), science or engineering (DSC or D Eng), and ministry (D Min)" (Belasco et al., 2014, p. 480). Similarly, the University of California *Graduate Student Well-Being Survey Report* found that financial confidence was relatively less indicative of life satisfaction for students in science, technology, engineering, and mathematics (STEM) fields than for those in humanities, social sciences, and professional fields, for which it was the second strongest predictor (University of California, 2017). Webber and Burns propose that diminished graduate assistantships are partly to blame, with evidence showing the "average total assistantship amounts in 2016 were lower and fewer students received assistantships than in 2000" (2020, p. 12). Such massive debt "has substantial, negative effects on physical health, mental health, and long-term financial health. Unfortunately, these effects are worse for marginalized individuals" (Wilcox et al., 2019, p. 9). Research indicates that Black/African American students are more profoundly impacted than other groups, and that impact is growing (Belasco et al., 2014; Pyne & Grodsky, 2020; Webber & Burns, 2020; Wilcox et al., 2019). International students are also more likely to report financial issues than domestic students (Hyun et al., 2007). While it is worrying that "nearly 40% of borrowers [are] expected to default on their student loans by 2023" (Webber & Burns, 2020, p. 2), the long-term impact of trying to pay off crushing debt is profoundly troubling. Some researchers liken the student debt crisis to indentured servitude, noting that due to returning to school, consolidation or refinancing the length of a loan term "frequently extends to 30 years...until retirement age" (Williams, 2008, p. 74).

Stress and Mental Health

In addition to financial concerns, one of the most common stressors for graduate students is, unsurprisingly, academics (University of California, 2017). The University of California *Graduate Student Well-Being Survey Report* found that overall health was the strongest predictor of depression among graduate and professional students followed by academic preparation. A majority of students are affected by curricular stress, and the negative effects are more prevalent in women (Amanya et al., 2018; Chapell et al., 2005; Evans et al., 2018; Mallinckrodt & Leong, 1992) and trans* and gender nonconforming (TGNC) students (Evans et al., 2018). Miller (2018) attributes the elevated stress in members of minoritized groups to systemic oppression. Evans et al. indicate graduate students are six times more likely to experience anxiety and depression than the general population, with 41% and 39%, respectively, of graduate students scoring moderate to severe (2018, p. 282). Other studies report similar results for various subpopulations. Stecker (2004), who found significant levels of depression, stress, and substance abuse among graduate and professional students at a medical school, notes that those most at risk were second year female students who were married with children. Similarly, Evans et al. (2018) report among the graduate trainee population that TGNC and female graduate students are significantly more likely than male counterparts to experience anxiety and depression (see also Mallinckrodt & Leong, 1992). It should also be noted that international students, many of whom are graduate students, report mental health needs at the same rate as domestic students and are "significantly less likely to use counseling services" (Hyun et al., 2007, p. 116). This may be due to cultural stigma, lack of awareness, or possible financial constraints.

Career prospects were found to be the strongest predictor of life satisfaction for academic doctoral and professional students across all disciplines (except STEM fields, for which it was the second strongest predictor) (University of California, 2017, pp. 36–37). The COVID-19 pandemic led to the "quickest month-over-month increase in unemployment rates and the highest overall unemployment rate since the [Current Population Survey] data started being collected in 1948" (Falk et al., 2021, p. 2). The impact of career uncertainty, especially in light of increasing student debt, will undoubtedly lead to significant stress and mental health concerns for current and recent graduate and professional students. For a fuller discussion of advising, mentorship, and career pathways for post-baccalaureate students, see Chapter 5.

Sexual Harassment

Financial pressures may be among the reasons that graduate students are vulnerable to sexual harassment. Rosenthal et al. (2016), in a study of rates of sexual harassment of graduate students, state that roughly 35% of both female and male students reported either student or faculty/staff harassment, but not both, and 31% of females and 13.9% of males reported harassment by both a student and faculty/staff member. Female students were 1.64 times more likely to report at least one instance of sexual harassment by faculty than male students. Looking at sexual harassment by program type, female law students were 1.58 times more likely than other female students to experience harassment from a faculty/staff member (1.5× for student harassment). Unsurprisingly, female students felt significantly less safe than male students. A study by the National Academies of Sciences, Engineering, and Medicine found similar results with "almost half of women in medical school or enrolled as a graduate student in a college of medicine reported having experienced some form of sexual harassment" (National Academies of Sciences, Engineering, and Medicine, 2018). Examining graduate students in their dual role as student and teacher, and contrapower vs. traditional sexual harassment, Mohipp and Senn found that male graduate students without teaching experience perceived contrapower harassment as less serious, and a lack of support for feminism was related to victim blaming (2008, pp. 1260–1271).

Cantalupo and Kidder (2018) analyzed litigated cases and Office for Civil Rights (OCR) complaints by students in graduate school from 1998 to 2016 and found that more than half of the perpetrators were serial harassers, noting that in several of the cases, "the faculty member's…tendencies…appear to be 'open secrets'" (p. 869). Cantalupo and Kidder (2018) identify four major areas of concern regarding the vulnerability of graduate students to faculty sexual harassment: the length and structure of academic programs, including the small community the students and faculty inhabit; the power differential between students and faculty, including harassment via quid pro quo and hostile environment; the personal and professional harm experienced by graduate students, especially the negative health effects, and the cultural damage to the academy, especially by serial harassers; and finally, the impact on bystanders.

Another area in need of attention in research and scholarship is the sexual harassment of nonbinary and lesbian, gay, bisexual, transgender, and queer/questioning (LGBTQ+) graduate and professional students. The Association of American Universities' *Report on the AAU Campus Climate Survey on Sexual Assault and Misconduct* does identify TGQN (transgender women and men, nonbinary/genderqueer, gender questioning, or gender not listed) as a variable. The report notes 14.5% of TGQN graduate and professional students reported nonconsensual sexual contact with approximately 33% of the perpetrators being faculty or an instructor (which was a higher percentage than reported by both men and women) and approximately 20% of perpetrators being a coworker (Cantor et al., 2020).

Unionization

One method that some graduate and professional students have used to improve their conditions and disrupt the power differential is unionization. There has been an increase in unionization efforts in recent years and awareness of the need for more protections for graduate student employees (GSEs) (Cain, 2017; Discenna, 2017; Hu et al., 2013; Singh et al., 2006). As Discenna puts it:

> The movement to unionize among GSEs has emerged largely as a response to the exploitation of their labor in light of their diminished opportunities for future academic employment in an academic labor market widely acknowledged to be producing fewer and fewer stable, secure positions under the aegis of the neoliberal assault on higher education.
>
> (2017, p. 80)

The issue is complex and stakeholders go far beyond the walls of the institution.

In most states, public sector employees are prohibited from engaging in a strike. Some states, including Georgia, Texas, Virginia, and the Carolinas, have also made collective bargaining illegal for public sector employees (Sanes & Schmitt, 2014). Barriers to graduate student unionization even include the federal government (Langin, 2019). Even when union tools such as strikes and collective bargaining are not illegal, the university may stand in the way, claiming that "due to their status as students, they cannot simultaneously be employees of the institutions for which they work" (Discenna, 2017, p. 80). Additionally, while graduate students are, in cases of gender (*Washington v. Jackson State University*, 2006) and age (*Becker v. Washington State University*, 2011) discrimination, not considered to be employees under the "compensated purpose test" (Fossey & Eckes, 2015, p. 163), they are considered employees if they perform services in return for compensation. The Boston Medical Center case (*Boston Medical Center*, 1999) applies only to private, nonsectarian institutions, but more universities are recognizing collective bargaining agreements for graduate assistants. This is likely due to universities' increasing dependency on graduate students as "relatively cheap sources of qualified labor, for teaching and related work" (Singh et al., 2006, p. 69). Overall, GSEs at both public and private institutions are shifting toward unionization efforts to protect their rights and influence institutional governance (Hu et al., 2013).

Graduate program faculty, particularly program coordinators and program/department chairs, is well advised to be aware of relevant labor law and to consult frequently with colleagues in Human Resources and Legal Counsel regarding labor issues. The same applies to matters related to discrimination, harassment, and Title IX (Briant, 2016). For a discussion of graduate student unionization's role in student engagement, see Chapter 6.

BELONGINGNESS

Strayhorn (2012), citing the work of Hagerty et al., asserts, "Sense of belonging is a basic human need and fundamental motive, sufficient to drive human behavior...important for human functioning and a critical factor in the psychological wellbeing of individuals" (p. 9). Graduate students' sense of belonging has not only been found to impact retention and completion rates, but also graduate students' interest in pursuing a research or faculty career in academia (Ostrove et al., 2011). Professional socialization, discussed later in this chapter and in greater detail in Chapter 5, is a central function of post-baccalaureate education, and a sense of belongingness is both an important component of and outcome of success in such a program (O'Meara et al., 2017; Weidman et al., 2001). Linley et al. (2016) note the informal interactions with faculty that play an important role in connecting students with the broader campus community.

Sense of belonging can have a significant impact on student success, retention, and quality of life for all graduate students, but students who identify as members of minoritized groups are at greater risk of feeling "marginalized, unsupported, or unwelcome" (Strayhorn, 2012). O'Meara et al. found that underrepresented

47

minority (URM) graduate students were more likely to experience microaggressions, though their analysis also noted that URM students did not differ from non-URM students "in how academic environments (i.e. professional relationships, microaggressions, and microaffirmations) affected their sense of belonging" (O'Meara et al., 2017). It is important when considering socialization, belonging, and student success to heed the insights of Yosso (2005) and not slip into the pitfall of conceiving minoritized students as having a deficit of cultural capital. The deficit is in a system (and individuals) who fail to recognize the value of all forms of cultural capital and not just those favored by the majority and undergirding privilege. Noting both that the majority is context dependent and that this list is therefore incomplete, examples of minoritized groups might include students who identify as disabled; Black, Indigenous, or People of Color (BIPOC); women; lesbian, gay, bisexual, trans*, queer, or other sexual orientation or gender identity (LGBTQ+); international; and parents. We will address issues of belonging for graduate students who identify as members of these groups, but are mindful that identities are intersectional and so the experiences of any individual in these groups will reflect the richness of their identities and the context in which they are operating.

Belongingness is not only important for graduate and professional students while they are in their program, but, at least when it comes to academia, it is also important for their career advancement (O'Meara et al., 2017). Research indicates that academic self-concept, which is affected by a sense of belonging, has a significant impact on academic career commitment (Ostrove et al., 2011; Ülkü-Steiner et al., 2000). Austin (2002) describes the transition from student to professional academic as a socialization process that includes "observing, listening, and interacting with faculty, peers, family, and friends," but notes that most students do not have faculty mentors to guide them (p. 104). As sense of belonging has such a lasting effect on graduate and professional students, it is imperative that faculty, program coordinators/chairs, and administrators develop assessments and programs to identify and address the needs of students who do not feel a sense of belonging.

Students with Disabilities

Approximately 12% of graduate students have a disability (National Center for Educational Statistics, 2016). Obermark notes, "Graduate students should not be on the periphery when considering the intersections of disability and higher education; in fact, they are often the innovative leaders in this conversation" (2019, p. 182). One of the most prominent aspects of belongingness and students with disabilities is in relation to disclosure. For some students, disclosure is not optional as their disability is visible or prominent, but for many students, disclosure is "not a singular event" (Kerschbaum et al., 2017, p. 1), it is a "continual process of evaluation, negotiation, and reevaluation" (Stewart & Collins, 2014, p. 26). Indeed, a study by Verdinelli and Kutner (2016) revealed that many graduate students with disabilities chose online programs so their disability remained invisible to the instructors, classmates, or even disability services. Some of the participants in the study felt that by not revealing, they were putting themselves on equal footing (despite equity issues) with their classmates and avoiding stigma. Similarly, Venville et al. reveal students felt that keeping the disability to themselves diminished "the power of the illness, and others, over the self" (as cited by Pearson & Boskovich, 2019, p. 9). Obermark's participants described the need to "'adjust,' 'adapt,' be 'very able,' 'accommodate' themselves, 'learn something regardless,' or 'muddle through... and figure it out.' These words belie the invisible but substantial labor of the reverse accommodation...[ironically making] disability and difference itself increasingly invisible as well" (2019, p. 194).

Carter et al. (2017) state:

> disabled graduate students must navigate a complex web of power. The connections among academic norms and rituals; institutional policies; hierarchies of race, nation, class, gender, and sexuality; and the corporeality of our bodies present circumstances that are distinct from the struggles of disabled undergraduate students or disabled faculty members.
>
> (2017, p. 96)

Stodden and Conway note that graduate students with disabilities are sometimes faced with the choice of succeeding in either their coursework or academic employment opportunities (2003, p. 16). However, involvement is not limited to the ability to participate as a graduate instructor or research assistant. Students may not even be fully aware of the equitable access available to them. One study found fewer than half of graduate teaching assistants (GTAs) (35%) and even fewer faculty (18%) reported announcing that arrangements are available for students with disabilities. In addition, only 34% of GTAs and 18% of faculty even included the availability of accommodations in the syllabus (Bruder & Mogro-Wilson, 2010).

Intersectionality also plays a role. In Carter et al.'s (2017) qualitative inquiry, a neurodivergent participant discussed how they had difficulties participating within the LGBTQ+ community: "Staying out late, being at shows or clubs, or even going to Pride impacts my bodymind, and I soon decided these activities weren't 'worth it.' As a result, I've felt disconnected and alienated from my community" (2017, p. 107). Thankfully that participant was able to connect with a "neuro-queer community" that they could identify with and develop a stronger sense of belonging.

BIPOC

The use of BIPOC as an acronym is the subject of critique (Garcia, 2020). Our usage of it is not intended to conflate the experiences of minoritized, colonized, and oppressed peoples. Where research refers to a specific population, we will use the language of the authors.

Inclusion for BIPOC begins before admission. Traditional recruitment methods "may exclude entire communities because of both proximity and cultural unease" (Young & Brooks, 2008, p. 397). Even after admission, BIPOC students are frequently excluded, either implicitly or explicitly, from the larger campus community. Campuses have "socially, physically, or programmatically made them think that they do not belong, are not welcome, and are not expected to succeed" (Cheatham & Phelps, 1995, p. 93). The lack of belonging is echoed by the participants of Windchief et al.'s (2018) study on developing an Indigenous mentoring program for Native graduate students in STEM as well as in Limas's (2019) study of Latinx graduate student experiences, Solórzano's (1998) study of Chicana and Chicano graduate students, and Nadal et al.'s (2010) research on the experiences of Filipino American graduate students. ChixApkaid (2013) additionally describes the need for Native students to be represented on committees at all levels and the need for campus-wide support networks. Writing on marginality for graduate students of color, Gay (2004) describes "the absence of a critical mass of peers and professors from their own ethnic groups places psycho-emotional burdens on graduate students of color that are different from those that affect European Americans" (p. 268).

Students need to see themselves represented in the faculty (Cheatham & Phelps, 1995; Cooke et al., 2020; Evangelista et al., 2020; Hubain et al., 2016; Nadal et al., 2010; Windchief et al., 2018). Additionally, it is important that BIPOC not be coerced into being spokespersons for their entire culture, ethnic group, or color of their skin (Cheatham & Phelps, 1995; Gay, 2004; Hubain et al., 2016; Robinson, 2013). Inclusion needs to be anti-racist (Clark & Hurd, 2020; Najdowski et al., 2020; Young & Brooks, 2008) and deliberately incorporated into the curriculum to "center the voices of marginalized and oppressed individuals" (Najdowski et al., 2020, p. 11).

Women

Fox (2001) asserts, "Academic women have already survived barriers of selection—both self-selection...and selection by institutions" (p. 656). Even after admission, Russo et al. (1985) found that "women, particularly in professional training programs traditionally dominated by men, report significantly more faculty hostility and social isolation" (as cited by Mallinckrodt & Leong,

1992, p. 717). Mallinckrodt and Leong's study additionally supported the finding that women have less social support in their graduate programs than men. While not directly associated with belonging, there is also the issue of "role strain," where women have competing expectations (Benshoff et al., 2015). Additionally, LaFollette (2016), in studying doctoral student mothers in a professional psychology program, notes that women "leak" out of the academic pipeline at rates much higher than men, citing high workloads and perceived lack of institutional support (at both the graduate and postgraduate level).

Examining graduate women of color and peer relationships at majority white urban institutions, Apugo, citing research, describes the experiences as "isolating, treacherous, and psychologically taxing" (2017, p. 361)—a point also made by Robinson (2013)—and notes microaggressive behavior that "involved GMBW [Graduate Millennial Black Women] going unnoticed, underestimated, silenced, and having their ideas dismissed or passed off" (2017, p. 362). Moses (1989) notes, "Black female students are often excluded from the informal and social aspects of their departments and institutions—sometimes by white women as well as by white men" (p. 4).

LGBTQ+

What people who identify as members of the LGBTQ+ need most is community (Couillard & Higbee, 2018, p. 15). As implied by Couillad and Higbee, this community can be difficult to find or join, especially when considering intersectional identities. Miller (2018) found that those with disabilities who are also in the LGBTQ+ community viewed their identities as parallel, with some noting that both are stigmatized. At least one participant described disability discrimination within the gay community. There are additional stressors for LGBTQ+ people of color as well (Nadal, 2019). Goldberg et al.'s (2019) study revealed a majority of TGNC graduate students felt concern for their safety on campus. Another study found that 57% of graduate and undergraduate students at the University of Nevada, Reno, had experienced discrimination due to their sexual identity (Haley, 2017). Carter et al. shared the story of a trans*-masculine student who had to abandon their gender identity in order to qualify for certain scholarships (2017). Graduate assistants in Catalano and Tillapaugh's study felt that the university did not fully support them, but rather they were just trying to show they have diversity without committing—exemplified by their requirement to work "within the norms of sexuality and gender, while [being] expected to change campus climate and support students experiencing oppression" (2020, p. 10). Parr (2020) found that sexual or gender minority and racial or ethnic minority students had significantly lower scores on belonging and flourishing than their cisgendered, heterosexual, and white counterparts, respectively. While Linley et al. (2016) note the importance of inclusive language, Nadal's research shows the importance of network and coalition building within one's community, not to wait for academia to invite you to the table, quoting "one of the mantras of LGBTQSOC is: 'If you don't get invited to the table, build your own table'" (2019, p. 15).

International Students

International students may also struggle with a sense of belonging (Glass et al., 2015). One participant in Phelps's (2016) study referred to having a "liminal world" (p. 8). Multiple participants discussed not feeling a sense of belonging in any particular place in the world. Trice (2004) finds that students who were the most similar to U.S. students were most likely to interact with U.S. students (i.e., western European, fluent in English, familiar with U.S. culture, etc.), but interaction does not necessarily equate to a sense of belonging. Even if it did, it leaves out the majority of the world and certainly the majority of international students in the United States (who predominantly come from India and China, representing 53% of the total international student population combined) (Institute of International Education, 2020). That noted, Glass's study revealed that international graduate students' interactions with professors improved their sense of belonging (2015, pp. 358–359). They may face additional difficulties due to parenting: "Parenthood is an often invisible aspect of doctoral student lives, and parents embarking on international study comprise unique iterations of life in transnational social spaces which serves to expand the global social imaginary for future generations" (Phelps, 2016, p. 9).

Parents

Graduate students who are pregnant or parenting can feel socially isolated from their peers (Larkins, 2015; Springer et al., 2009; Wladkowski & Mirick, 2019). Part of the reason for this may be due to nonparent students having more negative stereotypes regarding pregnancy and motherhood (Shafir, 2005). Although sometimes subtle, "there are constant reminders in the social and physical environment of the university that graduate student parents and their children do not truly belong" (Springer et al., 2009, p. 5). Moreover, participants in Larkins's study of pregnant graduate students also found themselves reevaluating their relationship with their advisor, finding they were primarily a source for course schedules and procedures rather than mentors, affecting their overall satisfaction and sense of support. Lack of institutional support is a recurring theme for pregnant and parenting graduate students (see Brown & Nichols, 2013; DuBransky, 2014; Hill,

2020). Bosch (2013), describing the work of Lynch, describes the dual role of student and mother and the practice of downplaying "their maternal role at university, and…their student role outside university" (p. 59) to ensure success in both roles. Cuny and Aspray, in their article on recruitment and retention of women graduate students in computer science and engineering, describe the importance of campus childcare options and family friendly departmental policies for both male and female students (2002, p. 172). Mentorship also plays an important role in assisting pregnant and parenting students not just complete their programs, but also feel supported, understood, and comfortable (Wladkowski & Mirick, 2019).

The *Family Friendly Campus Toolkit* (Program Evaluation and Research Group (PERG) at Endicott College, 2020) provides an excellent framework for supporting pregnant and parenting students. Additionally, The American Council on Education's (n.d.) website is a helpful resource to learn about supporting the needs of specific student populations.

ESTEEM

Maslowian esteem can be divided into esteem for oneself (dignity) and desire for reputation (respect) from others (McLeod, 2020). This section will focus on esteem through the lenses of power and celebration. In the life of a graduate student, "Balance is the power or means to decide" (Brus, 2006, p. 35). Professors and administrators need to be aware of the types of challenges in students' lives and work to give them the "power or means" to succeed even given those challenges. In this regard, departmental culture is tantamount (Ferreira, 2003; Hirt & Muffo, 1998). There is a wide array of potential challenges for graduate students both inside and outside the institution. While there is a limited amount that can be done regarding life outside the institution, in some cases, the institutional factors have been described as dehumanizing (Pierson, 2018).

The contributions of graduate students to their campus communities, both academic and social, too often go unrecognized. However, this is not to say they go unnoticed. It may rather be the case that appreciation goes unexpressed. In thinking about graduate esteem, advisors and administrators should remember to "Celebrate students, their backgrounds and achievements" (Strayhorn, 2012, p. 103). These efforts do not need to be costly to be impactful. They simply need to be deliberate, heartfelt, and ongoing.

COGNITIVE

Curiosity and a yearning for knowledge are generally considered prerequisites of post-baccalaureate students. We will focus on professional development, mentoring, and their roles in helping students develop in their disciplines. For a further discussion of advising and mentoring, see Chapter 5.

Professional Development

Weidman et al. (2001) rightly point out, "Whether support is financial, tutorial, social, or emotional, the needs of all students must be considered in the socialization and professionalization process" (p. 95). Weidman et al. (2001), drawing on the work of Thornton and Nardi, identify four stages of socialization of graduate students: anticipatory, formal, informal, and personal, with three core elements: knowledge acquisition, investment, and involvement. Rizzolo et al. (2016) and Duchney et al. (1997) propose similar professional development models that center on continuing one's education in their field or as it relates to job readiness, developing peer and mentor relationships, and finding balance. Moreover, Cheatham and Phelps note that when teaching and research assistantships are available, minority students improve academically and in satisfaction, though in general, at predominantly white institutions, they are dissatisfied due to the lack of opportunity (1995, p. 94). Duchney et al. feel that professional development should be an integral and a structured part of an academic program. Even with these models, however, there is "little clarity about exactly what professional development is and how it is achieved and enhanced" (Duchney et al., 1997, p. 87). An important aspect of professional development is mentoring.

Mentoring

Linley et al. (2016) explain that mentors are not just providing training in the field and academic advising, they are confidants and advocates. International students with involved advisors were less likely to report significant stress or emotional problems in the last year (Hyun et al., 2007, p. 116). Mentors, in a more tangible and direct way than coursework, show students how to succeed in their field. They help the students see themselves as professionals and teach them how to function independently. Mentors directly contribute to agency. Numerous studies have described the need for mentorship to support BIPOC graduate students (Najdowski et al., 2020; Windchief et al., 2018). Thomas et al. (2007) warn, however, against the notion that students of color should only be mentored by faculty of color. Nesheim et al. (2006) also point to the need for support for persistence and retention. On the flip side, Nelson and Berube observe, "Those faculty members who do little or no graduate training thus have an almost parasitic relationship to graduate-student employment: Their own salaries are sustained by exploiting teaching assistants" (as cited in Discenna,

2017, p. 86). Gilmore et al. (2016) also write about faculty perceptions of supporting graduate student success. Speaking of doctoral students, faculty located the issues within students, pointing primarily to motivation. Motivation is highly personalized, thus emphasizing the need for local and frequent assessment. Mentors should seek to develop that confidant relationship, so that they can better understand and assist their mentees.

AESTHETIC

Aesthetics in the Maslowian sense relates not just to beauty but also to form and balance (McLeod, 2020), which we relate to the importance of place and space, which is explored in detail in Chapter 8. It is recommended that instructors and campus administrators follow Universal Design for Learning (Couillard & Higbee, 2018; Damiani & Harbour, 2015; Pearson & Boskovich, 2019; Terras et al., 2015):

> With universal design in education, instructors can try to design curricula for a broad range of users from the beginning rather than changing everything or adding on individual accommodations later each time a different student shows up in a course.
>
> (Damiani & Harbour, 2015, p. 410 citing McGuire & Scott, 2006;
> Rose et al., 2006)

Couillard and Higbee, in particular, note the importance of intersectionality and interdependence in regards to expanding universal design (UD) to include students of varying gender identities and sexual orientations (see Universal Design for Learning Center, 2020).

Couillard and Higbee discuss the importance of physical space in UD. They expand UD beyond students with disabilities and classroom instruction to include the LGBTQ+ community advocating for inclusive restrooms, locker rooms, and housing. Barton et al. (2002) additionally address the resource and service needs of graduate and professional students in libraries. As with other needs, some students may or may not be able to take full advantage of what is available: "I mostly find that students with disabilities *underutilize* resources and accommodations, especially in professional settings in which they are struggling to be seen as comparable to their nondisabled peers" (emphasis theirs) (Olkin, 2009, p. 83).

UD grants access to learning materials and resources in such an equitable way that begins to address some of the systemic barriers which limit so many of our students. While UD is just one dimension of the post-baccalaureate experience, it is one which permeates all corners of the campus and classroom. As educators and administrators, we must make every effort to keep our classes and campuses from hindering our students. By designing curricula and campuses for everyone, we create an environment where students have the opportunity to unlock their full potential.

SELF-ACTUALIZATION

Self-actualization refers to realizing one's own potential. The culmination of this is role, identity formation, and agency. These important aspects, however, can be derailed by imposterism.

Role and Identity Formation

Graduate and professional students frequently struggle with role and identity formation (see the work of Weidman et al. (2001) on socialization). They have already achieved something noteworthy, but in their fields they are still learning and developing. Role transitions can be particularly difficult if the role from which the student is transitioning and the role into which they are transitioning are substantially different from one another: for example, the role variance for military-affiliated students who are entering graduate study (a transition which, to date, has received scant attention in the literature). These issues are further compounded when considering intersectional identities. It is much more difficult to see oneself as part of a department or field when there are few (or none) that you can identify with. There may also be problematic viewpoints within institutions. Jonas Zdanys, while he was Associate Dean of the Graduate Schools of Arts and Sciences at Yale, stated, "Being a graduate student is being caught between college and adulthood" (Discenna, 2017, p. 85). Discenna rightly contends that this type of statement infantilizes GSEs: "Graduate students are frequently both teachers and students; still this duality doesn't give them more leeway, it gives them less" (Sharnoff, 1993, p. 7). Almost half of all teaching assistants are fully responsible for one or more courses (Benjamin, 2002). One study by Saxe et al. (2017) found that interprofessional workshops can help PharmD and Advanced Practice Nursing (APN) students develop an increased perception of importance for the other discipline. Extrapolating from these results could suggest that by developing a better understanding of other's roles, one comes to better understand their own role. Role and identity formation may be further hindered by career prospects, with one report showing just 53% of graduate and professional students being "upbeat" about their postgraduate prospects (University of California, 2017). With role and identity formation in mind, researchers note the importance of the mentor/mentee relationship and the positive relationship between belonging and academic self-concept (Austin, 2002; Curtin et al., 2013; Damiani & Harbour, 2015; Glass et al., 2015). Young and Brooks (2008) list mentoring as one of the keys to supporting graduate students of color.

Agency

The mentoring experience is important for developing students' competency and perceived level of autonomy "toward a variety of tasks, not just those purely centered in research, teaching, or service alone" as well as a successful graduate experience (Cass et al., 2017). Studies additionally show that increasing graduate student confidence and self-efficacy increases interest in pursuing a faculty path (McConnell et al., 2018). Pierson (2018) describes the importance of "inclusion into the preexisting culture formed by department members." She emphasizes the "tenuousness and scarcity of agency" that GTAs have and urges departments to consider the ways that agency is undermined or subverted. Agency is what allows graduate to see themselves as (burgeoning) professionals.

Imposterism

Role and identity formation as well as the development of agency can both be disrupted by imposterism. The concerns of first-generation students in graduate and professional education, in regards to what is often referred to imposter syndrome or imposter phenomenon, is well documented in the literature, including explorations of intersectional identities as they relate to the first-generation experience (Gardner & Holley, 2011; Holley & Gardner, 2012; Leyva, 2011; Lounsbery, 2014; Lubrano, 2004; Moua, 2018; Scruggs, 2019; Vasil & McCall, 2018). Chakraverty, in his study of Black doctoral and postdoctoral students in STEM, linked the imposter phenomenon to six themes: "(1) Being the only-one, (2) Lack of belonging, (3) Stereotyping, micro-aggression and judgment, (4) External appearances, (5) Feeling like the 'diversity enhancers,' and (6) Complications of intersecting identities" (2020, p. 433–434). One of his participants, in describing institutional disadvantages for Black students, eloquently noted: "Some of them [disparities] are subtle and some of them are not so subtle. These disparities, they're cumulative. They widen over time. They have a multiplier effect and you never get caught up" (2020, p. 444). The feelings this student expressed are strongly related to the need of belongingness. Students from the Linley et al. (2016) study discuss the importance of professors who are members of their own community. Ewing et al. (1996) found that academic self-concept and racial identity relate to imposter feelings, though when academic self-concept is omitted, worldview is a stronger predictor than racial identity.

57

TRANSCENDENCE

Transcendence refers to motivation beyond one's self, including religion, spirituality, sex, aesthetics, and even the pursuit of science (McLeod, 2020). It is in this realm that self-care lies. "Self-care is the ongoing practice of self-awareness and self-regulation for the purpose of balancing psychological, physical, and spiritual needs of the individual" (Carter & Barnett, 2014, p. xiii). Institutionally, supporting graduate students' transcendence needs may look like campus spaces for prayer and meditation, green spaces to experience nature, and health centers that provide support and education regarding sexual health. Moreover, as graduate students approach the end of their programs, they increasingly become mentors to other graduate students (generativity). This pivot is because they want to give back/pay forward or possibly provide the support that they were lacking, now that they are a bit less in full-on survival mode and realize they have the ability to help other people. While these needs are, from an institutional perspective, secondary to safety, belongingness, esteem, and the others, they are still important for graduate success.

CONCLUSION

We have used a Maslowian framework to highlight the needs of graduate students across programs and degree types. Other chapters of the book will offer deeper insight into specific issues. One of the key takeaways from this overview should be that graduate students' needs are diverse, complex, and interconnected. Indeed, evidence suggests that, following ecological systems theory, alleviating one issue can lead to improvement in other areas of concern. Of course, the converse is also true. Practitioners and researchers must be mindful and take a holistic approach and frequently assess their students' needs individually and programmatically. The Basic Needs program, available on a number of campuses in the University of California system, is an example of one such holistic approach (*Basic Needs*, 2021). In conclusion, we share the following four frameworks offered in the literature of supporting the success of graduate students. We believe they can be really helpful across a wide array of students, academic programs, and types of institutions.

Pontius and Harper (2006) suggest seven principles for good practice in graduate student engagement. They are:

- Continuously strive to eradicate marginalization among underrepresented populations
- Provide meaningful orientation to the institution beyond academic units
- Invest resources in communication with graduate and professional students

- Facilitate opportunities for community building and multicultural interaction across academic units
- Partner with academic schools and departments to create engagement plans for students
- Enhance career and professional development
- Systematically assess satisfaction, needs, and outcomes

One might operationalize the principles by focusing on the specific areas of action identified by Young and Brooks, building on Freeman and others:

> Effective support includes an interrelated set of complex and protean factors. Such factors include (a) the diversity and alignment of curricular offerings, (b) recruitment and retention of faculty of color, (c) procurement and availability of financial assistance, (d) effective mentoring, provision of networking opportunities, and (e) assistance in interpreting the hidden curriculum of educational institutions and graduate programs that can reproduce and perpetuate inequity.
>
> (2008, p. 396)

Though Young and Brooks were exploring supporting graduate students of color, these factors are applicable across the board.

More technically focused is the recommendation from Grapin et al. endorsing the use of multitiered systems of support (MTSS) (2015). The MTSS approach aligns with ecological systems theory which:

> posits that individuals and their environments are mutually reinforcing and inextricably linked. Thus, problems experienced by the individual (e.g. adjustment, social, emotional, and academic difficulties) are conceptualized as a discordance between individual factors (e.g., existing knowledge and skills) and environmental factors (e.g., institutional demands and supports).
>
> (Grapin et al., 2015, p. 343)

A simple step is to explicitly invite students to take part in existing programs and services. Rooted in a public health model of prevention and intervention as well as problem-solving methodology, the three tiers are:

- Primary: all students, range of positive outcomes (e.g., academic writing support)
- Secondary: targeted for those with elevated risk (e.g., groups for stress workshops); and
- Tertiary: individualized, intensive, specialized (Grapin et al., 2015).

The fourth and final framework hearkens back to the list of principles from Pontius and Harper (2006). As a function of necessity, we have offered broad and generalized comments. Really doing powerful work, however, has to be localized: you can build on scholarship, but it must be applied at the local level. It is essential therefore that institutions develop comprehensive, thoughtful, and ongoing programs of assessment focused on the needs and experiences of graduate students on their campus. The case studies in Chapters 4–9 describe specific examples of meeting post-baccalaureate student needs in practice; for an in-depth discussion of assessment, see Chapter 9. Simply collecting data and piling it on a shelf is insufficient. A genuine commitment and follow-through are necessary to help ensure the needs of graduate students are met.

REFERENCES

Amanya, S. B., Nakitende, J., & Ngabirano, T. D. (2018). A cross-sectional study of stress and its sources among health professional students at Makerere University, Uganda. *Nursing Open*, 5(1), 70–76. https://doi.org/10.1002/nop2.113

American Council on Education. (n.d.). *Meeting the needs of underserved students*. Retrieved November 21, 2020, from https://www.higheredtoday.org/policy-research/student-support-success/meeting-needs-underserved-students/

Apugo, D. L. (2017). "We all we got": Considering peer relationships as multi-purpose sustainability outlets among millennial Black women graduate students attending majority white urban universities. *The Urban Review*, 49(2), 347–367. https://doi.org/10.1007/s11256-017-0404-2

Austin, A. E. (2002). Preparing the next generation of faculty: Graduate school as socialization to the academic career. *The Journal of Higher Education*, 73(1), 94–122. https://doi.org/10.1080/00221546.2002.11777132

Barton, H., Cheng, J., Clougherty, J. F., Persson, D. M., Walters, C., & Washington-Hoagland, C. (2002). Identifying the resource and service needs of graduate and professional students. *Libraries and the Academy*, 2(1), 125–143. https://doi.org/ 10.1353/pla.2002.0014

Basic Needs. (2021). *Berkeley basic needs*. https://basicneeds.berkeley.edu/

Becker v. Washington State University, 266 P. 3d ____ (Wash: Court of Appeals, 3rd Div. 2011).

Belasco, A. S., Trivette, M. J., & Webber, K. L. (2014). Advanced degrees of debt: Analyzing the patterns and determinants of graduate student borrowing. *The Review of Higher Education*, 37(4), 469–497. https://doi.org/10.1353/rhe.2014.0030

Benjamin, E. (2002). How over-reliance on contingent appointments diminishes faculty involvement in student learning. *Peer Review*, 1995, 4–10.

Benshoff, J. M., Cashwell, C. S., & Rowell, P. C. (2015). Graduate students on campus: Needs and implications for college counselors. *Journal of College Counseling*, 18(1), 82–94. https://doi.org/10.1002/j.2161-1882.2015.00070.x

Bosch, B. (2013). *Women who study: Balancing the dual roles of postgraduate student and mother* [Unpublished doctoral thesis, Edith Cowan University]. Retrieved from https://ro.ecu.edu.au/theses/592

Boston Medical Center. (1999). 330 N.L.R.B. 152. Retrieved from https://casetext.com/admin-law/boston-medical-center-corp

Briant, T. L. (2016). Title IX and graduate and professional students: How student affairs professionals can guide disclosure considerations. *Common Purpose: 2016 NASPA Annual Conference: The Annual Knowledge Community Conference Publication.* Retrieved from https://www.naspa.org/images/uploads/main/2016KCPublication.pdf

Brown, V., & Nichols, T. R. (2013). Pregnant and parenting students on campus: Policy and program implications for a growing population. *Educational Policy, 27*(3), 499–530. https://doi.org/10.1177/0895904812453995

Bruder, M. B., & Mogro-Wilson, C. (2010). *Student and faculty awareness and attitudes about students with disabilities.* http://scholarspace.manoa.hawaii.edu/handle/10125/58440

Bruening, M., Argo, K., Payne-Sturges, D., & Laska, M. N. (2017). The struggle is real: A systematic review of food insecurity on postsecondary education campuses. *Journal of the Academy of Nutrition and Dietetics, 117*(11), 1767–1791. https://doi.org/10.1016/j.jand.2017.05.022

Brus, C. P. (2006). Seeking balance in graduate school: A realistic expectation or a dangerous dilemma. In M. J. Guentzel & B. E. Nesheim (Eds.), *Supporting graduate and professional students: The role of student affairs (New Directions in Student Services)* (Vol. 115, pp. 31–46). Jossey-Bass. https://doi.org/10.1002/ss.214

Cain, T. R. (2017). Campus unions: Organized faculty and graduate students in U.S. higher education. *ASHE Higher Education Report, 43*(3), 7–163. https://doi.org/10.1002/aehe.20119

Cantalupo, N. C., & Kidder, W. C. (2018). A systematic look at a serial problem: Sexual harassment of students by university faculty. *Utah Law Review, 2018,* 671. https://heinonline.org/HOL/Page?handle=hein.journals/utahlr2018&id=697&div=&collection=

Cantor, D., Fisher, B., Chibnall, S., Harps, S., Townsend, R., Thomas, G., Lee, H., Kranz, V., Herbison, R., & Madden, K. (2020). *Report on the AAU campus climate survey on sexual assault and misconduct.* The Association of American Universities, Westat. https://www.aau.edu/sites/default/files/AAU-Files/Key-Issues/Campus-Safety/Revised%20Aggregate%20report%20%20and%20appendices%201-7_(01-16-2020_FINAL).pdf

Carter, A. M., Catania, R. T., Schmitt, S., & Swenson, A. (2017). Bodyminds like ours: An autoethnographic analysis of graduate school, disability, and the politics of disclosure. In *Negotiating Disability: Disclosure and Higher Education* (pp. 95–113).

Carter, L. A., & Barnett, J. E. (2014). *Self-care for clinicians in training: A guide to psychosocial wellness for graduate students in psychology.* Oxford University Press.

Cass, C., Kirn, A., Tsugawa, M. A., Perkins, H., Chestnut, J. N., Briggs, D. E., & Miller, B. (2017, June 24). *Board # 18: Improving performance and retention of engineering graduate students through motivation and identity formation.* ASEE Annual Conference & Exposition. https://peer.asee.org/board-18-improving-performance-and-retention-of-engineering-graduate-students-through-motivation-and-identity-formation

Catalano, D. C., & Tillapaugh, D. (2020). Identity, role, and oppression: Experiences of LGBTQ resource center graduate assistants. *Journal of Student Affairs Research and Practice,* 1–13. https://doi.org/10.1080/19496591.2019.1699104

Chakraverty, D. (2020). The impostor phenomenon among Black doctoral and postdoctoral scholars in STEM. *International Journal of Doctoral Studies, 15,* 433–460. https://doi.org/10.28945/4613

Chapell, M. S., Blanding, Z. B., Silverstein, M. E., Takahashi, M., Newman, B., Gubi, A., & McCann, N. (2005). Test anxiety and academic performance in undergraduate and graduate students. *Journal of Educational Psychology, 97*(2), 268–274. https://doi.org/10.1037/0022-0663.97.2.268

Cheatham, H. E., & Phelps, C. E. (1995). Promoting the development of graduate students of color (EJ545750). *New Directions for Student Services, 72*, 91–99. ERIC. https://eric.ed.gov/?id=EJ545750

ChiXapkaid, M. P. (2013). How institutions can support Native professional and graduate students. In S. C. Lowe, S. J. Waterman, J. Garland, & H. J. Shotton (Eds.), *Beyond the asterisk: Understanding Native students in higher education* (pp. 125–138). Stylus Publishing, LLC. http://ebookcentral.proquest.com/lib/olemiss/detail.action?docID=3037603

Clark, U. S., & Hurd, Y. L. (2020). Addressing racism and disparities in the biomedical sciences. *Nature Human Behaviour, 4*(8), 774–777. https://doi.org/10.1038/s41562-020-0917-7

Cook, S., & Gaylord, I. (2018). Navigating graduate school: Resource guide for undocumented students. *Immigration Law & Policy Practicum Projects, 1*, 52. https://digitalcommons.law.scu.edu/cgi/viewcontent.cgi?article=1002&context=stu-immigration

Cooke, N., Warren, K., Brown, M., & Jackson, A. (2020). It starts at home: Infusing radical empathy into graduate education. *Journal of Critical Library and Information Studies, 3*(Radical Empathy in Archival Practice (Pre-Prints)), 1–23. https://scholarcommons.sc.edu/libsci_facpub/295

Couillard, E. K., & Higbee, J. (2018). *Expanding the scope of universal design: Implications for gender identity and sexual orientation.* https://doi.org/10.3390/EDUCSCI8030147

Cuny, J., & Aspray, W. (2002). Recruitment and retention of women graduate students in computer science and engineering: Results of a workshop organized by the computing research association. *ACM SIGCSE Bulletin, 34*(2), 168–174. https://doi.org/10.1145/543812.543852

Curtin, N., Stewart, A. J., & Ostrove, J. M. (2013). Fostering academic self-concept: Advisor support and sense of belonging among international and domestic graduate students. *American Educational Research Journal, 50*(1), 108–137. https://doi.org/10.3102/0002831212446662

Damiani, M., & Harbour, W. (2015). Being the wizard behind the curtain: Teaching experiences of graduate teaching assistants with disabilities at U.S. universities. *Innovative Higher Education, 40*(5), 399–413. https://doi.org/10.1007/s10755-015-9326-7

Delisle, J., Phillips, O., & Van der Linde, R. (2014). *The graduate student debt review: The state of graduate student borrowing.* New America Education Policy Program.

Discenna, T. A. (2017). *Discourses of denial: The rhetoric of American academic labor.* Routledge.

DuBransky, T. D. (2014). *Employed graduate student mothers: The benefits, challenges, and perspectives of women fulfilling student, family, and worker roles* (UMI 3682891) [Doctoral dissertation, University of California, Santa Barbara]. ProQuest Dissertations Publishing.

Duchney, K., Alletzhauser, H. L., Crandell, D., & Schenider, T. R. (1997). Graduate student professional development. *Professional Psychology: Research and Practice, 28*, 87–91. https://doi.org/10.1037/0735-7028.28.1.87

Enright, R. (2018, May 24). *Why Maslow's self-actualization theory is not quite right.* Psychology Today. https://www.psychologytoday.com/blog/the-forgiving-life/201805/why-maslows-self-actualization-theory-is-not-quite-right

Evangelista, D. A., Goodman, A., Kohli, M. K., Bondocgawa Maflamills, S. S. T., Samuel-Foo, M., Herrera, M. S., Ware, J. L., & Wilson, M. (2020). Why diversity matters among those who study diversity. *American Entomologist, 66*(3), 42–49. https://doi.org/10.1093/ae/tmaa037

Evans, T. M., Bira, L., Gastelum, J. B., Weiss, L. T., & Vanderford, N. L. (2018). Evidence for a mental health crisis in graduate education. *Nature Biotechnology, 36*(3), 282–284. https://doi.org/10.1038/nbt.4089

Ewing, K. M., Richardson, T. Q., James-Myers, L., & Russell, R. K. (1996). The relationship between racial identity attitudes, worldview, and African American graduate students' experience of the imposter phenomenon. *Journal of Black Psychology, 22*(1), 53–66. https://doi.org/10.1177/00957984960221005

Falk, G., Carter, J. A., Nicchitta, I. A., Nyhof, E. C., & Romero, P. D. (2021). *Unemployment rates during the COVID-19 pandemic: In brief* (p. 16). Congressional Research Service. https://fas.org/sgp/crs/misc/R46554.pdf

Farahbakhsh, J., Ball, G. D. C., Farmer, A. P., Maximova, K., Hanbazaza, M., & Willows, N. D. (2015). How do student clients of a university-based food bank cope with food insecurity? *Canadian Journal of Dietetic Practice and Research: A Publication of Dietitians of Canada = Revue Canadienne De La Pratique Et De La Recherche En Dietetique: Une Publication Des Dietetistes Du Canada, 76*(4), 200–203. https://doi.org/10.3148/cjdpr-2015-020

Farahbakhsh, J., Hanbazaza, M., Ball, G. D. C., Farmer, A. P., Maximova, K., & Willows, N. D. (2017). Food insecure student clients of a university-based food bank have compromised health, dietary intake and academic quality. *Nutrition & Dietetics, 74*(1), 67–73. https://doi.org/10.1111/1747-0080.12307

Ferreira, M. (2003). Gender issues related to graduate student attrition in two science departments. *International Journal of Science Education, 25*(8), 969–989. https://doi.org/10.1080/09500690305026

Fossey, R., & Eckes, S. (Eds.). (2015). *Contemporary issues in higher education law* (3rd ed.). Education Law Association.

Fox, M. F. (2001). Women, science, and academia: Graduate education and careers. *Gender & Society, 15*(5), 654–666. https://doi.org/10.1177/089124301015005002

Gallegos, D., Ramsey, R., & Ong, K. W. (2014). Food insecurity: Is it an issue among tertiary students? *Higher Education, 67*(5), 497–510. https://doi.org/10.1007/s10734-013-9656-2

Garcia, S. E. (2020, June 17). Where did BIPOC come from? *The New York Times.* https://www.nytimes.com/article/what-is-bipoc.html

Gardner, S. K., & Holley, K. A. (2011). "Those invisible barriers are real": The progression of first-generation students through doctoral education. *Equity & Excellence in Education, 44*(1), 77–92. https://doi.org/10.1080/10665684.2011.529791

Gay, G. (2004). Navigating marginality en route to the professoriate: Graduate students of color learning and living in academia. *International Journal of Qualitative Studies in Education, 17*(2), 265–288. https://doi.org/10.1080/09518390310001653907

Gilmore, J., Wofford, A. M., & Maher, M. A. (2016). The flip side of the attrition coin: Faculty perceptions of factors supporting graduate student success. *International Journal of Doctoral Studies, 11*, 419–439. Retrieved from http://www.informingscience.org/Publications/3618

Glass, C. R., Kociolek, E., Wongtrirat, R., Lynch, R. J., & Cong, S. (2015). Uneven experiences: The impact of student-faculty interactions on international students' sense of belonging. *Journal of International Students, 5*(4), 353–367. https://doi.org/10.32674/jis.v5i4.400

Goldberg, A. E., Kuvalanka, K., & Dickey, L. (2019). Transgender graduate students' experiences in higher education: A mixed-methods exploratory study. *Journal of Diversity in Higher Education, 12*(1), 38–51. https://doi.org/10.1037/dhe0000074

Goldrick-Rab, S., Baker-Smith, C., Coca, V., Looker, E., & Williams, T. (2019, April). *College and university basic needs insecurity: A national #RealCollege survey report* [report on annual survey results]. Hope Center for College, Community and Justice. Retrieved from https://tacc.org/sites/default/files/documents/2019-04/hope_realcollege_report.pdf

Goldrick-Rab, S., Richardson, J., Schneider, J., Hernandez, A., & Cady, C. (2018, April). *Still hungry and homeless in college* [report on annual survey results]. Wisconsin HOPE

Lab, Madison, WI. Retrieved from https://www.pdx.edu/student-access-center/sites/g/files/znldhr1891/files/2020-08/Wisconsin-HOPE-Lab-Still-Hungry-and-Homeless_0.pdf

Grapin, S. L., Lee, E. T., & Jaafar, D. (2015). A multilevel framework for recruiting and supporting graduate students from culturally diverse backgrounds in school psychology programs. *School Psychology International*, *36*(4), 339–357. https://doi.org/10.1177/0143034315592270

Guentzel, M. J., & Nesheim, B. E. (2006). Editors' notes. In M. J. Guentzel & B. E. Nesheim (Eds.), *New Directions for Student Services* [Special issue: Supporting graduate and professional students: The role of student affairs], *2006*(115), 1–3. https://doi.org/10.1002/ss.211

Haley, J. R. (2017). *OUTnumbered: Assessing the LGBTQ campus climate at the University of Nevada, Reno* [Thesis]. https://scholarworks.unr.edu//handle/11714/1977

Haskett, M. E., Kotter-Grühn, D., & Majumder, S. (2020). Prevalence and correlates of food insecurity and homelessness among university students. *Journal of College Student Development*, *61*(1), 109–114. https://doi.org/10.1353/csd.2020.0007

Haskett, M. E., Majumder, S., Kotter-Grühn, D., & Gutierrez, I. (2020). The role of university students' wellness in links between homelessness, food insecurity, and academic success. *Journal of Social Distress and Homelessness*, 1–7. https://doi.org/10.1080/10530789.2020.1733815

Hill, M. E. (2020). "You can have it all, just not at the same time": Why doctoral students are actively choosing singlehood. *Gender Issues*, 1–25. https://doi.org/10.1007/s12147-020-09249-0

Hirt, J. B., & Muffo, J. A. (1998). Graduate students: Institutional climates and disciplinary cultures. *New Directions for Institutional Research*, *1998*(98), 17–33. https://doi.org/10.1002/ir.9802

Holley, K. A., & Gardner, S. (2012). Navigating the pipeline: How socio-cultural influences impact first-generation doctoral students. *Journal of Diversity in Higher Education*, *5*(2), 112–121. https://doi.org/10.1037/a0026840

Hu, S., Henderson, C. E., & Iacino, J. (2013). Student governance and involvement in institutional leadership. In K. M. Craig & P. J. Schloss (Eds.), *Organization and administration in higher education* (p. 66). Routledge.

Hubain, B. S., Allen, E. L., Harris, J. C., & Linder, C. (2016). Counter-stories as representations of the racialized experiences of students of color in higher education and student affairs graduate preparation programs. *International Journal of Qualitative Studies in Education*, *29*(7), 946–963. https://doi.org/10.1080/09518398.2016.1174894

Hughes, R., Serebryanikova, I., Donaldson, K., & Leveritt, M. (2011). Student food insecurity: The skeleton in the university closet. *Nutrition & Dietetics*, *68*(1), 27–32. https://doi.org/10.1111/j.1747-0080.2010.01496.x

Hyun, J., Quinn, B., Madon, T., & Lustig, S. (2007). Mental health need, awareness, and use of counseling services among international graduate students. *Journal of American College Health*, *56*(2), 109–118. https://doi.org/10.3200/JACH.56.2.109-118

Kerschbaum, S. L., Eisenman, L. T., & Jones, J. M. (2017). *Negotiating disability: Disclosure and higher education*. University of Michigan Press.

LaFollette, J. R. (2016). *Matching moms: Understanding how doctoral student mothers in professional psychology programs experience training and the APPIC match* (UMI 10111943) [Doctoral dissertation, Indiana University]. ProQuest Dissertations Publishing.

Langin, K. (2019, September 20). Grad student unions dealt blow as proposed new rule says students aren't 'employees.' *Science*. https://web.archive.org/web/20201112042440/https://www.sciencemag.org/careers/2019/09/grad-student-unions-dealt-blow-proposed-new-rule-says-students-aren-t-employees

Larkins, E. L. (2015). *Pregnancy and the academy: A phenomenological exploration of the experience of pregnant graduate students* [Master's thesis, Oregon State University]. https://ir.library.oregonstate.edu/concern/graduate_thesis_or_dissertations/vh53x057m

Leyva, V. L. (2011). First-generation Latina graduate students: Balancing professional identity development with traditional family roles. *New Directions for Teaching and Learning, 2011*(127), 21–31. https://doi.org/10.1002/tl.454

Limas, I. (2019). *Latinx graduate students' experiences* (UMI 13862213) [Master's thesis, California State University, Long Beach]. ProQuest Dissertations Publishing.

Linley, J. L., Nguyen, D., Brazelton, G. B., Becker, B., Renn, K., & Woodford, M. (2016). Faculty as sources of support for LGBTQ college students. *College Teaching, 64*(2), 55–63. https://doi.org/10.1080/87567555.2015.1078275

Lounsbery, N. B. (2014). *Who am I? Who am I supposed to be? First generation graduate student experiences of identity negotiation* [Doctoral dissertation, South Dakota State University]. *Electronic Theses and Dissertations.* 269. https://openprairie.sdstate.edu/etd/269

Lubrano, A. (2004). *Limbo: Blue-collar roots, white-collar dreams.* Wiley.

Mallinckrodt, B., & Leong, F. T. L. (1992). Social support in academic programs and family environments: Sex differences and role conflicts for graduate students. *Journal of Counseling & Development, 70*(6), 716–723. https://doi.org/10.1002/j.1556-6676.1992.tb02154.x

Mallinson, D. J. (2020). Food insecurity among public administration graduate students. *Teaching Public Administration.* https://doi.org/10.1177/0144739420935964

Maslow, A. H. (1943). A dynamic theory of human motivation. *Psychological Review, 50*(4), 370–396. https://doi.org/10.1037/h0054346

Maslow, A. H. (1987). *Motivation and personality* (3rd ed.). Pearson Education.

McConnell, S. C., Westerman, E. L., Pierre, J. F., Heckler, E. J., & Schwartz, N. B. (2018). United States National Postdoc Survey results and the interaction of gender, career choice and mentor impact. *ELife, 7*, e40189. https://doi.org/10.7554/eLife.40189

McLeod, S. (2020, March 20). *Maslow's hierarchy of needs.* Simply Psychology. https://www.simplypsychology.org/maslow.html

Miller, R. A. (2018). Toward intersectional identity perspectives on disability and LGBTQ identities in higher education. *Journal of College Student Development, 59*(3), 327–346. https://doi.org/10.1353/csd.2018.0030

Mohipp, C., & Senn, C. Y. (2008). Graduate students' perceptions of contrapower sexual harassment. *Journal of Interpersonal Violence, 23*(9), 1258–1276. https://doi.org/10.1177/0886260508314299

Moses, Y. T. (1989). *Black women in academe. Issues and strategies* (ED311817). ERIC. https://eric.ed.gov/?id=ED311817

Moua, M. (2018). Navigating graduate education as a first-generation, Hmong American woman: An autoethnography. *Hmong Studies Journal, 19*(1). Retrieved from http://www.hmongstudies.org/MouaHSJ19.pdf

Munro, N., Quayle, M., Simpson, H., & Barnsley, S. (2013). Hunger for knowledge: Food insecurity among students at the University of KwaZulu-Natal. *Perspectives in Education, 31*(4), 168–179. https://hdl.handle.net/10520/EJC151336

Nadal, K. L. (2019). Queering and browning the pipeline for LGBTQ faculty of color in the academy: The formation of the LGBTQ scholars of color national network. *Journal of Critical Thought and Praxis, 8*(2), Article 2. https://doi.org/10.31274/jctp.8210

Nadal, K. L., Pituc, S. T., Johnston, M. P., & Esparrago, T. (2010). Overcoming the model minority myth: Experiences of Filipino American graduate students. *Journal of College Student Development*, *51*(6), 694–706. https://doi.org/10.1353/csd.2010.0023

Najdowski, A., Gharapetian, L., & Jewett, V. (2020). *Towards the development of antiracist and multicultural graduate training programs in behavior analysis.* PsyArXiv. https://doi.org/10.31234/osf. io/384vr

National Academies of Sciences, Engineering, and Medicines. (2018). *Sexual harassment of women: Climate, culture, and consequences in academic sciences, engineering, and medicine.* https://doi. org/10.17226/24994

National Center for Education Statistics. (2016). *National postsecondary student aid study, graduate.* https://nces.ed.gov/surveys/npsas

Nesheim, B. E., Guentzel, M. J., Gansemer-Topf, A. M., Ross, L. E., & Turrentine, C. G. (2006). If you want to know, ask: Assessing the needs and experiences of graduate students. In M. J. Guentzel & B. E. Nesheim (Eds.), *New Directions for Student Services* [Special issue: Supporting graduate and professional students: The role of student affairs], *2006* (115), 5–17. https://doi.org/10.1002/ss.212

Obermark, L. E. (2019). Making space for the misfit: Disability and access in graduate education in English. *College English*, *82*(2), 173–203. https://www.proquest.com/scholarly-journals/ making-space-misfit-disability-access-graduate/docview/2329717207/se-2?accountid= 14512.

Olkin, R. (2009). The three Rs of supervising graduate psychology students with disabilities: Reading, writing, and reasonable accommodations. *Women & Therapy*, *33*(1–2), 73–84. https:// doi.org/10.1080/02703140903404788

O'Meara, K. A. Griffin, K., Kuvaeva, A., Nyunt, G., & Robinson, N. T. (2017). Sense of belonging and its contributing factors in graduate education. *International Journal of Doctoral Studies*, *12*, 251–279. https://doi.org/10.28945/3903

Ostrove, J. M., Stewart, A. J., & Curtin, N. L. (2011). Social class and belonging: Implications for graduate students' career aspirations. *The Journal of Higher Education*, *82*(6), 748–774. https://doi.org/10.1080/00221546.2011.11777226

Institute of International Education. (2020). *Open doors report on international exchange.*

Parr, N. J. (2020). Differences in the age-varying association of school belonging with socioemotional flourishing among minority and non-minority college and university students. *Journal of American College Health*, 1–5. Advance online publication. https://doi. org/10.1080/07448481.2020.1808662

Patton-López, M. M., López-Cevallos, D. F., Cancel-Tirado, D. I., & Vazquez, L. (2014). Prevalence and correlates of food insecurity among students attending a midsize rural university in Oregon. *Journal of Nutrition Education and Behavior*, *46*(3), 209–214. https://doi. org/10.1016/j.jneb.2013.10.007

Pearson, H., & Boskovich, L. (2019). Problematizing disability disclosure in higher education: Shifting towards a liberating humanizing intersectional framework. *Disability Studies Quarterly*, *39*(1), Article 1. https://doi.org/10.18061/dsq.v39i1.6001

Phelps, J. M. (2016). International doctoral students' navigations of identity and belonging in a globalizing university. *International Journal of Doctoral Studies*, *11*, 1–14. https://doi. org/10.28945/3397

Pierson, C. (2018). *Neither teacher nor scholar: Identity and agency in a graduate teacher's life* [Master's thesis, University of Central Florida]. *Electronic Theses and Dissertations, 2004–2019.* 5994. https://stars.library.ucf.edu/etd/5994

Pontius, J. L., & Harper, S. R. (2006). Principles for good practice in graduate and professional student engagement. In M. J. Guentzel & B. E. Nesheim (Eds.), New Directions for Student Services [Special issue: Supporting graduate and professional students: The role of student affairs], 2006(115), 47–58. https://doi.org/10.1002/ss.215

Program Evaluation & Research Group (PERG) at Endicott College. (2020). Family friendly campus toolkit [Toolkit]. https://www.endicott.edu/family-friendly-campus-toolkit

Pyne, J., & Grodsky, E. (2020). Inequality and opportunity in a perfect storm of graduate student debt. Sociology of Education, 93(1), 20–39. https://doi.org/10.1177/0038040719876245

Rizzolo, S., DeForest, S. R., DeCino, D. A., Strear, M., & Landram, S. (2016). Graduate student perceptions and experiences of professional development activities. Journal of Career Development, 43(3), 195–210. https://doi.org/10.1177/0894845315587967

Robinson, S. J. (2013). Spoketokenism: Black women talking back about graduate school experiences. Race Ethnicity and Education, 16(2), 155–181. https://doi.org/10.1080/13613324.2011.645567

Rosenthal, M. N., Smidt, A. M., & Freyd, J. J. (2016). Still second class: Sexual harassment of graduate students. Psychology of Women Quarterly, 40(3), 364–377. https://doi.org/10.1177/0361684316644838

Sanes, M., & Schmitt, J. (2014, March). Regulation of public sector collective bargaining in the states [Report]. Center for Economic and Policy Research. Retrieved from https://core.ac.uk/download/pdf/71365218.pdf

Saxe, J. M., Balano, K., Wamsley, M., Nakajima, M., & Brock, T. (2017). Promoting role clarity for health professional students participating in an interprofessional behavior change counseling workshop. Journal of Allied Health, 46(2), 35E-37E.

Scruggs, A. (2019). A guidebook to assist more first generation graduate students: Overcoming the invisible barriers [Master's thesis, California State University, Northridge]. https://scholarworks.calstate.edu/downloads/dz010t462

Shafir, D. Z. (2005). Stereotypes among psychology graduate students toward peers who are pregnant/mothers (UMI 3195997) [Doctoral dissertation, Texas Woman's University]. ProQuest Dissertations Publishing.

Silva, M. R., Klenert, W. L., Sheppard, A. V., Cantrell, K. A., Freeman-Coppadge, D. J., Tsoy, E., Roberts, T., & Pearrow, M. (2017). The relationship between food security, housing stability, and school performance among college students in an urban university. Journal of College Student Retention: Research, Theory & Practice, 19(3), 284–299. https://doi.org/10.1177/1521025115621918

Sharnoff, E. (1993, December 27–30). Neither fish nor fowl: Graduate students, unionization, and the academy (ED375473) [Paper presentation]. Annual meeting of the Modern Language Association. Toronto, ON, Canada. ERIC. https://eric.ed.gov/?id=ED375743

Singh, P., Zinni, D. M., & Maclennan, A. F. (2006). Graduate Student Unions in the United States. Journal of Labor Research, 27(1), 55–73. http://umiss.idm.oclc.org/login?url=http://search.ebscohost.com/login.aspx?direct=true&db=s3h&AN=19651292&site=ehost-live&scope=sit

Solórzano, D. G. (1998). Critical race theory, race and gender microaggressions, and the experience of Chicana and Chicano scholars. International Journal of Qualitative Studies in Education, 11(1), 121–136. https://doi.org/10.1080/095183998236926

Springer, K. W., Parker, B. K., & Leviten-Reid, C. (2009). Making space for graduate student parents: Practice and politics. Journal of Family Issues, 30(4), 435–457. Article https://doi.org/10.1177/0192513X08329293

Stecker, T. (2004). Well-being in an academic environment. *Medical Education, 38*, 465–478. https://doi.org/10.1046/j.1365-2929.2004.01812.x

Stewart, D.-L., & Collins, K. (2014). CONSTRUCTING DISABILITY Case studies of graduate students and new professionals with disabilities in student affairs. *College Student Affairs Journal, 32*(1), 19–33.

Stodden, R. A., & Conway, M. A. (2003). Supporting individuals with disabilities in postsecondary education. *American Rehabilitation, 27*(1), 24–33. https://www.researchgate.net/profile/Robert-Stodden/publication/237814129_Supporting_Individuals_with_Disabilities_in_Postsecondary_Education/links/0c96052e1b10a6dfb7000000/Supporting-Individuals-with-Disabilities-in-Postsecondary-Education.pdf

Strayhorn, T. L. (2012). *College students' sense of belonging: A key to educational success for all students.* Routledge. https://doi.org/10.4324/9780203118924

Terras, K., Leggio, J., & Phillips, A. (2015). Disability accommodations in online courses: The graduate student experience (EJ1083812). *Journal of Postsecondary Education and Disability, 28*(3), 329–340. ERIC. https://eric.ed.gov/?id=EJ1083812

Thomas, K. M., Willis, L. A., & Davis, J. (2007). Mentoring minority graduate students: Issues and strategies for institutions, faculty, and students. *Equal Opportunities International, 26*(3), 178–192. https://doi.org/10.1108/02610150710735471

Trice, A. G. (2004). Mixing it up: international graduate students' social interactions with American students. *Journal of College Student Development, 45*(6), 671–687. https://doi.org/10.1353/csd.2004.0074

Ülkü-Steiner, B., Kurtz-Costes, B., & Kinlaw, C. R. (2000). Doctoral student experiences in gender-balanced and male-dominated graduate programs. *Journal of Educational Psychology, 92*(2), 296–307. https://doi.org/10.1037//0022-0663.92.2.296

Universal Design for Learning Center. (2020, August 31). UDL Center. https://medium.com/udl-center/learning-anywhere-anytime-and-for-anyone-back-to-school-during-covid-19-48d2dbc10bd8

University of California. (2017). *Graduate student well-being survey report.* https://www.ucop.edu/institutional-research-academic-planning/_files/graduate_well_being_survey_report.pdf

Verdinelli, S., & Kutner, D. (2016). Persistence factors among online graduate students with disabilities. *Journal of Diversity in Higher Education, 9*(4), 353–368. https://doi.org/10.1037/a0039791

Vasil, M., & McCall, J. M. (2018). The perspectives of two first-generation college students pursuing doctoral degrees in music education. *Journal of Music Teacher Education, 27*(2), 67–81. https://doi.org/10.1177/1057083717717464

Washington v. Jackson State University, 532 F. Supp. 2d ___ (Dist. Court, SD Mississippi 2006).

Webber, K. L., & Burns, R. (2020). Increases in graduate student debt in the US: 2000 to 2016. *Research in Higher Education.* https://doi.org/10.1007/s11162-020-09611-x

Weidman, J. C., Twale, D. J., & Stein, E. L. (2001). *Socialization of graduate and professional students: A perilous passage?* (ED457710) [(ASHE-ERIC Higher Education Report, 28(3), Jossey-Bass Higher and Adult Education Series]. ERIC. https://eric.ed.gov/?id=ED457710

Wilcox, M. M., Barbaro-Kukade, L., Pietrantonio, K. R., & Franks, D. N. (2019). It takes money to make money: Inequity in psychology graduate student borrowing and financial stressors. *Training and Education in Professional Psychology.* https://doi.org/10.1037/tep0000294

Williams, J. J. (2008). Student debt and the spirit of indenture. *Dissent, 55*(4), 73–78. https://doi.org/10.1353/dss.2008.0076

Windchief, S., Arouca, R., & Brown, B. (2018). Developing an Indigenous mentoring program for faculty mentoring American Indian and Alaska Native graduate students in STEM: A qualitative study. *Mentoring & Tutoring: Partnership in Learning, 26*(5), 503–523. https://doi.org/10.1080/13611267.2018.1561001

Wladkowski, S. P., & Mirick, R. G. (2019). Mentorship in doctoral education for pregnant and newly parenting doctoral students. *Journal of Women and Gender in Higher Education, 12*(3), 299–318. https://doi.org/10.1080/26379112.2019.1654394

Yosso, T. J. (2005). Whose culture has capital? A critical race theory discussion of community cultural wealth. *Race Ethnicity and Education, 8*(1), 69–91. https://doi.org/10.1080/1361332052000341006

Young, M. D., & Brooks, J. S. (2008). Supporting graduate students of color in educational administration preparation programs: Faculty perspectives on best practices, possibilities, and problems. *Educational Administration Quarterly, 44*(3), 391–423. https://doi.org/10.1177/0013161X08315270

PART II

STATE OF THE FIELD

Successful Strategies for Graduate and Professional Student Affairs

Chapter 4

Transition to Graduate and Professional School

Tammy Briant Spratling and Sarah Valdovinos

Student Affairs as a profession is inherently focused on the undergraduate experience, except for a few graduate and professional school professionals. This attention often leads to misconceptions about the unique characteristics and needs of graduate and professional students who are uniquely situated within the university environment, as discussed in Chapter 3. As a result, the graduate and professional student onboarding and orientation experience can be limited in scope and quality compared to the robust and integrated offerings available during a typical undergraduate orientation.

Access and engagement with student services and support, often through an orientation model, are key to increasing retention and persistence in a graduate program (Poock, 2004). Graduate and professional students are involved with the university in ways that are different compared to undergraduate students due to program-specific training and coursework, teaching assistantships, research output, departmental expectations, and academic engagement. However, graduate and professional students are still navigating a new experience and, as discussed in Chapter 3, face many similar challenges such as stress and anxiety, navigating university structures and resources, finding opportunities for connection, and networking amongst peers and the wider campus community. Stress and anxiety are common within the graduate student community (Hullinger & Hogan, 2014), and stressors such as finances, navigating academic expectations, family obligations, adjustments to a new location or new country in the case of international students, all impact the student experience.

Graduate and professional students are most successful when Student Affairs professionals understand and address the unique needs of these students and, in turn, advocate for specific programming that supports their onboarding needs. This chapter presents key elements of graduate and professional student onboarding and orientation, including planning, implementation, and assessment. Three case studies bring in real-time, transferable examples of data and evidence-based practice. This chapter then concludes with an exploration of pre- and post-orientation programming that provides holistic support for graduate and professional students.

KEY CONSIDERATIONS FOR ONBOARDING GRADUATE AND PROFESSIONAL STUDENTS

Graduate and professional school programs set similar yet distinct learning objectives and goals for their new student orientation programs. Consistent aspects include creating a sense of belonging, covering necessary logistics, and ensuring students are tooled for success. As admitted students matriculate into graduate and professional schools, elements from traditional undergraduate orientation programs can be tailored to graduate school orientation programs to create a comprehensive new experience. These programs are often separate and apart from undergraduate first-year experience programs and are decentralized from the main university. Individual professional schools, master's programs, and doctoral programs may coordinate their own student orientations. Where first-year programs may be run primarily by student affairs professionals, graduate and professional programs may be coordinated by both student affairs and academic affairs professionals. Involvement of faculty and academic advisors in orientation planning respects the heightened academic focus and rigor found in graduate and professional programs.

Fostering a Sense of Belonging

Orientation programs foster a sense of belonging for the student in their academic program and with other students in the program. A sense of belonging can positively impact pre-matriculation retention. In the authors' experience, the more students feel connected to the school or other students, the more likely they are to stick with their acceptance decision. Admissions professionals may create online portals or social media pages to encourage admitted students to connect with one another before orientation. Those coordinating graduate and professional school orientation can work with admissions professionals to purposefully transition these portals and pages to use during the academic program.

Many graduate and professional students are organized into cohorts. While social media may create space for connection upon admissions, orientation programs offer the first formalized opportunity for students to connect with their fellow cohort members. Student affairs professionals can cultivate a sense of connectedness and belonging amongst and between new students. Networking, team building, or icebreakers may be incorporated into official orientation

74

programming or arranged informally. Upper-level students may serve as peer advisors to help support new students. Having recently been in their shoes, upper-level students are best positioned to tell new students "what it is really like." Student affairs professionals may create formalized programs that train upper-level students as orientation leaders or "ambassadors" to teach new students all they need to know to be best prepared to start their program.

Covering Onboarding Logistics

Whether university-wide or departmentally focused, orientation for new graduate and professional students should offer robust and varied experiences for students to connect with the institution. Orientations should include opportunities for students to take care of university administrative matters when possible. Setting aside time during an orientation program or providing a checklist of action items can help students understand requirements, help graduate and professional students navigate their first experiences on campus, and establish timelines for completing necessary tasks before coursework begins. Some of these tasks include picking up a student ID card, enrolling in the student health plan, creating institutional email accounts and logins, and gaining access to important software and digital tools. Given the departmental-specific nature of graduate education, institutions should consider baseline requirements that all entering graduate students should complete in addition to departmental-specific needs.

There may also be logistical components that are best coordinated or executed by the centralized university. One example is compliance with federal laws such as the Violence Against Women Act (VAWA). Many universities maintain a centralized Title IX Office responsible for ensuring all students engage in the same sexual misconduct and violence prevention education. The centralized Title IX Office may require all university students to complete an online program or Title IX professionals may present in-person at all decentralized orientations. Consistent with federal law, the university will ensure all students receive the same training and are introduced to the same support resources. The centralized university may also coordinate graduate and professional new student orientation components such as overviews to campus life and university-wide services, campus emergency services, parking, and receiving student identification.

Ensuring Graduate and Professional Students are Tooled for Success

At the University of California, Los Angeles (UCLA), Graduate Student Orientation activities include many stakeholders from across the university, including student services and academic support programs. Graduate student orientation programs should include ample opportunity for engagement with university resources and support services. Some areas to consider include centers focused on counseling, research, teaching, and health, and student resource offices such as housing, career services, student activities, student union services, volunteer center, legal services, transportation offices, and community entertainment (on-campus theater, concerts, etc.), among others. Institutions should consider models for engagement to ensure students are well informed but also have the opportunity for direct engagement. A tabling fair, virtual resource fair, open house, resource guide, or resource website are some options to consider when engaging with university resource and support services. When offering a departmental- or school-specific orientation, consider partnering with university-wide orientation services if available to coordinate and reiterate important campus information and services. For example, if graduate and professional students consistently ask for more information about mental health services, identify whether the university-wide orientation offers a tabling fair, a tailored workshop, or other opportunities where graduate and professional students could receive additional support. Many university services are open to all university students. Encourage university partners to highlight when specific services or offerings are available to graduate and professional students, as many students assume these services are only open to undergraduates.

In addition to general university-wide services, identify ways to include them in programmatic efforts of affinity groups and specific resources. As an example, UCLA's Equity, Diversity, and Inclusion Day, a part of the graduate orientation programming, includes opportunities for students to connect with multiple community centers and organizations on campus. Affinity group-specific resources could include diversity/multicultural centers, programs for students with dependents, students who are Black, Indigenous, or People of Color (BIPOC), lesbian, gay, bisexual, transgender, and queer/questioning (LGBTQ+) students, undocumented students, first-generation students, and international students. These offices often not only provide their own programming and services but also offer essential community spaces for graduate and professional students to connect outside of their department and with communities in which they identify. In addition to inviting community-specific resources to the orientation, consider the ways in which broader university-wide resources can address the needs of diverse graduate and professional student communities. For example, the Professional Development Office may have a workshop about working with faculty advisors and could integrate information throughout about unique challenges the advisor relationship may bring for marginalized communities and how to overcome them. Institutions should also consider developing opportunities for affinity spaces such as student identity panels, networking hours, discussion groups, and student organization sessions focused on specific identities.

By design and necessity, graduate and professional school programs narrow in on specific academic pursuits and careers. For professional school graduates, these careers often have professional expectations and licensing requirements. Therefore, many graduate and professional programs are not only teaching substantive material but also "how to act like a lawyer, doctor, teacher, etc." Professional expectations are often first introduced during orientation as a programmatic theme. Students learn ethics, professionalism expectations, and skill development. At Stetson University College of Law, new students attend a professionalism lunch where they are introduced to important ethical considerations for law students and lawyers. Students may be required to take a professional oath like that found in their profession such as an oath of attorney for law students or the Hippocratic Oath for medical students. Student affairs professionals coordinating orientation experiences assist students in taking their educational pursuit as a serious first step to their future career.

Parental and Family Involvement

A key element found in many undergraduate first-year orientation programs is family member involvement, particularly parents. Many undergraduate colleges and universities develop concurrent orientation programs specifically designed for parents. Historically, there has been far less parental and family involvement at the graduate and professional level. However, those student affairs administrators creating graduate and professional programs should consider whether family involvement would contribute to student success. For instance, law and medical students struggle with mental health and are less likely to seek professional help (Organ et al., 2016; Selvaraj & John, 2020). Setting family expectations and tooling families with resources to help support their loved ones may serve an important and perhaps life-saving purpose. At Stetson University College of Law, an orientation welcome reception is open to family and friends to engage new students' support networks during the first step in their legal education. Graduate and professional school orientation is a perfect time to initiate family engagement.

CONSIDERATIONS FOR SPECIAL POPULATIONS

Students Who Transfer into Graduate and Professional Programs

While some graduate programs do not allow for transferring, it is a common practice in professional schools. Orientation efforts for professional school transfer students can range from completing a checklist to a full orientation program like that found in the academic program's initial matriculation. Professional school transfer students already have a track record for academic success. Therefore, learning objectives for these transfer student orientations are usually tailored to introductions to support services and exploring timely academic opportunities (such as upper-level electives, internships, and career planning). Additional professional school transfer orientation topics include registration, financial aid, housing information, student life, experiential learning, and career opportunities.

Students Who Commute and Distance Learners

Graduate and professional student affairs professionals may also consider commuter student orientation needs. Orientation programs for commuters at the graduate level can include networking events and programs that address their unique challenges. These programs may be coordinated through the graduate or professional school or a centralized Office of Commuter Services.

Students from Historically Underrepresented Groups

As discussed in Chapter 3, practitioners working with graduate and professional students should consider the unique needs of students who have not been historically represented in graduate and professional school programs when planning student orientation experiences. BIPOC experiences and stressors are compounded by systemic racism, isolation, lack of mentoring, microaggressions, hostile campus and departmental climate, identity stressors, mental health, and coping (Brunsma et al., 2017). LGBTQ+ students experience homophobia and transphobia, an unwelcoming campus climate, harassment, violence, and acts that invalidate their identity (Vaccaro, 2012). First-generation students may not know how to access the information to succeed and feel lost navigating a graduate program which is further compounded by family and support networks being unfamiliar with the graduate school experience (Lunceford, 2011). International students experience difficulty navigating a new home environment, cultural expectations, xenophobia, discrimination, and increased amounts of stress (Bang & Montgomery, 2013). Graduate and professional student affairs professionals can increase support for these students by tapping into centralized university resources or developing their own support systems.

Students with Assistantships

Some graduate programs require an assistantship as an academic requirement. In assistantships, students learn-by-doing in placements similar to what they will experience in their future careers. Where an assistantship is required, students usually interview for open positions. Frequently, placement supervisors and students rank their choices to be matched together. In Higher Education and Student Affairs graduate programs, assistantships may qualify as tuition where students work in the assistantship to cover the costs of their academic program. Unfortunately, in times when higher education funding is strained, it is these assistantship positions that are often first for budget cuts. Administrators supporting these graduate students should understand the unique academic implications for students who have had their assistantship eliminated due to budget constraints.

Assistantships and fellowships can continue orientation efforts to cultivate belonging. Student Affairs professionals serving graduate and professional students should coordinate their efforts with those who oversee these opportunities on campus. Case Study 1 discusses how the Rackham Merit Fellowship (RMF) at the University of Michigan (U-M) is an excellent example of how a fellowship can be used to cultivate belonging for graduate students.

CASE STUDY 1

By Emma Flores-Scott

Title: Rackham Merit Fellowship Connection

Institution: University of Michigan (large, public, research institution)

Problem of Practice: At University of Michigan (U-M), the Rackham Merit Fellowship (RMF) is a prestigious award designed to sustain the academic excellence and inclusiveness of the graduate student community. By offering financial assistance to those students who might not otherwise have access, this fellowship aims to reduce disparities in graduate education by encouraging the admission and funding of students who represent a broad array of life experiences and perspectives. The RMF community includes a higher percentage of former Pell recipients, underrepresented minority (URM) students, females, and first-generation college students compared to the general graduate student population at U-M. While funding is the cornerstone of the Fellowship, Rackham Graduate School has also developed dedicated programming for Fellows across all graduate disciplines. This case study highlights the goals and activities of the first point of engagement, a two-week orientation program for all incoming PhD Rackham Merit Fellows, and discusses the impact of the program on students' sense of belonging.

Evidence of the Problem: Although the research on graduate students' sense of belonging is limited, studies are beginning to show that it does have an impact on graduate student retention and success (O'Meara et al., 2017; Pascale, 2018; Strayhorn, 2018). While departments play an important role in cultivating a student's sense of belonging, graduate schools like Rackham are in the unique position of being able to bring students together from across campus to further facilitate their sense of belonging. The goal of RMF programming is to build community, connect students to on-campus resources, help students navigate their graduate experience, and to strengthen their sense of belonging.

Initiative: RMF Connection is a two-week orientation program for all entering RMF PhDs, and it takes place before the start of the fall semester. Throughout the two weeks, students participate in a series of professional development workshops on topics including staying organized and productive; optimizing wellness; establishing a positive relationship with their advisor; research-based strategies for overcoming imposter syndrome; money management; and academic writing. These workshops connect students to a variety of faculty and staff presenters and students are encouraged to view them as part of their broader network of support.

One major goal of the program is for students to get to know one another. Each workshop is interactive and students often break out into smaller groups for discussion. These groups are often interdisciplinary but some topics lend themselves better to more disciplinary-focused groupings. Additionally, every workshop culminates in a shared meal, which allows informal conversations to continue. Other community building activities include a campus tour, trivia night at a pizza restaurant, a day trip to Detroit, and a closing dinner that includes current RMFs.

A particularly important activity in this program is that all students are required to share their intellectual autobiography in the form of a five-minute presentation. The telling of "their story" encourages students to reflect on the experiences and motivating factors that led them to graduate school. The exercise of presenting their intellectual development to their peers helps to strengthen each student's self-awareness and academic self-efficacy as well as reaffirm each individual's experience. As the students continue in their degree program, they are encouraged to return to their intellectual autobiography as a tool to re-center and re-calibrate.

A PhD student's success is largely dependent on maintaining a productive and healthy relationship with their faculty advisor. In addition to providing a workshop on how to establish a positive relationship with their advisor, fellows attend a semi-formal dinner in which each student invites a faculty member to attend as their guest. Some students invite their formal faculty advisor. Others invite a faculty member they would like to get to know. The celebratory nature of the dinner provides students and faculty the opportunity to get to know each other in a more relaxed setting that emphasizes the role of mentorship in student success.

In a recent evaluation conducted by the Center for Education Design, Evaluation, and Research at U-M, RMFs were surveyed at the end of their first year to learn more about their experience. Researchers were able to compare students who did participate in RMF Connection with those that did not. The students that participated in RMF Connection reported higher levels of research self-efficacy, a smoother transition to U-M, a greater sense of belonging (especially with peers outside of their departments), and more clarity in their research area because of their access to resources such as faculty and peers.

Implications for Policy and Practice: Pre-semester programs like RMF Connection are easily adaptable and can provide students with the opportunity to meet other graduate students from across campus, build community, and broaden their support network. Brandes (2006) has argued that underrepresented graduate students may benefit from cross-disciplinary community building especially when they find themselves in departments that lack diversity, and this is the case for many Fellows. Given the diversity of our Fellows, RMF Connection has helped us to establish strong connections among students and with Rackham that students can rely on throughout their studies.

Case Study 1 References

Brandes, L. (2006). Graduate student centers: Building community and involving students. In M. J. Guentzel & B. Elkins Nesheim (Eds.), *New Directions for Student Services* [Special issue: Supporting graduate and professional students: The role of student affairs], *2006*(115), 85–99. https://doi.org/10.1002/ss.218

O'Meara, K. A., Griffin, K., Kuvaeva, A., Nyunt, G., & Robinson, T. (2017). Sense of belonging and its contributing factors in graduate education. *International Journal of Doctoral Studies, 12*, 251–279. https://doi.org/10.28945/3903

Pascale, A. B. (2018). Co-existing lives: Understanding and facilitating graduate student sense of belonging. *Journal of Student Affairs Research and Practice, 55*(4), 399–411. https://doi.org/10.1080/19496591.2018.1474758

Strayhorn, T. L. (2018). *College students' sense of belonging a key to educational success for all students* (2nd ed). Routledge.

PLANNING AND SUPPORTING A GRADUATE OR PROFESSIONAL STUDENT ORIENTATION

Planning a graduate or professional school student orientation takes a lot of time and coordination. A planning committee can assist with identifying who will cover what material as well as whether it will be accomplished within the program or by someone with a university-wide office. The planning committee will make critical decisions about content delivery, logistics, accessibility, and budgeting.

Forming a Planning Committee

Forming an orientation planning committee is one way to increase campus partnership and engagement around graduate student support and distribute workload and resources, particularly if your office does not have sufficient staffing or resources. When forming a committee, consider what needs the department has such as funding, logistical, curricular, space, food, printed materials, and sponsorships. Consider which offices or individuals should be present on the committee due to their current or needed engagement with graduate students (wellness services, departmental faculty/staff, Graduate School, Graduate Student Association, Student Affairs, Diversity, Equity and Inclusion Office, International Student Office, etc.).

Graduate and professional practitioners should formulate a leadership structure and scope of the work to meet its needs. Planning committees are a good way to increase engagement and connection from university partners around graduate student support (University of Washington, 2020). Student affairs professionals should determine the scope of the planning committee. For example, is this an advisory committee (group provides ideas, insight on content) or a working group (group has specific roles in the planning and implementation with actionable goals)? If the orientation is small scale, consider who within the department should have input into the planning process such as departmental staff, faculty, current students, or other campus partners. If the lead department is located within a larger school or division, consider partnering across departments to reduce costs and staffing needs.

Many institutions, including UCLA, engage students directly in the planning process, which can be an important way to center the graduate student experience while providing leadership and professional development opportunities to current students. Involvement could range from hosting focus groups composed of current students to better understand their experiences and needs, including students on the planning committee, or developing student positions designed to support direct planning and implementation efforts.

Establishing Content Delivery and Format

Content delivery and format are important considerations when implementing a successful orientation program. Learning objectives should guide decisions about program length and delivery methods. Whether the program is a half-day or weeks-long, in-person or remote, the program should effectively and efficiently meet learning objectives.

When developing an orientation program, graduate and professional school student affairs professionals may start by creating a list of everything new students should learn and experience for successful matriculation. Considerations include everything from receiving their student ID card to academic skill development. With a comprehensive list of necessary experiences and objectives, consider what format best fits each component. For instance, information about parking regulations could be delivered in a video, ensuring everyone receives the same information, but meeting faculty and upper-level students may best be in-person. Once it has been determined who will deliver each piece of the program, it can be determined whether the program should be delivered in-person, online, or in another way (such as incorporated into a class).

Accessibility

Orientation programs should be designed to be accessible to all students in the identities that they bring to the institution. In-person programs should be held in Americans with Disabilities Act (ADA)-compliant facilities and include only activities that allow all students to participate equitably. Online orientation programs should use accessible software platforms. Student affairs professionals should consider captioning, audio descriptions of visual information, descriptive transcripts, and sign language for online content. Offering the orientation program in languages other than the primary language of instruction should also be considered.

Budgeting Considerations

Budgeting considerations are also important when determining content delivery. In-person, full-day orientations can be more expensive. Full-day, in-person sessions require meal breaks and may require a food and beverage budget. Online orientations may require investment in third-party software. Some institutions may be able to call upon university resources to develop an online orientation portal. These homegrown software systems can be cost-efficient (University of Washington, 2020).

Graduate and professional school professionals should scale their orientation based on their budget and number of students served. If the institution is making budget cuts, moving from an in-person program to an online program may be a prudent cost-saving measure. Regardless of format, student affairs professionals should advocate for a budget that reflects outlined learning objectives and meets all needs of students matriculating into the program. For a fuller discussion of student needs, see Chapter 3.

Considerations for Virtual Orientations

Creating an online orientation requires understanding technology capabilities or partnering with those who have experience with online learning. An institution may have capability to use its own resources to build an online orientation portal. However, if the institution does not have the capability to build its own, student affairs professionals may consider purchasing orientation-specific, third-party software. Budgeting considerations may drive this decision.

Many companies have come into the market and are making more and more software available to higher education institutions. A benefit to third-party software is that it has been developed by professionals to specifically meet higher education institutions' online learning needs. Student Affairs professionals should ensure that the software is accessible and practices inclusivity.

The University of Washington's (UW) award-winning online orientation program, discussed below in Case Study 2, serves as an excellent example and tool kit for other graduate and professional schools interested in creating an online orientation experience for their students.

Considerations for Distance Learners

For graduate and professional school programs with an online component or with long-distance commuters, special considerations should be made to ensure students are well connected and supported throughout the orientation experience. Consider the ways that students' ability to complete administrative and/or onboarding tasks (e.g., picking up an identification card) could be limited due to time constraints and see if special hours or alternative methods could be arranged to meet students' specific needs. Social and community engagement could be challenging for students that may have limited or no on-campus time and institutions should consider offering virtual community-building opportunities, programs that are asynchronous, access to online content and materials from orientation programs, and duplicate sessions offered at a variety of times. Information should be provided about how to access essential campus, academic, and research support services such as options for virtual services, extended hours, and online content.

Considerations for Assessment

Assessment is critical to ensuring orientation programs are successfully achieving learning objectives. Student affairs professionals serving graduate and professional students may consider creating their own pre-orientation and post-orientation surveys or using assessment built into third-party software. Qualitative and quantitative data will inform the student affairs professional on what is effective and what should be modified for future orientations. For additional support, student affairs professionals can turn to NODA (2018), the Association for Orientation, Transition, and Retention, which offers on-site evaluations for its clients through its Consulting Program (nodaweb.org). See Chapter 9 for an in-depth discussion of assessment.

CASE STUDY 2

By Katy DeRosier

Title: U501: Flipping the Orientation for Graduate and Professional Students

Institution: University of Washington (large, public, research institution)

Problem of Practice: At UW, we want our students to be successful from the start. And that means helping them even before they get here. It is not a foregone conclusion that students experience a smooth and successful transition to graduate school—a concerted effort drawing upon expertise across the University is needed to make this possible.

Evidence of the Problem: Prior to 2017, a comprehensive orientation to graduate school at UW did not exist. We knew that departmental and program orientations vary in quality and thoroughness, and are often not early enough for some incoming students, for instance, those in accelerated programs or those relocating from overseas. From this initial problem analysis, the Graduate School gained interest in creating an online orientation like U101, UW's version for undergraduates. We conducted extensive research to better understand first the need and then the content required for an effective orientation.

A graduate and professional student survey was developed and disseminated with the partnership of UW staff advisors on the Bothell, Seattle, and Tacoma campuses. A total of 229 students responded: 76 doctoral, 144 master's, eight professional, and one certificate. Questions included:

- What is something you would tell an incoming graduate student?
- Think back, if you can, to your very first day as a graduate student at UW. What is one thing you wish you would have known at the start of your graduate school experience?

Student focus groups were conducted to gather more in-depth information and allow for follow-up questions. A total of ten students participated. These groups and the survey informed the topics to address and signaled the tone; we learned relatability was paramount.

To ensure use and effectiveness of the content, staff and faculty input was included as the project was designed. All staff advisors from the three campuses were asked for input and invited to join an advisory group. The common themes that emerged for inclusion in U501 were class registration, funding, financial aid, teaching assistantships and research assistantships, how graduate school works, resources at the UW, and living in the Pacific Northwest. In addition to content about *how* to transition, a need to simply *welcome* students was identified. One of the learnings from U101 is that orientation does not happen at one moment or on one day. The ability to have ongoing access to information—including repeat viewing of videos, particularly with captions—ensures that information can be digested at the user's pace.

Initiative: We created U501, a self-guided, online resource used by graduate and professional students at all UW campuses that is intended to help prepare students who are starting their graduate studies. Incoming graduate and professional students, wherever they reside around the globe, may begin their transition to the UW by viewing the five modules. U501 is designed for various points of entry: students coming in at different levels of familiarity with graduate education overall, with the region, and with the University itself. To get the most out of U501, students may use it in preparation for their arrival, but it is also available throughout their time at the UW.

The online format allows the administrators immediate access to data from multiple sources, providing extensive data from which to determine the effectiveness of the overall project, each individual module, and even the specific videos within the modules. These metrics come from four sources: Canvas, the platform housing the modules; Vimeo, which provides access to the videos; Qualtrics, the survey software for user feedback (placed at the end of each module); and a UW netID that is required to log in and links to student information such as age, gender, ethnicity, and residency.

Since the 2017 launch, U501 has been a phenomenal success. At the three-year mark, our data shows 361,202 page views in Canvas; 64 average page views per enrolled user; 144,492 total video views; and 129 known countries from which videos have been accessed. Check out the U501 public version at grad.uw.edu/u501-public.

Implications for Policy and Practice: U501 is particularly helpful for international students who may not be familiar with the United States or the Pacific Northwest. For students who are the first in their families to pursue a graduate degree, U501 answers questions they may not have thought to ask.

Graduate and professional student staff and faculty also benefit from U501. The module content and access was designed so staff can not only direct their students to the entire orientation, but also to individual modules they find especially helpful in their own orientations and materials:

- Staff and faculty can pick and choose certain modules to direct their students through Canvas Commons.
- Staff and faculty were also given access to a video library outside of Canvas, which houses the 90 short videos; they can link directly to specific videos. For example, some advisors intend to have their students watch the "Staff & Faculty Advisors: Who They Are and What They Do" video before a one-on-one meeting so they can make the best use of their time together.

UW discovered it is a leader among peer institutions in developing and offering an online orientation for incoming graduate and professional students. In fact, U501 won the 2017 Educational Testing Service/Council of Graduate Schools (ETS/CGS) Award for Innovation in Promoting Success in Graduate Education (Council of Graduate Schools, 2017). With part of the award funds, we developed the U501 Toolkit, an online guide—with no cost—for other universities interested in enhancing or creating their own online orientations. Particularly with the onset of the COVID-19 pandemic, online orientations are more necessary than ever. The U501 Toolkit has allowed us and other universities to develop online orientations that inspire graduate students to engage immediately and fully in all that graduate education has to offer. Need help building your orientation? Follow the steps in the U501 Toolkit at depts.washington.edu/u501.

Case Study 2 References

Council of Graduate Schools. (2017, December 7). University of Washington receives ETS/CGS award for innovation in promoting success in graduate education. *Author.* Retrieved from https://cgsnet.org/university-washington-receives-etscgs-award-innovation-promoting-success-graduate-education

PRE- AND POST-ORIENTATION PROGRAMMING

Many people think of orientation programs beginning immediately prior to matriculation; however, early orientation can be used to retain admitted students. Programs may opt to provide orientation materials soon after acceptance and engage admitted students immediately when their excitement is high. According to Taub and Komives (1998), this is a time that admitted students can build unrealistic expectations that lead to involuntary or voluntary retreat or withdrawal once the student has matriculated. Early orientation can serve to build realistic expectations and paint a clearer picture of what students can expect in the program. Early orientation programming may include providing program publications, making personal contact with social media or phone calls, transmitting program culture, and creating a sense of community (Taub & Komives, 1998).

Engaging the admitted student early can also foster connection and belonging during a vulnerable time, reinforcing their admission decision. Use of an online early orientation portal or software allows admissions or student affairs professionals to track engagement. When an admitted student is not engaging with the early orientation portal, student affairs or admissions professionals can reach out to ensure the admit is still committed to attending the program. If their commitment is wavering, admissions professionals can work to reconnect them. Where graduate and professional schools are competing for students, early orientation can also be used as a strategy to retain high performing admittees who could be poached by higher ranking programs.

Extended or Continued Orientation

Traditionally, orientation programs take place at the beginning of the first year or perhaps throughout the first year of a program. Although orientation as a concept makes sense during the first year, so much information can be overwhelming and forgotten by student attendees. Offering an extended orientation which offers similar sessions, topics, and engagement after the first year of study and during critical stages of the graduate or professional school program is one model to address retention and continued support. If the material is academic in nature, student affairs professionals should work with the faculty to ensure it aligns with their academic goals.

Claremont Graduate University (CGU) created a reorientation program to address concerns around PhD completion rates. Case Study 3 outlines data collection and then program creation and implementation for their successful reorientation program.

CASE STUDY 3

By Christine Kelly

Title: ReOrientation: From Student to Scholar

Institution: Claremont Graduate University (private, graduate-only, R2: doctoral research institution)

Problem of Practice: In 2015, CGU launched ReOrientation, a program designed to help doctoral students move more quickly from the completion of coursework to the completion of their dissertation. It grew from discussions among the Directors of the Career Development Office, Preparing Future Faculty, the Center for Writing and Rhetoric, and Dean of Students centered on why students were not progressing toward degree completion and how the offices could contribute to help students navigate this part of the PhD process. Further, faculty expressed concerns that students were "falling off the map" after coursework and sought to understand this phenomenon.

Evidence of the Problem: The Reorientation committee surveyed post coursework students to discover their perceived barriers to completion. Students identified multiple academic barriers: lack of clarity of how to prepare for qualifying exams; write dissertation proposals and dissertations; lack of preparation to conduct independent scholarship; not understanding how to work with their advisor; isolation; and lack of clear career goals/knowledge of how to achieve those goals. There were additional personal barriers: work commitments, family obligations, financial pressures and health challenges that impacted degree completion. The committee also discovered that students lacked knowledge of the resources available to assist them at this stage of the process. These resources were presented at New Student Orientation; however, this was often three or more years prior to entering the post coursework phase, thus the title of the program: ReOrientation.

Initiative: All students who have completed 48 units are invited to participate. Advisors are asked to recommend participation to their advisees. Program Coordinators, support offices, and faculty (beginning in year three) are also invited to the event. All students complete a survey when they register that asks for their stage in the process, advisor's name, work/teaching experience during program, career goals/preparation, questions for the faculty panelists, and expectations for the day. They complete a post-event survey and a follow-up survey at six months and one year after the event.

The goals of ReOrientation were based on findings from the survey. The most important goal was to help students individualize a structured road map to help them navigate the stage from coursework to dissertation completion. This involved providing the cultural capital many students lack about navigating the scholarly process. The committee sought to scaffold the process for immediate and future success by helping students develop strategies for effective self-management and academic management so they can work optimally to complete their degrees, while also developing professionally to successfully move into careers in academia and beyond.

Students also indicated reluctance to speak to faculty, thus the committee wanted to connect students with professors and step ahead peers to help them develop a network of resources and support and possibly to find a group of peers they can work with in studying for quals and writing their proposals and dissertations. The committee believed these goals would ultimately decrease time to degree.

The program changed minimally over the first four years and included sessions about career planning, research, writing, financial aid, and a faculty panel. In year five, the program was reinvented to incorporate more working sessions so participants would leave with the start of a concrete plan. The year five programming best hits the goals the committee set out to accomplish and students left with a more concrete plan than in prior years. Programs in year five included:

1. Strategies for moving from coursework to completion: Faculty panel
2. Designing your timeline to completion: Process mapping and introduction to ImaginePhD tools
3. Doing the dissertation: Writing after course work and organizing research tools
4. Beyond the dissertation: Career planning strategies, creating your scholarly persona
5. Negotiating progress upward and inward: Motivation, time management, and managing burnout
6. Your timeline for completion: Using the career exploration tools in ImaginePhD and creating your outline of a completion plan

Implications for Policy and Practice: The committee has tracked the outcomes over the past five years and has evidence of the success of the program based on participant feedback. Students consistently reported that the faculty panel and the discussion on self-care were most useful to them. Immediately after the event, most agreed that participation in ReOrientation showed them resources to better manage the process, helped them feel more confident about completing their degree in a timely manner, and helped them feel less isolated. Further, immediately after the event, most reported increased confidence in their ability to proactively approach completion and career development, complete their degree in a timely manner, use resources available to them, and approach faculty for assistance. The committee also conducted follow-up surveys with participants six months and one year after the event. Respondents reported taking steps toward finishing, designing a completion plan, engaging with Career Development, Center for Writing and Rhetoric and/or Preparing Future Faculty offices, and approaching a faculty member for help.

Students need a roadmap to help them navigate the post coursework process. Participants cited a lack of knowledge of how to proceed and a belief that everyone else knew the process as a major barrier. This often prevented them from asking for help. It helped them learn that their advisors experience very similar challenges in their PhD programs. A program like this normalizes these feelings and provides students with the knowledge they need to successfully complete their PhD.

CONCLUSION

This chapter reviewed key considerations for onboarding graduate and professional school students. Student affairs professionals who support graduate and professional students should understand the unique characteristics of their experience and create an onboarding experience that reflects the meaningful nuances and differences that graduate and professional students bring to their academic program. At their core, graduate and professional orientation programs should achieve three objectives: (1) foster a sense of belonging within the program; (2) cover necessary onboarding logistics; and (3) ensure graduate and professional students are tooled for academic and professional success.

Much like undergraduate populations, graduate and professional school programs attract students from a variety of different backgrounds and experiences. Onboarding and orientation experiences should consider the unique needs of transfer, commuter, distance, and historically underrepresented students. Orientation experiences and professionals developing the orientation programs should also consider students who have assistantships or fellowships as part of their academic program. Finally, this chapter provided tactical support for developing a graduate or professional school student orientation. Assessment was recommended to drive decisions on building the program as well evaluating ongoing effectiveness. This chapter also explored thinking of orientation holistically by considering early onboarding/orientations as well as extended or continued orientations.

REFERENCES

Association for Orientation, Transition and Retention in Higher Education (NODA). (2018). *Educational Outreach: NODA External Review Program* [PDF file]. Retrieved from https://cdn.ymaws. com/www.nodaweb.org/resource/resmgr/docs/noda_consulting_program_info.pdf

Bang, H., & Montgomery, D. (2013). Understanding international graduate students' acculturation using Q methodology. *Journal of College Student Development*, 54(4), 343–360. https://doi. org/10.1353/csd.2013.0066

Brunsma, D. L., Embrick, D. G., & Shin, J. H. (2016). Graduate students of color. *Sociology of Race and Ethnicity, 3*(1), 1–13. https://doi.org/10.1177/2332649216681565

Hullinger, M., & Hogan, R. L. (2014). Student anxiety: Effects of a new graduate student orientation program. *Administrative Issues Journal Education Practice and Research.* https://doi.org/10.5929/2014.4.2.3

Lunceford, B. (2011). When first-generation students go to graduate school. *New Directions for Teaching and Learning, 2011*(127), 13–20. https://doi.org/10.1002/tl.453

Organ, J. M., Jaffe, D., & Bender, K. M. (2016). Suffering in silence: The survey of law student well-being and the reluctance of law students to seek help for substance use and mental health concerns. *Journal of Legal Education, 66*(1), 116–156. Retrieved from http://www.jstor.org/stable/26402424

Poock, M. C. (2004). Graduate student orientation practices: Results from a national survey. *Journal of Student Affairs Research and Practice, 41*(3). https://doi.org/10.2202/1949-6605.1356

Selvaraj, S., & John, V. (2020). Taking care of medical students: The pillars of future healthcare. *Brazilian Journal of Psychiatry, 43*(1). https://doi.org/10.1590/1516-4446-2020-1037

Taub, D. J., & Komives, S. K. (1998). A comprehensive graduate orientation program: Practicing what we preach. *Journal of College Student Development, 39*, 394–398. http://dx.doi.org/10.1353/csd.2006.0027

University of Washington. (2020). Making the pitch. *U501: Graduate School Orientation Toolkit* [toolkit]. Retrieved from https://depts.washington.edu/u501/the-pitch/making-the-pitch/

Vaccaro, A. (2012). Campus microclimates for LGBT faculty, staff, and students: An exploration of the intersections of social identity and campus roles. *Journal of Student Affairs Research and Practice, 49*(4), 429–446. https://doi.org/10.1515/jsarp-2012-6473

Chapter 5

Graduate Student Success and Socialization

Stephanie K. Eberle, Jamie Heck, Angie Cook, and Dawn Loyola

Over the last 30 years graduate education has faced significant political, financial, and social challenges. In response, it evolved into increased professional degree programs, diversified student demographics and degree types, and an entirely new purpose: specifically moving from academic job preparation to acquisition and application of expertise in myriad fields. As discussed in Chapter 3, research on student success traditionally focused on undergraduate student outcomes and needs, many of which do not similarly translate to graduate populations. This chapter highlights considerations for graduate student success that depart from undergraduate best practices, and instead embrace the dynamic nature of graduate education. Important factors in graduate student success include the roles of advising and mentorship, development of campus-wide support strategies that mirror the efforts in undergraduate persistence, academic integrity, graduate career support, and graduate core competencies. Such considerations allow graduate educators to create intentional and transformational learning environments that respond to the complexities of today's graduate populations.

GRADUATE STUDENT SUCCESS FACTORS

Building Persistence

Persistence factors contribute significantly to the success of graduate students as they transition from the less independent culture of undergraduate education. While undergraduates may struggle with insufficient academic readiness and abilities, graduate student persistence predominantly depends on external factors (Gansemer-Topf et al., 2006) such as family responsibilities, financial concerns, integrating academics with full-time employment, battling personal illness, and caring for dependents or ailing loved ones. Multi-faceted external stressors and responsibilities cause academic stress to reach a tipping point. Institutions must

DOI: 10.4324/9781003121671-7

educate themselves on graduate student challenges and pursue ways to mitigate them. Consider, for example, deadline flexibility for individuals in crisis, accessible mental health resources that reflect graduate student experiences, tutoring and technology support, childcare, financial aid and financial counseling, identity centers and affinity spaces, and student advocacy through representation on decision-making groups. Cohen and Greenberg (2011) found that family and personal support structures are significant factors for student persistence, especially in part-time master's programs. At the undergraduate level, educators try to build student independence from parental involvement. At the graduate level, educators must design educational experiences that welcome and include families.

According to Felder and St. John (2014), success within any organization first depends on socialization into the social and cultural mores within it. Doing so for graduate students by program, department, college, and/or institution increases persistence (Pontius & Harper, 2006). Historically, retaining graduate students was the responsibility of individual departments or colleges rather than a university-wide support system (Gansemer-Topf et al., 2006). Institutions often assume that graduate students already know how to navigate higher education given their undergraduate degree experience (Pontius & Harper, 2006), but socialization within graduate school vs. undergraduate training significantly differs (Felder & St. John, 2014). Educators must inform graduate students of available resources and advocate for graduate student support on a campus-wide scale, involving both the same offices that support undergraduate students and those unique to graduate specialization. For career integration, educators should consider how to support student involvement in professional organizations, such as funds for conferences or academic writing support for publications. For each strategy, educators must make a conscious effort to equitably reach students in all program types—doctoral, master's, professional, and certificate—and keep in mind their constituents' unique internal and external strengths and constraints.

BIPOC Student Persistence

In fall 2019, 25% of first-time graduate students identified as Black, Indigenous, Persons of Color (BIPOC), and BIPOC students represent a growing proportion of the graduate student population nationally, growing at faster rates than white graduate students (Okahana et al., 2020). Despite these gains, BIPOC students remain underrepresented within graduate education, leading to feelings of isolation and identity-related stress (Okahana et al., 2020; Verschelden, 2017). These challenges combine with the common mental health challenges that all graduate students encounter, causing BIPOC students to arrive at graduate education with depleted bandwidth for overcoming obstacles (Verschelden, 2017).

Felder and St. John (2014) stress the importance of African Americans recognizing the plausibility of their aspirations despite external pressures. Graduate educators encourage an empowering environment through both cultural representations across the university and via specialized services which allow marginalized populations to connect within their own communities (Felder & St. John, 2014). Graduate educators must critically examine every stage of the graduate student experience—from recruitment to matriculation to graduation—and implement strategies to address the unique needs of marginalized student populations. Consider recruitment of diverse and representative faculty, curriculum redesign with an anti-racism framework, and in-depth equity training for students, staff, and faculty (Effland and Hay, 2018; Gordon et al., 2016). Below, Case Study 1 provides a deeper look into the ways institutions can engage their graduate students' ideas and leadership in efforts to support diverse student populations.

Specialized support services, increased representation within faculty, staff, and students, and affinity spaces also contribute positively to a sense of belonging and persistence for women, older adults, parents/caregivers, lesbian, gay, bisexual, transgender, and queer/questioning (LGBTQ+) individuals, first-generation students, students with disabilities, veterans, and other historically marginalized populations (Brus, 2006). Educators must discover new and effective strategies for removing barriers to student access and success without further burdening marginalized populations.

Managing Mental Health Concerns

Graduate students, being older, more experienced, and often adult learners, experience more complex life circumstances than commonly seen with traditionally aged undergraduate students (Gansemer-Topf et al., 2006), which strains mental health and negatively impacts persistence. In addition to personal factors, graduate education often perpetuates unhealthy values: competitive environments, vulnerability viewed as weakness, unhealthy work-life balance, and lack of adequate mentorship and support (Benshoff et al., 2015; Di Pierro, 2017). In a 2016 *The Atlantic* article, Patterson urged institutions to acknowledge and address their contributions to student mental health challenges: "In exploring what exacerbates mental-health issues among graduate students, it may be wise to shift the focus away from labeling graduate students 'deficient' to investigate how institutions themselves may be causing attrition" (para. 3). In addition to increased mental health services for graduate students through counseling, support groups, and faculty/staff training, institutions must critically assess their pervading cultures and cultivate environments that respond to and support students' complex lives and needs.

Socialization of Academic Honesty and Integrity Standards

Amid the many factors affecting graduate student success is prior exposure and overall understanding of academic integrity practices. Therefore, institutions must include related content into their early socialization efforts in the form of sufficient training, support services, and extended resources (Thompson et al., 2017). Such frameworks provide graduate students with the knowledge, awareness, and assistance warranted for continued refinement of their writing and research skills throughout the entirety of their graduate enrollment and beyond.

Education on the academic integrity, values, and ethical practices necessary for graduate student success begins early in a student's academic studies (Marsh & Campion, 2018); higher education institutions share responsibility with the students themselves for promoting and developing these standards (Hanbidge et al., 2020). Myriad strategies exist within higher education to do so. First, institutions' academic integrity standards must be established and communicated to stakeholders (Gallant, 2008; Jamieson, 2008; Pecorari, 2008; Sefcik et al., 2020; Simonson et al., 2003). Student affairs professionals play key, collaborative roles in ensuring academic integrity via purposeful training to graduate students and faculty, encouraging continuous skill refinement. Faculty and student affairs professionals alike use platforms such as course syllabi, handbooks, relevant websites, and community pages within learning management systems to reiterate, maintain, and disperse expectations.

Best practices recommend strategically creating stand-alone coursework housed in the institution's learning management system (Lowe et al., 2018), incorporating academic integrity training into orientation activities (Din et al., 2018), and regularly updating standards. Enforcement of established compliance policies, procedures, and sanctions create the structure for both faculty and student affairs professionals to ensure academic integrity standards are upheld (Sefcik et al., 2020). Importantly, close support through advising and mentoring ensures both proper socialization into academic expectations and the oversight necessary to ensure compliance and understanding.

ACADEMIC SOCIALIZATION AND SUPPORT

Factors Impacting Advising and Mentoring

Socialization within the graduate sphere is twofold: both an introduction into how to be a successful graduate student and instruction and modeling of professional expectations within a given field (Golde, 1998). Further, graduate students' advanced life experiences imply unique advising and mentoring needs. Course planning advising exists within graduate training, but because of graduate students' previous educational (and sometimes work) experience, advisors may assume students are more confident and independent than they are. Advising remains important, especially for first-generation students and/or those without support and understanding from their family and community network. Unlike undergraduates, funding agencies view them as independent, so funding opportunities vary (Sheehy & Kerr, 2019). If they do not finish training, they are left with neither a degree nor a job: a very precarious position. Graduate school is also fraught with high-stakes academic milestones in the form of entrance exams, written and oral qualifying exams, and public defenses, in addition to potential experiential requirements such as practicums, internships, and clinical rotations. They may simultaneously work full time and attend school, paying out-of-pocket or through loans. In some cases, financial assistantships are the only means for students to meet full-time enrollment requirements (Fagen & Wells, 2000; Golde, 1998), yet they also present significant time constraints (Ampaw & Jaeger, 2012; Kim & Otts, 2010) via applying for and/or meeting the demands of these supports. The constant balancing act of graduate school requires both academic advising and personal and professional mentoring approaches.

Tinto finds that stage of training impacts this balance as well (Tinto, 1993). In the first transitioning stage of Tinto's model of doctoral retention, socialization into the university setting is key. Ensuring appropriate academic competencies becomes central in the second candidacy phase. The final dissertation completion phase centers on socialization into a particular academic specialty and career (Tinto, 1993). As such, faculty and graduate administrators often alternate between their advising and mentoring roles; adequate involvement is required for successful progression throughout (Felder & St. John, 2014).

What is the difference between advising and mentoring? *Advising* typically focuses on the specifics of program completion, ensuring students meet requirements and reach the competencies necessary for success in their field (Marcdante & Simpson, 2018). The ability of the advisor to connect students to individualized resources and provide feedback is imperative to navigating complex university systems and to building student confidence. This is especially true of first-generation students without previous understanding of these structures (Riggs, 2014) and of adult learners reacclimating to a system that has significantly changed since their last experience. Academic advising takes place in "situations in which an institutional representative gives insight or direction to a college student about an academic, social, or personal matter. The nature of this direction might be to inform, suggest, counsel, discipline, coach, mentor, or even teach" (Kuhn, 2008, p. 3). *Mentoring* centers around the holistic development of the student throughout and beyond their program—the academic, personal, professional, and career aspects affecting or affected by their work. Marcdante and Simpson (2018, p. 227) state mentoring is a role wherein "experiential wisdom is offered to help build the many aspects of a learner's career."

Setting boundaries is an important skill for advisors and mentors as well as understanding when to handle a student issue personally vs. referring them to counseling or other services. It is vital to remember that the advising role differs from counseling roles, and advisors do not diagnose. Refer to a counselor when:

- Empathy and resources are not enough
- Working together could damage the student
- You or the student feel physically and/or psychologically unsafe
- This student is taking up significantly more time/resources than others
- Specific training is needed to best help the student

Remember, empathy is not relating to someone just like you; it is relating to the experience of others through compassion and making space for their narrative. If you do not know how your student feels or what they want, ask and listen.

Building Effective Mentoring Relationships

Mentoring encompasses a community of perspectives from peers, faculty, alumni, and staff. Effective faculty mentoring immensely influences graduate students' overall academic and career success (Fallatah et al., 2018), productivity (Hund et al., 2018), and sense of belonging (Holloway-Friesen, 2021). It also positively contributes to students' mental health, and recruitment and retention (Hund et al., 2018). A successful mentoring relationship not only develops student academic competencies and field socialization, it also contributes to the overall retention of graduate students within the institution (Golde, 2005; Lovitts, 2001).

Common attributes associated with effective mentoring include shared interests, active engagement in and commitment from the mentor and mentee in the relationship, and open communication (Barrett et al., 2017). Unfortunately, adequate and ongoing faculty mentoring training to help foster purposeful interactions and conversations with graduate students is lacking (Hund et al., 2018), which contributes to ineffective and inconsistent mentoring approaches. With communication being a vital part of mentoring, faculty need preparation and assurance in providing feedback. Without formalized training, faculty may simply draw from personal experiences as a resource to guide their approaches and hone their skills (Amundsen & McAlpine, 2009). Creating standards of excellence and expectations between the mentor and mentee help establish

99

norms and consistency in mentoring practices within departments and institutions (Barnes & Austin, 2009). SUNY-Stony Brook University's Institute for Advanced Computational Science (IACS), for example, applies improvisation techniques to training faculty and student mentors/mentees. See Case Study 2 for a description of this program in practice.

Mentoring not only applies to the faculty/advisor-student relationship; peer relationships also provide the support and socialization necessary for success (Sullivan, 1991). Peer mentoring (student-student) fosters social engagement, community building, and continued learning (Bemker & Leibold, 2018). The peer-peer relationship positively impacts academic success, leadership development, and graduate student retention (Alcocer & Martinez, 2017); it further provides emotional support (Geesa et al., 2018). This relationship equally benefits mentees and mentors as "mentors relate to the social, emotional, and academic life balances of mentees, mentors provide support and reassurance to mentees, mentors guide mentees to focus on the future, and mentors gain personal and professional growth" (McConnell et al., 2019, p. 86). In addition, peer-peer mentoring relationships offer student mentors the opportunity to develop leadership skills and diversify their professional experience (McConnell et al., 2019), both valuable rewards for mentors.

Alumni networks and connecting students with alumni mentors in the same or related fields is another meaningful strategy, especially for marginalized populations or those underrepresented in their professional field. This frees time and funding within departments lacking both. It also creates ongoing, positive relationships between institutions and their former students as they transition into their chosen careers.

Using Individual Development Plans to Discuss and Evaluate Progress

Individual development plans (IDPs) inform and increase the quality of conversations between doctoral students and their advisors/mentors. The forms contain questions about academic and professional progress, goals, and competency; personal concerns affecting progress; and career interests and preparation. Programs at Stanford Biosciences (n.d.b) and University of California, San Francisco (UCSF) (n.d.) follow a development model that adjusts questions according to a student's year in program. Some departments also supplement with the myIDP assessment (Hobin et al., 2012) or a self-assessment, such as the one offered by the American Psychological Association (n.d.) to help students align their interests, skills, and values with those of their future careers.

Students use these forms to both reflect on their interests and set goals with their advisors. Discussing IDP content with advisors is imperative to program success and socialization into future careers. Practitioners must ensure these conversations are motivational, student-led, and end with concrete feedback and next steps (Vincent et al., 2015). Successful IDP programs include faculty, student, and administrator feedback from inception to launch and include training for both faculty and students on giving/receiving feedback and setting goals and expectations. Some professional fields, such as psychology, incorporate practicum or internship advisor feedback as well.

SOCIALIZATION INTO FUTURE CAREERS

Factors Impacting Career and Professional Development

Historically, graduate student socialization efforts are centered on career preparation for linear paths to specific jobs: academia for PhDs and professional careers for business, law, healthcare, or technical fields (Felder & St. John, 2014). Graduate career support was therefore left to advisors and services were limited to job search help in said fields, without exploring broader opportunities and fit. This leaves a legacy of variable mentoring quality, which contributes to the current graduate student mental health crisis. Evans et al. (2018) find that the majority of graduate students suffering from anxiety or depression do not believe their advisors are assets to their careers. And, while career awareness increases throughout training, in-depth understanding of options and direction remains opaque, even years later (Gibbs et al., 2015).

For PhD students, the prioritization of academic positions is partially to blame for this confusion. In 2006, Lehker and Furlong discussed the need to prepare graduate students for careers outside of academia because faculty positions are declining (National Institutes of Health [NIH] Biomedical Research Workforce Working Group Report, 2012). Even in professional schools, the assumption that students already understand the breadth of options available within their field and their place within these pervades. Post-training career options are wide-ranging, and programs increasingly support professional students looking to advance in their careers or to transition to new opportunities. Institutions must frame career services with more inclusive, empathetic understanding of student needs and provide equally diverse and responsive support for career exploration opportunities (Lehker & Furlong, 2006), including focused discussions about the breadth of options and intentional language about the changing value of graduate education. Stanford Biosciences, for example, uses "career of choice" to re-center the holistic experience of training, replacing the "academia" vs. "non-academia" dichotomy that preferences one career choice over another (Stanford Career of Choice Philosophy, n.d.a). See Case Study 3 for an initiative at the Regis College Doctorate of Higher Education Leadership program, where a freshly designed capstone course provides students with opportunities for in-depth career reflection and planning.

Graduate training itself presents new perspectives and opportunities to define and explore interests, values, and new skills. For example, a student may enter law school to improve ethical corporate policies and find themselves attracted to environmental law instead. The strong training-career connection makes systemic integration imperative for students' ability to translate their training into real-world experiences (Dey & Cruzvergara, 2019). Career centers are already shifting from student services to academic services departments for seamless offerings (NACE, 2019), and professional schools often provide specialized services. Train-the-trainer opportunities such as that offered by the National Institutes of Health (NIH Office of Intramural Training and Education, 2020) address this growth by preparing noncareer center administrators to address basic academic and career development issues. As such, the career center of the future is an inclusive community of partners beyond career specialists (Dey & Cruzvergara, 2019).

Practitioners often perceive career support as advice and application review, which addresses students' stated needs but dismisses the developmental nature of career identity. A student may present with a curriculum vitae (CV) question, for example, but hold underlying personal and career anxieties. Career theories evolved over time to address this incongruence, encouraging practitioners to both empower active exploration (Krumboltz & Levin, 2004) and uncover themes in students' personal success narratives (Savickas, 2013). When used early, these approaches allow students to try out various options throughout training and to more intentionally target career opportunities in applications and interviews later on.

Strategies to help graduate students define and create meaning range from career exploration and assessment tools (e.g., ImaginePhD, myIDP, and Career Leader—all online) to immersion coursework and network connection opportunities (alumni mentoring, career fairs, panels, and similar activities). For noncareer center professionals, the latter opportunities, especially with department alumni, are key, as are professional development opportunities such as the Graduate Career Consortium (GCC), National Postdoctoral Association (NPA), and The Group on Graduate Research, Education, and Training (GREAT).

A trend is increasing within many graduate and professional programs to show how students are being prepared for the future workforce (NIH, National Research Service Award [NRSA] Requirements; Dey & Cruzvergara, 2019). Responding requires that graduate professionals make alumni career data visible and accessible. It further requires new approaches for measuring career success. Among promising practices are exploring time to career, impact, and evaluating the number of connections made at events.

Coaching and Advising International and Undocumented Students

While the graduate career landscape seems generally difficult, international and undocumented students face unique roadblocks. Variations in visa status mean international students are restricted from working in different sectors for certain time limits or even from working at all. In some cases, international students' home countries paid for their graduate training in exchange for their return home. Undocumented students simultaneously experience stress from employment needs and potential deportation.

Unless we work in international affairs offices or possess unique training in the details of international law, our work remains at the support and resource referral level. This includes empathic listening, empowerment to make life-impacting decisions, and ensuring access to proper resources and connections. Helping students find career opportunities, for example, might entail:

- working with them to find companies who previously hired alumni;
- considering companies with bases in the United States; and/or
- deciding among staying in the United States, returning home, or going to another country for employment.

Finding Postdoctoral Positions

Currently, postdoctoral positions are practically required in most science, technology, engineering, and mathematics (STEM) fields and are increasingly common in other fields, including humanities (Brown, 2011). These positions allow trainees to re-specialize where needed, develop independence as educators, and advance their research and network. Postdoctoral fellowships help prepare trainees for research careers, both in and outside academia. However, as the length of positions increases and the number of academic research positions decreases, the linear pipeline to these jobs is disrupted (Fuhrmann et al. 2017). When coaching students regarding pursuit of postdoctoral positions, advisors should address the following:

- How sure is the student of their career-of-choice?
- What competencies and experiences are needed for their career-of-choice?

103

- What competencies will a postdoctoral fellowship build?
- Is a postdoc position the only way to build these competencies?
- Are they using the postdoc as a placeholder because they do not know what else to do?

Core Competencies for Graduate Students

Core competencies are those seen as broadly requisite by the majority of leaders in a particular field. Studying and understanding competencies defines interdisciplinary standards; provides a common vocabulary among administrators, employers, and students; sets guidelines for training and supporting students; and informs methods for measuring these efforts (NACE, n.d.).

Each field defines its own set of competencies for success which are often outlined by their primary professional associations. More generally, the National Association of Colleges and Employers (NACE, n.d.) recommends eight core competencies based on consistent, annual data collected across various fields. These include:

- Critical Thinking/Problem-Solving
- Oral/Written Communications
- Teamwork/Collaboration
- Digital Technology
- Leadership
- Professionalism/Work Ethic
- Career Management
- Global/Intercultural Fluency

Unfortunately, students rate their competency in these areas higher than employers rate them (Blumenstyk, 2019). Because academic development translates directly into career development, both academic and career administrators are responsible for integrating core competencies into their education and for providing students with the feedback, experience, and support necessary for accurate self-evaluation (Fuhrmann et al. 2017). The IDPs discussed above and experiential learning provide opportunities for this integration.

Experiential Learning Promising Practices

While graduate students today consider a broader span of career opportunities than before (Fuhrmann et al. 2017), finding work that is closely related to their area of training remains important to students (NSF, 2015). This is true of doctoral students, who seek understanding of skill transferability in myriad careers as well as professional, master's, and certificate students hoping to directly apply their new education to a fulfilling position. Each population benefits from greater self-awareness and exposure to the array of opportunities in their fields. Experiential learning practices increase students' knowledge and confidence in their career choices (Schnoes et al., 2018) and increase employability (Saltikoff, 2017). The competencies gleaned from these experiences contribute to academic success as well. For example, project management internships translate into stronger collaborations and goal setting within class cohorts as well.

The most common experiential learning opportunities include:

- *Practicum requirements*: projects, assignments, and/or employment, ranging from short to long term, built into academic training and requirements to directly specialize, master, better understand, and make connections in a field; also rotations, residency (MD), apprenticeship.
- *Internships*: short-term employment in an organization which provides field-specific training, mentorship, and professional connections.
- *Immersion coursework*: employer/alumni, faculty, and administrator partnerships to teach students field-specific competencies through lecture, case studies, professional connections, and final projects.
- *Industry collaborations*: short-term research projects with industry connections to both contribute to and learn from the organization.

To best benefit students, these offerings should provide feedback from a mentor or mentors on performance and fit with their chosen career, include assignments that provide direct experience with work content, introduce day-to-day life on the job, and provide opportunities to connect with others in the field.

CONCLUSION

As the make-up of today's graduate populations increased and changed, so did the value of graduate education and the approaches necessary to support it. Competitive landscapes, funding constraints, and the rise of professional degree programs mean the definition of graduate student success no longer centers around one linear career path. Longer training times, work-education-life balance issues, and the changing make-up of graduate cohorts imply that traditional undergraduate-centered socialization methods are not as useful. Graduate students bring their own unique mental health concerns into training, and that training conveys its own core competencies and academic standards. Graduate programs, therefore, require inclusive, community-based practices that integrate experiential learning, intentional academic advising, and holistic mentoring into the fabric of their offerings. Graduate students should be able to define and follow their own definitions of success; our job is to provide the early socialization, education, and resources that empower them to do so.

Below are three cases that bring some of the content discussed in this chapter to life. The three cases include: (1) Diversity, Equity, and Inclusion; (2) Advising; and (3) Career Development.

CASE STUDY 1

By Jessica C. Moronez, Kayleigh Anderson-Natale, and Hillary Jenks

Title: Institutionalizing Peer Support and Advocacy to Promote Equity and Inclusion at the Graduate Level

Institution: University of California, Riverside (large, public, research institution)

Problem of Practice: While structural racism is endemic to higher education, its impact is especially acute at the graduate level (Brunsma et al., 2017). Even at the University of California, Riverside (UCR)—a Hispanic-Serving Institution nationally recognized for its effectiveness in educating Black and Latinx undergraduates—a significant demographic difference exists between graduate and undergraduate student populations. Current enrollment indicates just 39.2% of UCR graduate students identify as members of historically underrepresented minorities compared to 85.6% of undergraduates.

Evidence of the Problem: Nationally, efforts to address this disparity (e.g., McNair Scholars, Mellon Mays Fellows) initially focused on barriers to entry, such as academic preparation and funding (Griffin & Muniz, 2015). However, barriers to persistence are also significant problems requiring targeted interventions (Ramirez, 2017; Slay et al., 2019; Trent et al., 2020). These barriers—inclusive of microaggressions, intersectional discrimination, and other manifestations of a hostile campus climate—negatively impact retention and completion among historically underrepresented as well as other "non-traditional" students. A campus racial climate framework (Griffin et al., 2012; Hurtado et al., 1999; Milem et al., 2005) is particularly relevant to addressing issues impacting persistence, as it accounts for the interaction of both external (government policies, historical factors) and internal (compositional diversity, psychological and behavioral climate, institutional structure) factors.

Initiative: Diversity and Inclusion Academic Liaison (DIAL) role for peer support and advocacy in addressing barriers to persistence: Officers of the UCR Graduate Student Association (GSA) and Graduate Division leadership began discussing options for improving campus climate through institutional change in 2015. Recognizing the value of peer support and advocacy in addressing barriers to persistence (Lorenzetti et al., 2019; Roumimper & Falk, 2019), the GSA partnered with the Graduate Division to create an innovative new graduate student position: the DIAL. The Graduate Division funds the position at a teaching assistantship level for a minimum of two years, to reach out to other campus units for assistance in funding the position beyond that time frame, and to provide relevant training and support, including sexual violence/sexual harassment training and diversity training. The Graduate Division also provides a consultation system for individualized one-on-one DIAL support. The GSA oversees the position, a small programming budget, and incorporates the DIAL into its governance structure (for instance, by inviting DIAL to executive board meetings and creating a student advisory committee).

The first graduate student hired into the position, Kayleigh Anderson-Natale, was a PhD candidate in Education, with previous experience administering the campus graduate student mentorship program and working in domestic abuse and rape crisis counseling. Drawing on her background and responding to the needs of the Title IX office, the first campus partner to provide additional funding for the position, Anderson-Natale focused primarily on issues related to sexual harassment/sexual violence (SVSH) and gender discrimination during her two-year tenure. Resulting from her efforts, the required SVSH training is offered and certified for hundreds of graduate students during orientation and confidential office hours are offered through the Campus Advocacy, Resources, and Education (CARE) office, another early funding partner. Workshops on diversity-related subjects such as "Out in the Academy" and "First-Generation Faculty" are also provided. Finally, a new, annual graduate student campus climate survey now allows the Graduate Division and GSA access to consistent, renewable, self-reported data on this topic for the first time.

The second DIAL, Jessica Moronez, a PhD candidate in Sociology with a research and programming background related to women of color and the carceral state, expanded the position's outreach in new directions. As a result, a partnership with UCR's Ethnic and Gender offices offers quarterly Grad Students of Color mixers, regularly attracting 80–90 graduate students. The mixers also provide opportunities to obtain student feedback used by the Ethnic and Gender offices to inform their graduate student programming and to introduce administrators to the concerns of graduate students from underrepresented minority (URM) populations. Collaborations with UCR's new Vice Chancellor for Diversity, Equity, and Inclusion also offer training to departments seeking communication and climate improvements. Finally, student success data are analyzed, producing a report identifying areas where underrepresented students drop out, take longer to finish, or otherwise encounter institutional barriers. As a result, the DIAL position attracts the support of the Vice Chancellor of Student Affairs, and a three-year Memorandum of Understanding (MOU) institutionalizing funding for the position was signed by all campus sponsors in 2019. Isabela Perez, a PhD candidate in Psychology, is the third DIAL as of this publication.

Implications for Policy and Practice: UCR's DIAL promotes collaboration among multiple campus partners in supporting underrepresented graduate students while putting graduate students themselves in a campus leadership role. This position indicates one possible path towards transformational change (Chang, 2002) that other institutions may wish to pursue in addressing barriers to persistence among underrepresented graduate students and plugging "leaks" in the pipeline leading to a more diverse and inclusive professoriate.

Case Study 1 References

Brunsma, D. L., Embrick, D. G., & Shin, J. H. (2017). Graduate students of color: Race, racism, and mentoring in the white waters of academia. *Sociology of Race and Ethnicity, 3*(1), 1–13. https://doi.org/10.1177/2332649216681565

Chang, M. (2002). Preservation or transformation: Where's the real educational discourse on diversity? *The Review of Higher Education, 25*(2), 125–140. https://doi.org/10.1353/rhe.2002.0003.

DeCuir-Gunby, J. T., Johnson, O. T., Edwards, C. W., McCoy, W. N., & White, A. M. (2020). African American professionals in higher education: Experiencing and coping with racial microaggressions. *Race Ethnicity and Education, 23*(4), 492–508. https://doi.org/10.1080/13613324.2019.1579706

Griffin, K. A., & Muniz, M. (2015). Rethinking the structure of student recruitment and efforts to increase racial and ethnic diversity in doctoral education. *International Journal of Doctoral Studies, 10*, 199–216. Retrieved from http://ijds.org/Volume10/IJDSv10p199-216Griffin0749.pdf

Griffin, K. A., Muñiz, M. M., & Espinosa, L. (2012). The influence of campus racial climate on diversity in graduate education. *The Review of Higher Education, 35*(4), 535–566. https://doi.org/10.1353/rhe.2012.0031

Hurtado, S., Milem, J., Clayton-Pedersen, A., & Allen, W. (1999). Enacting Diverse Learning Environments: Improving the Climate for Racial/Ethnic Diversity in Higher Education (ED430514). *ASHE-ERIC Higher Education Report, 26*(8). ERIC. https://eric.ed.gov/?id=ED430514

Lorenzetti, D. L., Shipton, L., Nowell, L., Jacobsen, M., Lorenzetti, L., Clancy, T., & Paolucci, E. O. (2019). A systematic review of graduate student peer mentorship in academia. *Mentoring & Tutoring: Partnership in Learning, 27*(5), 549–576. https://doi.org/10.1080/13611267.2019.1686694

Milem, J. F., Chang, M. J., & Antonio, A. L. (2005). *Making diversity work on campus: A research-based perspective.* Association American Colleges and Universities.

Ramirez, E. (2017). Unequal socialization: Interrogating the Chicano/Latino(a) doctoral education experience. *Journal of Diversity in Higher Education, 10*(1), 25–38. https://doi.org/10.1037/dhe0000028

Roumimper, K. R., & Falk, A. F. (2019). Peer support of graduate students of color through a formal graduate student association. In S. Wisdom, L. Leavitt, & C. Bice (Eds.), *Handbook of research on social inequality and education* (pp. 111–129). IGI Global.

Slay, K. E., Reyes, K. A., & Posselt, J. R. (2019). Bait and switch: Representation, climate, and tensions of diversity work in graduate education. *The Review of Higher Education 42*(5), 255–286. https://doi:10.1353/rhe.2019.0052

Trent, F., Dwiwardani, C., & Page, C. (2020). Factors impacting the retention of students of color in graduate programs: A qualitative study. *Training and Education in Professional Psychology* (Advanced Online Publication). https://doi.org/10.1037/tep0000319

CASE STUDY 2

By Jennifer R. McCauley

Title: Mentoring in Science Training and Research to Inform Decisions (STRIDE): A Workshop Model Supporting Empathic Mentoring Relationships Through Improvisation and Active Listening

Institution: Institute for Advanced Computational Science (IACS) at Stony Brook University (large, public, research institution)

Problem of Practice: Mentoring is a fundamental component of education. Having strong mentoring relationships contributes to one's overall success in STEM programs (Kendricks et al., 2013). This is especially true for URM students as mentoring increases academic achievement, enrollment, and retention (Wilson et al., 2010). The trust, empathy, and support necessary for effective mentoring relationships is readily developed through mentor and mentee shared experiences of navigating the academic world as members of their underrepresented group (Patton, 2009). Having underrepresented identities in upper-level academia creates difficulty for these students to identify an allied mentor (Patton, 2009). One strategy for increasing retention of underrepresented students in academia is mentor training for existing faculty, especially those mentoring underrepresented students (Carroll & Barnes, 2015).

Evidence of the Problem: Many studies find trainings adopted by institutions and companies aimed at solving problems of racial discrimination, unconscious bias, and sexual harassment are ultimately ineffective and, in some cases, exacerbate the problem (Dobbin & Kalev, 2018; National Academies, 2018). These trainings generally adhere to a knowledge deficit model, a concept first established in the science communication field based on the premise that provision of more information regarding a topic (e.g., science, diversity, or sexual harassment) leads to positive behavioral and attitude changes in those receiving the information (Bak, 2001; Simis et al., 2016). This model is ineffective because people often do not process information rationally, especially surrounding politically or culturally charged topics such as race or gender (Bak, 2001). If the goal is eliciting behavior change, skills-based trainings (e.g., bystander intervention or behavior modeling training) are generally more effective than knowledge-based trainings (National Academies, 2018). Effective trainings focus on equipping participants with specific skills relevant to certain scenarios and provide opportunities to practice these skills in a controlled environment.

Initiative: Improvisation-based workshop to build empathy in mentoring relationships in support of academic equity: Improvisational theater techniques or "improv" effectively develop communication, listening, empathy, and negotiation skills. Improv allows audience connections through deep listening—turning focus toward others and facilitating collaboration (Bernstein, 2014). We designed an interactive, improvisation-based workshop to teach effective communication in mentoring relationships and to build empathy for underrepresented students in academia. The training aims to both improve mentoring relationships and to increase participation and success of URM students in STEM.

SUNY-Stony Brook University offered the workshop three times as part of an overall mentoring initiative undertaken by the Science Training and Research to Inform Decisions (STRIDE) program. The workshop incorporates improv techniques initiated by the Alan Alda Center for Communicating Science at Stony Brook University as well as group discussions, small group activities, and role-playing. STRIDE stems from a $3 million National Science Foundation (NSF)-funded graduate STEM training program, housed within the university's IACS. The program trains scientists to better communicate their research to decision-makers and the public. The STRIDE program is interdisciplinary and committed to recruiting URM students. The STRIDE mentoring model pairs students with STRIDE faculty mentors and peer mentors and requires participation in the *Mentoring in STRIDE* workshop to facilitate effective mentor-mentee relationships.

Following introductions, workshop participants are randomly divided into small groups of three to four, where they list good mentoring qualities. The whole group discusses each list, noting repeated themes. To facilitate shared perspectives, faculty and students take turns answering the question *What worries you?* Student worries include successful degree completion, getting a job, work-life balance, paying bills, and project funding. Faculty then share their concerns, which include supporting students financially, work-life balance, being a good scientist, and giving the right advice to students. The exercise builds empathy between faculty and students, who quickly realize they share many of the same concerns and commonalities.

After discussions, participants are guided through several applied improv exercises, including "Yes, and….," which separates participants into pairs to discuss a simple opinion statement. In round 1, partner A states the opinion statement (e.g. "Summer is better than winter") and partner B responds with "No" and supporting evidence. Partners take turns for two minutes. In round 2, partners A and B discuss a topic starting each statement with "Yes, but…," and in round 3, they start with "Yes, and…." This exercise introduces a critical concept in improv: for dialogue to flow effectively, each individual accepts the others' perspective (the *yes*) and adds something that advances the conversation productively (the *and*) (Spolin, 1963). This concept transforms conversations from conflictual to collaborative and constructive. In this exercise, workshop participants practice active listening within productive and respectful disagreements by focusing on their partner's words rather than their own thoughts.

Critical discourse is imperative to the inherently unequal faculty advisor-student relationship. If students believe their only option is acquiescence, both the relationship and research are damaged. This dynamic traumatizes URM students, especially given their already underrepresented position within academia and society as a whole. The "Yes, and…" exercise teaches participants how to make disagreements constructive. Students learn to listen to and address advisors' concerns while advisors acknowledge and remain open to students' thought processes.

The second half of the workshop focuses on diversity. The group brainstorms a list of obstacles to diversity they personally observed, which leads to a lively discussion of potential solutions. The final component of the workshop consists of several role-playing exercises, including students playing the role of advisor and vice versa. The role-plays teach students how to set healthy boundaries, learning when a firm "no" is more appropriate than a "Yes, and…."

Implications for Policy and Practice: Participant feedback specifically mentions the role-plays and group discussions. The interaction between faculty and students is particularly valuable because it allows for honest dialogue and empathy between the two groups. Overall, survey responses demonstrate that the majority of participants benefit from the interactive structure, improv exercises, and empathic approach built into the workshop. This outcome supports that mentoring and diversity are effectively addressed using an interactive, skills-based training format (National Academies, 2018).

The workshop achieved our goal of imparting specific skills that greatly improve mentoring and it supported two of the major goals of the STRIDE program: building effective mentoring structures and increasing inclusion and representation within the program. This workshop advanced several of the overarching goals of the Stony Brook Diversity Plan as well: to "support the development of a campus climate that values diversity, equity, and inclusion…" and to "expand educational… efforts to ensure that Stony Brook students have the ability to thrive as members of the campus community" (Stony Brook University, n.d., p. 6). Additionally, the outcomes of this workshop support the Diversity Initiative from the Office of Diversity and Inclusion at NSF, which aims to "cultivate a culture that encourages collaboration, flexibility, and fairness to enable individuals to contribute to their full potential and further retention" (NSF, n.d., para. 4).

Case Study 2 References

Bak, H.-J. (2001). Education and public attitudes toward science: Implications for the "Deficit Model" of education and support for science and technology. *Social Science Quarterly 82*, 779–795. https://doi.org/10.1111/0038-4941.00059

Bernstein, R. (2014). Communication: Spontaneous scientists. *Nature*, 505, 121–123. https://doi.org/10.1038/nj7481-121a

Carroll, M. A., & Barnes, E. F. (2015). Strategies for enhancing diverse mentoring relationships in STEM fields. *International Journal of Evidence Based Coaching and Mentoring*, 13, 58–69.

Dobbin, F., & Kalev, A. (2018). Why doesn't diversity training work? *Anthropology Now*, 10(2), 48–55. https://doi.org/10.1080/19428200.2018.1493182

Kendricks, K. D., Nedunuri, K. V., & Arment, A. R. (2013). Minority student perceptions of the impact of mentoring to enhance academic performance in STEM disciplines. *Journal of STEM Education*, 14, 38–46.

National Academies of Sciences, Engineering, and Medicine. (2018). *Sexual harassment of women: Climate, culture, and consequences in academic sciences, engineering, and medicine.* The National Academies Press. https://doi.org/10.17226/24994.

National Science Foundation (NSF). *NRT-DESE: Interdisciplinary graduate training to understand and inform decision processes using advanced spatial data analysis and visualization.* Award# 1633299.

National Science Foundation (NSF) (n.d.). *Diversity initiatives: Overview.* Retrieved from https://www.nsf.gov/od/odi/diversity.jsp

O'Connell, C., McCauley, J., & Herbert, L. (2021). Improvisation-based workshop to build empathy in mentor-mentee relationships and support academic equity. *Journal of Student Affairs Research and Practice*, https://doi.org/10.1080/19496591.2020.1842747

Spolin, V. (1963). *Improvisation for the theater: A handbook of teaching and directing techniques.* Northwestern University Press.

Simis, M. J., Madden, H., Cacciatore, M. A., & Yeo, S. K. (2016). The lure of rationality: Why does the deficit model persist in science communication? *Public Understanding of Science*, 25(4), 400–414. https://doi.org/10.1177/0963662516629749

Stony Brook University. (n.d.). *Plan for Equity, Inclusion, and Diversity.* Retrieved from www.stonybrook.edu/commcms/cdo/pdfs/divplan_092816.pdf

Wilson, A., Sanner, S., & McAllister, L. (2010). An evaluation study of a mentoring program to increase the diversity of the nursing workforce. *Journal of Cultural Diversity*, 17, 144–150.

CASE STUDY 3

By Heather N. Maietta

Title: Dissertation to Publication and other Postgraduate Career Pursuits: A Career Development Capstone Course for Doctoral Students

Institution: Doctorate of Higher Education Leadership Program at Regis College (private, Catholic institution)

Problem of Practice: Graduate programs cultivate student growth by developing problem-solving and critical-thinking skills. Typically, this transformation happens over the course of several years, while students simultaneously manage programmatic obligations, such as research, writing, presenting, and teaching, as well as non-programmatic commitments to career, family, and community. While managing multiple roles provides solid career progression, it limits career planning opportunities. Additionally, many graduate programs offer inadequate professional development offerings, leaving graduates underprepared for faculty roles and expectations (Adams, 2002; Austin, 2002; Helm et al., 2012) or workforce demands (Nyquist & Wulff, 2000).

Evidence of the Problem: Career development is fundamental to the success of doctoral studies in myriad ways. Access to faculty and staff advisors provides opportunities to discuss professional development and career goals (Campbell et al., 2005; King, 2003; Nyquist & Wulff, 2001) and early and consistent career mentoring contributes to increased persistence and earlier degree completion (Moran Craft, 2016; Roksa et al., 2018).

Initiative: In fall 2018, the Regis College Doctorate of Higher Education Leadership program repurposed a core leadership course into a capstone course focusing on career development and applications of the Dissertation in Practice (DiP). The course offers students intentional application of knowledge and skills gained from the DiP to both their current positions and future career aspirations. Because adults are less inclined to engage in learning unless it is meaningful (Merriam & Cafferella, 2020), the course encourages students to sustain and enlarge their work through several activities directly related to their research interests and current occupational roles.

Step one established objectives through program stakeholder input, a key component to successful design processes (Magleby et al., 2001). Student feedback reveals the following interest areas: career reflection, postgraduate career identification, professional skills and document development, publication education and support, and long-term career decision-making strategies. The following course objectives are:

- Gain deeper understanding of potential nonacademic career options outside of higher education; how the EdD provides value to these options
- Analyze the range of roles available for employment across an institution that fully engage with desired life design

- Explore and prepare for academic and nonacademic careers through resource and portfolio building
- Evaluate the vast array of professional networks to identify those most appropriately aligned with desired career goals
- Create an engagement plan that maximizes investment
- Build a professional suite of marketing materials that showcase one's brand capacity across myriad industries and occupations

The following activities address course objectives:

- *This I Believe* Essay: Using Bandura's (1977, 1997) social cognitive career theory as a lens, students construct a personal *This I Believe* podcast essay based on reflection of their doctoral journey and core values as scholarly practitioners.
- Backcasting Goal Setting Activity: Using Robinson's (1992) design research technique, Backcasting, and Asana or Trello software, students set a postgraduate scholarly publication submission target and timeline.
- Design Your Life: Looking at Schlossberg's (1984) adults in transition theory and using the doctoral-designed customer relationship management (CRM) platform ImaginePhD, students engage in values, skills, strengths, and interest assessment.

Other notable activities include creating a professional ePortfolio using Wix.com, a vita/professional resume, and conducting a series of informational interviews. Additionally, several guest speaker topics are incorporated:

- Mapping Your Career During Uncertain Times: Chaos Careers
- The Ins and Outs of Search Firms
- Happenstance in Your Career Search: Looking for Opportunities Where Opportunities Don't Exist
- Dissertation to Publication and Other Publishing Strategies
- You're a Doctor Now, Act Like It: Executive Presence

Other discussion topics include career advancement necessities, job search and hiring inequities, and pivoting during an unhealthy or unproductive career trajectory.

Career Integration: Crites' (1978) model of career maturity includes accurate self-appraisal, gathering occupational information, goal selection, planning, and problem-solving. The ability to engage in these activities increases career self-efficacy (Bandura, 1977, 1997; Betz et al., 2005; Taylor & Betz, 1983). Students in the course exercise self-efficacy exploration during the *This I Believe* podcast essay, vita and ePortfolio creation, and the ImaginePhD assessments. Through the *Design Your Life* activity, students reflect on their larger learning journey and gain understanding for how the EdD program prepared them for leadership and academic roles. Students use ImaginePhD to examine their accomplishments and goals against the Boyer model of scholarship (1990) and to discern past accomplishments and desired career direction.

Implications for Policy and Practice: The Regis EdD capstone course teaches students to capitalize on their professional knowledge, talents, and creativity. It also enhances their problem-solving skills, intellectual versatility, leadership, adaptability, and breadth of understanding of their dissertation research and the EdD program overall. Through carefully constructed activities, students reflect on how the DiP influences their role as scholar-practitioners in both their current professional setting and their desired future career path.

Case Study 3 References

Adams, K. A. (2002). What colleges and universities want in new faculty. *Preparing Future Faculty Occasional Paper* (ED472499). Association of American Colleges and Universities and Council of Graduate Schools. ERIC. https://files.eric.ed.gov/fulltext/ED472499.pdf

Austin, A. E. (2002). Preparing the next generation of faculty: Graduate school as socialization to the academic career. *The Journal of Higher Education, 7*(1), 94–122. https://doi.org/10.1080/00221546.2002.11777132

Bandura, A. (1977). Self-efficacy: Toward a unifying theory of behavioral change. *Psychological Review, 84,* 191-215. https://doi.org/10.1037/0033-295X.84.2.191

Bandura, A. (1997). *Self-efficacy: The exercise of control.* Freeman.

Betz, N. E., Hammond, M. S., & Multon, K. D. (2005). Reliability and validity of five-level response continua for the Career Decision Self-Efficacy Scale. *Journal of Career Assessment, 13,* 131–149. https://doi.org/10.1177/106907279600400103

Campbell, S. P., Fuller, A. K., & Patrick, D. AG. (2005). Looking beyond research in doctoral education. *Frontiers in Ecology and the Environment, 3*(3). 153–160. The Ecological Society of America. https://doi.org/10.2307/3868543

Crites, J. O. (1978). *Career Maturity Inventory.* CTB/McGraw Hill.

Helm, M., Campa, III, H., & Moretto, K. (2012). Professional socialization for the Ph.D.: An exploration of career and professional development preparedness and readiness for Ph.D. candidates. *Journal of Faculty Development, 26*(2). 5-23.

King, M. (2003). *On the right track: A manual for research mentors.* Council of Graduate Schools.

Magleby, S. P., Todd, R. H., Pugh, D. L., & Sorensen, C. D. (2001). Selecting Appropriate Industrial Projects for Capstone Design Programs. *International Journal of Engineering Education, 17*(4 and 5). 400-405.

Merriam, S. B., & Caffarella, R. S. (2020). *Learning in adulthood: A comprehensive guide* (4th ed.). Jossey-Bass.

Moran Craft, C., Augustine-Shaw, D., Fairbanks, A., & Adams-Wright, G. (2016). Advising doctoral students in education programs. *NACADA Journal, 36*(1). 54-65. https://doi: 10.12930/NACADA-15-013

National Science Foundation, National Center for Science and Engineering Statistics. (2019). *Doctorate Recipients from U.S. Universities: 2018.* Special Report NSF 20-301 https://ncses.nsf.gov/pubs/nsf20301/

Nyquist, J. D., & Wulff, D. H. (2000). *Re-envisioning the Ph.D.: Recommendations from national studies on doctoral education.* University of Washington. https://depts.washington.edu/envision/project_resources/national_recommend.html

Nyquist, J. D., Austin, A., Sprague, J., & Wulff, D. H. (2001). *The development of graduate students as prospective teaching scholars, a four-year longitudinal study: Final report* [report]. University of Washington, Center for Instructional Development and Research.

Robinson, J. B. (1982). Energy backcasting: A proposed method of policy analysis. *Energy Policy, 10*(4), 337–344. https://doi.org/10.1016/0301-4215(82)90048-9

Roksa, J., Feldon, D. F., & Maher, M. (2018). First-generation students in pursuit of the PhD: Comparing socialization experiences and outcomes to continuing-generation peers. *The Journal of Higher Education, 89*(5), 728–752. https://doi.org/10.1080/00221546.2018.1435134

Schlossberg, N. K. (1984). *Counseling adults in transition.* Springer.

Taylor, K. M., & Betz, N. E. (1983). Applications of self-efficacy theory to the understanding and treatment of career indecision. *Journal of Vocational Behavior, 22*(1), 63–81. https://doi.org/10.1016/0001-8791(83)90006-4

Wulff, D. H., Austin, A. E., Nyquist, J. D., & Sprague, J. (2004). The development of graduate scholars as teaching scholars: A four-year longitudinal study. In D. H. Wulff, & A. E. Austin (Eds.). *Paths to the professoriate: Strategies for enriching the preparation of future faculty* (Chapter 3). Jossey-Bass.

REFERENCES

Alcocer, L. F., & Martinez, A. (2018). Mentoring Hispanic students: A literature review. *Journal of Hispanic Higher Education, 17*(4), 393–401. https://doi.org/10.1177/1538192717705700

American Psychological Association. (n.d.). *APA's resource for individual development plans.* Retrieved from https://www.apa.org/education/grad/individual-development-plan

Ampaw, F. D., & Jaeger, A. J. (2012). Completing the three stages of doctoral education: An event history analysis. *Research in Higher Education, 53*, 640–660. https://doi.org/10.1007/s11162-011-9250-3

Amundsen, C., & McAlpine, L. (2009). 'Learning supervision': Trial by fire. *Innovations in Education and Teaching International, 46*(3), 331–342. https://doi.org/10.1080/14703290903068805

Barnes, B. J., & Austin, A. E. (2009). The role of doctoral advisors: A look at advising from the advisor's perspective. *Innovative Higher Education*, *33*(5), 297–315. https://doi.org/10.1007/s10755-008-9084-x

Barrett, J. L., Mazerolle, S. M., & Nottingham, S. L. (2017). Attributes of effective mentoring relationships for novice faculty members: Perspectives of mentors and mentees. *Athletic Training Education Journal*, *12*(2), 152–162. https://doi.org/10.4085/1202152

Bemker, M., & Leibold, N. (2018, September). Peer mentoring: A key to success in online graduate nursing education [Conference session]. Leadership Connection Conference, Indianapolis, IN. www.sigma.nursingrepository.org/bitstream/handle/10755/16378/Bemker_J01_92850_1.pdf?sequence=1&isAllowed=y

Benshoff, J. M., Cashwell, C. S., & Rowell, P. C. (2015). Graduate students on campus: Needs and implications for college counselors. *Journal of College Counseling*, *18*(1), 82–94. https://doi.org/10.1002/j.2161-1882.2015.00070.x

Blumenstyk, G. (2019, April). Career ready education: Beyond the skills gap, tools and tactics for an evolving economy [Report]. *Chronicle of Higher Education*.

Brown, R. (2011, August 28). Postdoctoral fellowships in the humanities gain importance in career paths. *Chronicle of Higher Education*. Retrieved from https://www.chronicle.com/article/postdoctoral-fellowships-in-the-humanities-gain-importance-in-career-paths/?cid2=gen_login_refresh&cid=gen_sign_in

Brus, C. P. (2006). Seeking balance in graduate school: A realistic expectation or a dangerous dilemma? *New Directions for Student Services, 2006*(115), 31–45. http://doi.org/10.1002/ss.214

Cohen, M. A. O., & Greenberg, S. (2011). The struggle to succeed: Factors associated with the persistence of part-time adult students seeking a master's degree (EJ967811). ERIC. *Continuing Higher Education Review*, *75*, 101–112. https://files.eric.ed.gov/fulltext/EJ967811.pdf

Dey, F., & Cruzvergara, C. Y. (2019, November 6). Five future directions in university career services. *LinkedIn*. Retrieved from https://www.linkedin.com/pulse/five-future-directions-university-career-services-farouk-dey/

Din, M., Malik, H. D., & Afzal, S. (2018). Contribution of ethical integrity in escalating academic integrity among university students. *The Journal of Humanities and Social Sciences*, *26*(2), 115.

Di Pierro, M. (2017). Mental health and the graduate student experience. *The Journal for Quality and Participation, 40*(1), 24–27. https://search.proquest.com/docview/1895913017?accountid=2909

Effland, K. J., & Hays, K. (2018). A web-based resource for promoting equity in midwifery education and training: Towards meaningful diversity and inclusion. *Midwifery, 61*, 70–73. https://doi.org/10.1016/j.midw.2018.02.008

Evans, T. M., Bira, L., Gastelum, J. B., Weiss, L. T., & Vanderford, N. L. (2018, March). Evidence for a mental health crisis in graduate education. *Nature Biotechnology, 36*(3), 282–284. https://doi.org/10.1038/nbt.4089

Fagen, A., & Wells, K. S. (2000). *National doctoral program survey* [Survey]. National Association of Graduate and Professional Students.

Fallatah, H. I., Soo Park, Y., Farsi, J., & Tekian, A. (2018). Mentoring clinical-year medical students: factors contributing to effective mentoring. *Journal of Medical Education and Curricular Development*, *5*. https://doi.org/10.1177/2382120518757717

Felder, P. P., & St. John, E. P. (Eds.) (2014). *Supporting graduate students in the 21st century: Implications for policy and practice.* AMS Press, Inc.

Fuhrmann, C. N., Halme, D. G., O'Sullivan, P. S., & Lindstaedt, B. (2017). Improving graduate education to support a branching career pipeline: Recommendations based on a survey of doctoral students in the basic biomedical sciences. *CBE—Life Sciences Education, 10*(3). https://doi.org/10.1187/cbe.11-02-0013

Gallant, T. B. (2008). *Academic integrity in the twenty-first century: A teaching and learning imperative.* Josey-Bass.

Gansemer-Topf, A. M., Ross, L. E., & Johnson, R. M. (2006). Graduate and professional student development and student affairs. *New Directions for Student Services, 2006*(115), 19–30. https://doi.org/10.1002/ss.213

Geesa, R. L., Lowery, K., & McConnell, K. (2018). Mentee perspectives of a first-year mentoring program for educational doctoral (EdD) students. *International Journal of Doctoral Studies, 13*, 471–495. https://doi.org/10.28945/4148

Gibbs, Jr., K. D., McGready, J., & Griffin, K. (2015). Career development among American biomedical postdocs. *CBE Life Sciences Education, 14*(4). https://doi.org/10.1187/cbe.15-03-0075

Golde, C. M. (1998). Beginning graduate school: Explaining first year doctoral attrition. In M. S. Anderson (Ed.), *The experience of being in graduate school: An exploration* (New Directions for Higher Education, 101, pp. 55–64). Jossey-Bass.

Golde, C. M. (2005). The role of the department and discipline in doctoral student attrition: Lessons from four departments. *Journal of Higher Education, 76*(6), 669–700. https://doi.org/10.1080/00221546.2005.11772304

Gordon, W. M., McCarter, S. A., & Myers, S. J. (2016). Incorporating antiracism coursework into a cultural competency curriculum. *Journal of Midwifery & Women's Health, 61*(6), 721–725. https://doi.org/10.1111/jmwh.12552

Hanbidge, A. S., Tin, T., Zaharuk, G., & Tsang, H. (2020). Building awareness of academic integrity with badges: Canadian university context. In Montoneri, B. (Ed.), *Academic misconduct and plagiarism: Case studies from universities around the world* (p. 89). Rowman & Littlefield.

Hobin, J. A., Fuhrmann, C. N., Lindsteadt, B., & Clifford, P. S. (2012, September 7). You need a game plan. *Science Careers* [newsletter published by *Science*]. https://doi.org/10.1126/science.caredit.a1200100

Holloway-Friesen, H. (2021). The role of mentoring on Hispanic graduate students' sense of belonging and academic self-efficacy. *Journal of Hispanic Higher Education, 20*(1), 46–58. https://doi.og/10.1177/1538192718823716

Hund, A. K., Churchill, A. C., Faist, A. M., Havrilla, C. A., Love Stowell, S. M., McCreery, H. F., & Scordato, E. S. (2018). Transforming mentorship in STEM by training scientists to be better leaders. *Ecology and Evolution, 8*(20), 9962–9974. https://doi.org/10.1002/ece3.4527

Jamieson, S. (2008). One size does not fit all: Plagiarism across the curriculum. In R. M. Howard & A. E. Robillard (Eds.), *Pluralizing plagiarism* (pp. 77–91). Boynton/Cook Publishers.

Kim, D., & Otts, C. The effect of loans on time to doctorate degree: Differences by race/ethnicity, field of study, and institutional characteristics. *The Journal of Higher Education, 81*(1), 1–32. https://doi.org/10.1080/00221546.2010.11778968

Krumboltz, J. D., & Levin, A. S. (2004). *Luck is no accident: Making the most of happenstance in your life and career.* Impact Publishers.

Kuhn, T. (2008). Historical foundations of academic advising. In V. N. Gordon, W. R. Habley, & T. J. Grites (Eds.), *Academic advising: A comprehensive campus process* (pp. 3–16). Jossey-Bass.

Lehker, T., & Furlong, J. S. (2006). Career services for graduate and professional students. *New Directions for Student Services, 2006*(115), 73–83. https://doi.org/10.1002/ss.217

Lovitts, B. E. (2001). *Leaving the ivory tower: The causes and consequences of departure from doctoral study.* Rowman & Littlefield.

Lowe, M. S., Londino-Smolar, G., Wendeln, K. E., & Sturek, D. L. (2018). Promoting academic integrity through a stand-alone course in the learning management system. *International Journal for Educational Integrity, 14*(1), 13. https://doi.org/10.1007/s40979-018-0035-8

Marcdante, K., & Simpson, D. (2018). Choosing when to advise, coach, or mentor. *Journal of Graduate Medical Education, 10*(2), 227–228. https://doi.org/10.4300/JGME-D-18-00111.1

Marsh, J. D., & Campion, J. (2018). Academic integrity and referencing: Whose responsibility is it? *Journal of Academic Language and Learning, 12*(1), A213–A226. Retrieved from https://journal.aall.org.au/index.php/jall/article/view/546

McConnell, K., Geesa, R. L., & Lowery, K. (2019). Self-reflective mentoring: Perspectives of peer mentors in an education doctoral program. *International Journal of Mentoring and Coaching in Education, 8*(2), 86–101. https://doi.org/10.1108/IJMCE-07-2018-0043

NACE. (2019). Trends continue for career services' location, reporting structure. *Author.* Retrieved from https://www.naceweb.org/career-development/trends-and-predictions/trends-continue-for-career-services-location-reporting-structure/

NACE Core Competencies Defined. (n.d.). Retrieved November 2020, from, https://www.naceweb.org/career-readiness/competencies/career-readiness-defined/

National Institutes of Health (NIH). (n.d). NRSA institutional predoctoral training grants program description and guidelines. *Author.* Retrieved from https://www.nigms.nih.gov/training/instpredoc/pages/predoctrainingdescription.aspx

National Institutes of Health (NIH) Biomedical Research Workforce Working Group Report. (2012). Retrieved from http://biomedicalresearchworkforce.nih.gov/background.htm

National Institutes of Health (NIH) Office of Intramural Training & Education. (2020). Preparing to teach and advise biomedical grad students and postdocs around career and professional development: A train-the-trainers event. *Author.* Retrieved from https://www.training.nih.gov/train_the_trainers_2020

National Science Foundation (NSF). (2015). Revisiting the STEM workforce: A companion to science and engineering indicators 2014. *Author.* Retrieved from https://nsf.gov/pubs/2015/nsb201510/nsb201510.pdf

Okahana, H., Zhou, E., & Gao, J. (2020, October). *Graduate enrollment and degrees: 2009 to 2019* [report]. Council of Graduate Schools. https://cgsnet.org/publication-pdf/6486/CGS_GED19_Report_final2.pdf

Patterson, T. (2016, July 6). Why do so many graduate students quit? *The Atlantic.* https://www.theatlantic.com/education/archive/2016/07/why-do-so-many-graduate-students-quit/490094/

Patton, Lori D. (2009). My sister's keeper: A qualitative examination of mentoring experiences among African American women in graduate and professional schools. *The Journal of Higher Education, 80*(5), 510–537. https://doi.org/10.1080/00221546.2009.11779030

Pecorari, D. (2008). *Academic writing and plagiarism: A linguistic analysis.* Continuum.

Pontius, J. L., & Harper, S. R. (2006). Principles for good practice in graduate and professional student engagement. *New Directions for Student Services, 2006*(115), 47–58. https://doi.org/10.1002/ss.215

Riggs, L. (2014, December 31). First-generation college goers: Unprepared and behind. *The Atlantic.* https://www.theatlantic.com/education/archive/2014/12/the-added-pressure-faced-by-first-generation-students/384139/?gclid=Cj0KCQiAh4j-BRCsARIsAGeV12CPxDz-X82-1nVm04dAfaWF4ajUv81Q-h9igTqeGVVlSfqsm_9WvA0aAuVCEALw_wcB

Saltikoff, N. (2017, May 1). The positive implications of internships on early career outcomes. *NACE Journal*. https://www.naceweb.org/job-market/internships/the-positive-implications-of-internships-on-early-career-outcomes/

Savickas, M. L. (2013). The theory and practice of career construction. In S. Brown, & R. Lent (Eds.) *Career development and counseling: Putting theory and research to work* (2nd ed. pp. 147–183). Wiley.

Schnoes, A. M., Caliendo, A., Morand, J., Dillinger, T., Naffziger-Hirsch, M., Moses, B., Gibeling, J. C., Yamamoto, K.R., Lindstaedt, B., McGee, R., & O'Brien, T.C. (2018). Internship experiences contribute to confident career decision making for doctoral students in the life sciences. *CBE Life Sciences Education*, *17*(1 ar16), 1–14. https://doi.org/10.1187/cbe.17-08-0164

Sefcik, L., Striepe, M., & Yorke, J. (2020). Mapping the landscape of academic integrity education programs: What approaches are effective? *Assessment & Evaluation in Higher Education*, *45*(1), 30–43. https://doi.org/10.1080/02602938.2019.1604942

Sheehy, K., & Kerr, E. (2019, June 19). 4 differences between grad and undergrad loans. *U.S. News and World Report*.

Simonson, M., Smaldio, S., Albright, M., & Zvacek, S. (2003). *Teaching and learning at a distance* (2nd ed.) Prentice Hall.

Stanford Biosciences. (n.d.a). *Career of choice*. Retrieved from https://biosciences.stanford.edu/current-students/idp/ https://biosciences.stanford.edu/current-students/career/

Stanford Biosciences. (n.d.b) *Individual Development Plans*. Retrieved from https://biosciences.stanford.edu/current-students/idp/

Sullivan, T. A. (1991). Making the graduate curriculum explicit. *Teaching Sociology*, *19*, 408–413. https://doi.org/10.2307/1318208

Thompson, L. W., Bagby, J. H., Sulak, T. N., Sheets, J., & Trepinski, T. M. (2017). The cultural elements of academic honesty (EJ1125650). *Journal of International Students*, *7*(1), 136–153. ERIC. https://files.eric.ed.gov/fulltext/EJ1125650.pdf

Tinto, V. (1993). *Leaving college: Rethinking the causes and cures of student attrition* (2nd ed.). University of Chicago Press.

University of California, San Francisco (UCSF). (n.d.) *Individual development plans*. Retrieved from https://mentoring.ucsf.edu/idps

Verschelden, C. (2017). *Bandwidth recovery: Helping students reclaim cognitive resources lost to poverty, racism, and social marginalization*. Stylus Publishing.

Vincent, B. J., Scholes, C., Staller, M. V., Wunderlich, Z., Estrada, J., Park, J., Bragdon, M. D. J., Lopez Rivera, L., Biette, K. M., & DePace, A. H. (2015). Yearly planning meetings: Individualized development plans aren't just more paperwork. *Molecular Cell*, *58*(5), 718–721. https://doi.org/10.1016/j.molcel.2015.04.025

121

Chapter 6

Graduate Student Engagement and Campus Programming

Mariann Sanchez and Trista Beard

Student affairs practitioners have long been involved in the holistic care and development of students on college and university campuses. The model in which this work has been done for decades has aimed to assist residential students and young adults making the transition through higher education from adolescence to adulthood to join society as college-educated, civically minded world citizens. Student affairs specialists who focus on the cocurricular engagement and well-being of graduate and professional students (GAPS) are harder to find, and focused training has been limited. Graduate student programming is often managed by specific academic units, fails to connect students widely to their peers, and reflects varying levels of departmental priorities. Academic units rarely allocate sufficient resources to adequately address many basic issues such as housing, counseling and wellness, and career development, let alone sponsor opportunities for engagement.

Programs for graduate students are often most successful when delivered through partnerships between student affairs and academic affairs professionals (Nesheim et al., 2007). Cross-unit collaborations to design intentional programs and workshops have proven successful in improving communication and overall systems of support for GAPS. Forming and sustaining collaborations with campus partners can promote centralized communication efforts, which leads to enhanced information-sharing and increased awareness and access to existing resources. This chapter highlights a variety of promising practices designed to support graduate students' engagement and holistic development and will make a case for implementing inclusive and purposeful campus-wide engagement opportunities for GAPS.

HOLISTIC STUDENT DEVELOPMENT

Many studies conducted on GAPS' experiences focus on retention (Bain et al., 2011; Di Pierro, 2012), academic writing (Jimenez y West et al., 2011; Walter &

DOI: 10.4324/9781003121671-8

Stouck, 2020), use of online tools (King, 2014), relationship to faculty mentoring (Lechuga, 2011; Lunsford et al., 2017), and student development in a specific academic context, like nursing (Gazza & Hunker, 2014), engineering (Crede & Borrego, 2014), and social work (Fakunmoju et al., 2016). Considering students' social class, Ostrove et al. (2011) found graduate students' sense of belonging was impacted by their financial struggles and had correlation to academic self-concept and career aspirations, regardless of academic field.

What is absent from the literature on strategies to support graduate students is a holistic and developmental approach that considers the student first before the academic training. This chapter focuses on the engagement of graduate students across university-wide resources designed to build community, equity, and inclusion. GAPS are a hugely diverse group of students. The Council of Graduate Schools reported 1.8 million students enrolled in master's degree, doctoral, and graduate certificate programs in 2016, with 75% of those students in master's programs and about 25% seeking doctoral degrees, which include the PhD, but also PsyD, DSW, EDD, JD, and MD, among other professional doctorates (Okahana & Zhou, 2016). The GAPS population is spread across a dozen academic fields and even more demographic markers: 57% women, 43% men, 60.7% White, 12% Black/African American, 11% Latino, 7% Asian/Asian-American, 6% race/ethnicity not reported, 3% multiracial, 81% U.S. Citizens or permanent residents, 19% temporary residents, and 58% enrolled full time. What the national data does not tell student affairs professionals is how many of the graduate students on the campus are parents, how many are undocumented, how many are food and/or housing insecure, and how many are working full-time jobs.

Having access to disaggregated data at the institutional level informs decisions and program development on each campus. Centralized program options and developmental activities will allow students space to share their unique experiences of the campus climate and their academic program and will illuminate barriers to their success that can then be addressed. Student affairs professionals are often the campus leaders in cocurricular programming, student development curriculum, and community-building activities, but on many campuses, centralizing graduate student support is a territorial battle.

Central to the mission of Graduate and Professional Student Programs and Services (GPSPS) is the necessity to connect students with appropriate resources through collaboration with campus partners and experts when services are not centrally provided by a GPSPS Office (CAS, 2019). Where centralization is not an option, it could be beneficial to create a graduate student success network composed of different schools that serve GAPS to discuss trends and all-campus student services. Doing so may assist in organizing advocacy efforts. Where advisors of graduate students often have a "council" or collegial group across departments, students may not have explicit pathways to build interdepartmental connections; all the more reason to implement campus-wide engagement opportunities to foster a common student identity among GAPS.

ONBOARDING

As detailed in Chapter 4, the tone of a University's engagement culture is typically set in the onboarding process, such as during Orientation. This time frame is critical to introduce students to campus resources, help acclimate them to the culture, and facilitate a sense of belonging to their new community. Multilayered onboarding structures can provide support for GAPS entering higher education with varying degrees of familiarity with the graduate environment. Certain schools have begun exploring the creation of Graduate Summer Bridge Programs to acclimate students to the academic and social norms of their departments and schools. Targeted programs can be incredibly beneficial for students who identify as Black, Indigenous, or People of Color (BIPOC), first-generation, low income, or hold other marginalized identities, as these often feel underprepared going into their graduate programs. These programs can go deeper into graduate school preparation by exploring themes around the hidden curriculum, imposter syndrome, making the most of an academic advisor, and financial wellness. Having support systems in place and familiarizing GAPS to these early on can help set up students of different backgrounds for success.

The importance of matriculating GAPS with marginalized identities became incredibly apparent during the Coronavirus (COVID-19) pandemic. COVID-19 exposed several realities for universities and provided new opportunities to better support minoritized student populations. COVID-19 reinforced the value of virtual onboarding processes for all GAPS, regardless of when they matriculate, to accompany orientation activities. As campuses had to pause or limit their in-person classes and onboarding activities, GAPS' onboarding efforts were directly impacted. The absence of detailed campus tours inhibited GAPS' visualization of becoming community members. Additionally, campuses had to shorten their orientation programs and limit socialization programs, thus resulting in the unintended disconnect of the students to campus and to each other. This is not to say, however, that COVID-19 had only negative effects on onboarding. COVID-19 forced campuses to revisit their marketing efforts, revamp their websites, adopt new platforms, and streamline their communication channels. One of the greatest benefits of virtual components is that they supplement in-person activities. For example, creating new onboarding pages filled with 2–3-minute videos detailing different resources accessible to incoming and current students anytime results in easier access for GAPS that have full-time jobs and/or other personal responsibilities. Additionally, streamlining communications reduced the campus geography specifically for larger institutions that have satellite campuses and siloed professional schools. If campuses are intentional about using near-peer models for the execution of their onboarding efforts, these new lessons learned can also contribute to new and productive mentoring relationships.

MENTORING

Studies consistently show that quality mentorship is one of the most consistent indicators of graduate student success (Spalter-Roth & Erskine, 2007). While quality mentorship can positively impact persistence in graduate programs, a lack of mentorship or poor mentorship, especially combined with financial strains, contributes to student attrition (Glover, 2019). In the previous chapter, mentorship models that support graduate students are highlighted. Using mentorship as an engagement tool for GAPS is an important strategy to add to the portfolio of institutional options to support professional, identity, and psychosocial development across disciplines. A discipline-specific model of mentoring for the "field" is a time-tested, but by no means the only, model and does a disservice to holistic approaches.

GAPS are also connected to mentors through campus career center programs, first-gen offices, multicultural centers, and other resources designed to serve *all* students. Peer mentoring programs and alumni networks are particularly useful for providing mentors and models who should be encouraged to take a skills-based approach to mentorship and lessen the focus on industry matching. Alumni mentors are uniquely positioned to provide intimate knowledge on the transition from graduate school to working life, balancing work/school and family, and navigating early career pivotal moments as well as negotiating cultural differences between school, professional, and community spaces. These connections are especially important for GAPS from underrepresented racial and class groups, who may experience a cultural divide between the institutional community and their home life.

GAPS also benefit from serving as mentors. The opportunity to engage graduate students in mentoring of peers and undergraduates is underutilized at many universities, often due to the academic silos of program demands, schedules, outside responsibilities, and school culture. Umbrella organizations like graduate student government (GSG), volunteer centers, wellness centers, and career services can draw on the talented pool of graduate students to assist in coaching undergrads in study skills, goal-setting, and help-seeking practices. Although the concern for adding to the unpaid labor of graduate students is not to be understated, learning objectives for both mentees and mentors should be carefully considered. Peer mentoring, alumni mentoring, and connections between affinity or identity groups should be utilized to offer career and social-emotional support across disciplines and connect fellow graduate students to resources that support holistic well-being.

WELLNESS

Rising mental health concerns for GAPS are well documented in recent national studies (ACHA, 2019; Woolston, 2019). A global study involving thousands of graduate students, the majority of whom were in PhD programs, showed that graduate students suffer from extreme rates of mental health concerns—six times that of the general population: 41% showed moderate to severe anxiety and 39% moderate to severe depression, with minority students having significantly higher rates than their peers (Evans et al., 2018). While Chapter 7 dives deeper into student well-being and outcomes, the focus here is on students' engagement in a variety of wellness initiatives. Wellness resources such as counseling services, mental health check-ins, and health center access are instrumental for graduate student success and well-being.

There is great potential to partner with counseling and mental health services on various efforts: creation of a student success coaching program, the development of a Graduate Student Support Group, and practicum hours for Master of Arts in Clinical Mental Health Counseling. Nearly every university with graduate programs offers a support group and/or group counseling opportunities specifically for graduate students under the counseling and mental health division of their student health center. Student Affairs professionals can mirror this model of support groups across intersectional identities to facilitate community-building around wellness. Such groups may include international GAPS, women in graduate school, lesbian, gay, bisexual, transgender, and queer/questioning (LGBTQ+) and nonbinary GAPS, men of color in graduate school, graduate student parents, and other special and intersecting communities. Where counseling centers often offer group therapy options for international students or graduate students as a monolithic group, student affairs professionals have the ability to be more nimble and address student needs as they arise, creating International Graduate Student Tea Time or Mindfulness Parenting for Graduate Students, for example. This approach puts a focus on positive practices that reinforce self-care, allows for more peer connections outside the academic department, and provides a nonclinical setting for students to share their experiences across the university.

Outside of clinical group therapy, student affairs staff should offer peer-led support groups that are unstructured, such as drop-in gatherings with a theme or as weekly meetings over a period during the semester (often five to six weeks) with an intentional curriculum covering life skills and wellness-related topics. Facilitators may be staff from cultural centers, religious life, career center, mindfulness or meditation leaders, learning centers, GSG, health promotion, international student services, or other campus partners that are charged with supporting students across the institution (as opposed to those who are bound to provide service in a particular academic unit). The most inclusive programs are developed in collaboration among departments and will have the best chance of reaching a wide swath of graduate students.

Wellness-centered programs are a wide enough umbrella to cover a broad range of topics. Guided by positive psychology practices, program facilitators (who are not trained psychologists) can still teach the soft skills needed to self-regulate and persist in graduate school. A wellness focus puts students at the center of the curriculum, as well as staying connected to the mission of the student affairs field: to cultivate and care for the whole student. Positive psychology is a framework that educators can use in coaching and support programs to focus the learning on positive aspects of development: what works, what motivates the student, where can one improve (Sheldon & King, 2001). This approach keeps the locus of control with the student and builds up self-efficacy skills, such as recalling past successes, resilience to hardships and obstacles, and a stronger ability to cope with pressures and reduce negative self-talk (Fredrickson, 2001).

Incredibly important to GAPS' overall wellness is the support of physical wellness programs. These can be done in collaboration with Campus Recreation departments, Fitness Centers, and Outdoor Adventures Offices. As enrolled students, GAPS once again have access to fitness facilities, on-site swimming pools, free or subsidized fitness classes, and intramural or club sports. According to the American College Health Association's National College Health Assessment (ACHA, 2019), 4.2% of the GAPS assessed indicated that they had participated in Club Sports, while 8.7% had participated in Intramural Sports. On certain college campuses, intramural sports are more popular with the GAPS population than undergraduates, allowing for GAPS to form cohort or program-specific teams. Intramurals also offer international graduate students an opportunity to bridge home and host cultures through sports less common in the United States, such as cricket, netball, or hurling. GAPS involved in recreational activities have been found to perceive a stronger sense of community (Elkins et al., 2011).

Similarly, GAPS-exclusive outdoor outings and camping trips allow students to build their community while exploring natural habitats within their cities. COVID-19 limitations and restrictions highlighted the importance of supporting physical wellness programs for GAPS and their families, prompting campuses to create robust virtual wellness programs, that is, yoga, zumba, mindfulness, and meditation. These are also examples of the *student advantage* that GAPS have when re-enrolling into a university. With their ID card, they renew their student access to sporting events, theater performances, concerts, and lectures as well as campus visits by diplomats, spiritual leaders, authors, poets, and musicians, to name a few. These opportunities contribute to a vibrant and engaged campus life and a sense of belonging to a wider campus community.

SENSE OF BELONGING

As discussed in Chapters 3 and 8, sense of belonging contributes to the success of GAPS, and can be facilitated through active engagement and involvement in all facets of campus life. For graduate students, a strong sense of belonging has been found to impact completion rates, mediate the effects of microaggressions, and ease network-building within the student's department and across the campus (O'Meara et al., 2017). Microaggressions are "brief, everyday exchanges that send denigrating messages" to individuals because of their membership in a marginalized racial identity group (Sue et al., 2007, p. 273). A study conducted by University of Maryland found that graduate students' perceptions that they had ongoing mentors and positive experiences with others in their departments was more important to their sense of belonging than reported micro-affirmations or microaggressions, though they also played a role (O'Meara et al., 2017). Academic departments and faculty advisors have an enormous impact on a student's connection to the discipline and their self-concept as a member of a professional field (Curtin et al., 2013), but in order for GAPS to feel connected to the institution as a whole, more value can be added with assistance from student affairs and student life experts.

Student affairs staff can facilitate community-building and belonging with a variety of levers. Student affairs divisions can enrich the socialization processes of graduate and professional programs through intentional collaborations during orientations, for example, or informally through the creation of social events and activities geared toward GAPS. Student affairs professionals can develop programs and services to promote students' emotional, social, and cognitive development (Gansemer-Topf et al., 2006). Student engagement thus becomes a measure to evaluate GAPS' sense of belonging, persistence both in and out of the classroom, and institutional quality. Recent studies have focused on doctoral student attrition highlighting opportunities for Student Affairs to support GAPS more intentionally. Not only do schools lose talented and qualified students, they also forfeit enormous amounts of time and money invested in students through assistantships, fellowships, and professional development initiatives (Pontius & Harper, 2006).

Student engagement across the campus translates into success in retention, alumni connectedness, and even eventual donations. Alumni giving is now the largest source of voluntary support, accounting for over a quarter (26%) of philanthropy to higher education (Kaplan, 2019). Engagement is a valuable approach to developing GAPS' sense of belonging and community. However, universities must consider the long-term implications of common practices that affect belonging, such as lack of diversity in the student body and faculty, large classes, the use of adjuncts, the graduate cocurricular experience, and more, as these may have an effect on alumni engagement and giving (Drezner & Pizmony-Levy, 2020). The following case study highlights the power of fellowship programs to offer holistic support that connects students to each other and to the wider campus community.

CASE STUDY 1

By Trista Beard

Title: Building Community through Topping Fellows Program

Institution: University of Southern California (USC), a large, private, research university in the center of Los Angeles, with 46,000 students, of which 56% are graduate students.

Problem of Practice: Much of the work done in student affairs to increase a sense of belonging campus-wide for graduate students depends on activities that foster community. Graduate students speak about their experiences as if they are bound by their discipline or department. Because of barriers to integration and engagement mentioned throughout in this chapter, students struggle to navigate the university-wide resources and full menu of experiences open to them. Fellowship programs offer a unique opportunity for GAPS on campus to find community and belonging that is not specifically tied to their academic discipline.

Evidence of the Problem: While there is centralized training for academic advisors who serve both undergraduate and graduate students, there is no centralized Graduate Student Life office in academic or student affairs divisions. Each of the 20 professional schools has its own support services, offering academic and professional support, but engagement activities to build community among graduate students varies widely. Only GSG offers cocurricular activities that cut across the academic silos.

Initiative: In the absence of university-wide programming to support the academic, personal and professional growth of GAPS specifically, the University of Southern California's (USC) Topping Fellows Program (Topping) developed a pilot curriculum for first-generation, low-income graduate students. The fellowship program aims to ease the stress of transition to graduate school, engage students around the development of community, leadership, and well-being, and promote a shared identity as an emerging scholar, regardless of academic discipline. This is an example of what practitioners can do to support students more broadly, even in the absence of a current campus-wide initiative.

Every new Fellow is paired with a returning student, in a near-peer mentor model, to facilitate community-building and validation. Validation theory (Rendón, 1994) is the underlying theoretical framework for this program and drives the advising practices and the focus on social capital-building as well. Connecting students to others who have shared identities and/or lived experiences, including similar challenges, validates that the difficulties graduate students face are not individual shortcomings; they are part of the challenge of graduate school and can be overcome with appropriate interventions and support.

The Topping Fellows enter as a cohort each fall, and are selected based on the strength of their community awareness demonstrated through a history of service. Topping Fellows are also first-gen or low-income college grads, and so the program can increase equity by offering supplemental support for historically underrepresented groups in advanced degree programs as well as serve as a cross-campus model in graduate student development. Holistic advising and a pedagogical approach to exposing the hidden curriculum of graduate and professional school is recommended in using cocurricular support of professional students. Every Fellow is required to attend a retreat and welcome mixer in the week before fall term begins, which includes workshops on financial literacy, time management, and networking skills for graduate students.

Exposing GAPS to a variety of faculty and alumni not related to their field widens their support network and increases social capital. Due to COVID-19, a large majority of student support programs moved online. Instead of the annual formal mentorship luncheon where all Fellows bring an instructor or advisor they want to get to know better, the program pivoted to a week-long series of Faculty Spotlight discussions (online), where intimate conversations could be replicated in small groups and the graduate students could meet instructors outside of their department (with special attention paid to inviting faculty of color and first-generation graduates). Undergraduate scholarship recipients in the Topping program were also able to attend the faculty talks. Assessment revealed that graduate Fellows reported a higher realization of learning outcomes from faculty network-ing over the undergraduates. The scores were 14% higher on three items related to ability to interact with faculty and 12% higher on the two items related to feeling connected to the campus community. Programming already in place for undergraduates can be utilized for graduate student needs, with careful thought given to the developmental goals of GAPS.

Implications for Policy and Practice: Campus-wide programs designed to foster mentorship, networking, and build confidence, en-gagement, and belonging have an even greater impact on GAPS when designed intentionally to cultivate community. Professional schools often engage students around identity markers, such as race, ethnicity, gender, age, nationality, and class status. First-generation and low-income gradu-ate groups, such as those at Cornell (Hrichak, 2019), Duke (Daly, 2020), and University of California, Los Angeles (UCLA) (n.d.) are the latest it-eration of these student-led advocacy groups to make new spaces for stu-dents to engage in community-building. Encouraging cross-collaboration between student groups and institutional offices is essential for recogniz-ing intersectional identities and strengthening community bonds.

Case Study 1 References

Daly, J. (2020, January 28). *Duke FIRSTS builds a community for first-gen graduate stu-dents.* Duke Graduate School. Retrieved from https://gradschool.duke.edu/about/news/duke-f1rsts-builds-community-first-gen-graduate-students

Hrichak, K. (2019, November 20). New group supports first-generation and low-income students. *Cornell Chronicle.* Retrieved from https://news.cornell.edu/stories/2019/11/new-group-supports-first-generation-and-low-income-students

Rendón, L. I. (1994). Validating culturally diverse students: Toward a new model of learning and student development. *Innovative Higher Education, 19*(1), 33–51.

University of California, Los Angeles. (n.d.). First-Generation Graduate Student Council. Retrieved from https://firsttogo.ucla.edu/For-Graduate-Students/First-Generation-Graduate-Student-Council

IDENTITY DIALOGUES

Utilizing innovative community-building opportunities *across* programs and de-partments enhances the sense of belonging and overall success of a diverse and growing GAPS population. These can be programs or dialogue series facilitated by faculty and/or students focused on their multiple identities, the intersection of those identities, and how they influence their daily lives. The Office of Graduate

Student Life at University of San Diego (USD) has designed a multidimensional interactive dialogue series designed to uplift GAPS to explore themes unique to their graduate experience and identify tools to better manage challenges when they arise. This type of dialogue series can proactively engage GAPS and invites them to examine their multiple identities in spaces that will validate who they are and what they are experiencing. As USD is a faith-based institution, the partnership with the Graduate Ministry allows students to explore themes related to their spiritual and religious life. Similarly, the partnership with the University's Identity Centers and Wellness Office invites students to dive into a deep exploration of the intersection of their multiple identities, mental health and well-being. Programs include Black Grads Matter, First-Generation Graduate Student Dialogues, Graduate Women of Color, Theology on Tap, Latinx Socials, AAPI Community-Building Spaces, Native American Awareness, and others that also serve to uplift and validate their living experiences. Though facilitated dialogues may not mimic the acceptance level of larger society, they are important for institutions of higher education striving to give students the room to strengthen communication skills and develop an authentic self-identity. The safer students feel in the dialogue space, the more likely their time together will be increasingly productive (Giacomini & Schrage, 2009). These dialogues can also support specific efforts to celebrate diverse communities during Women's History Month and the National Heritage Months: African American, American Indian, Asian Pacific, Jewish, Hispanic, and LGBTQ. As institutions of higher education continue to diversify, it will be increasingly important for these institutions to create spaces on campus—physical and psychological—where students can explore their differences in a safe and effective way (DeBowes, 2006). Key to the success of facilitated dialogues is for facilitators to create intentional spaces that allow all participants' voices to be heard.

One framework that colleges and universities have adopted to create a meaningful dialogue space is a model called intergroup dialogue (IGD). This model has been adopted by campuses nationwide, including University of Washington, Arizona State University, University of Maryland, and University of Massachusetts; however, this approach can be best attributed to the University of Michigan (Chesler et al., 2005). The University of Michigan created a Program on Intergroup Relations (IGR) which centers on IGD as a model for social justice. IGD blends theory and experiential learning to facilitate students' learning about social group identity, social inequality, and IGR (Intergroup Relations, n.d.). Throughout the dialogues, facilitators assist participants in exploring issues of power, privilege, conflict, and oppression in an effort to break down intergroup barriers and build alliances between dialogue participants (Schoem et al., 2001). Since its inception, IGD has been used by student affairs practitioners for facilitation of dialogue with student leaders, student organizations, and campus programming.

IGDs are one way that institutions might fully reap the benefits of structural diversity by providing a safe, confidential, and facilitated opportunity for meaningful cross-group peer interaction (DeBowes, 2006). Participants are able to build trust, empathy and ally-ship, and move in a direction of personal growth.

Creating meaningful connections and strong relationships can be complicated in a virtual capacity. To this end, campuses have looked to restorative justice as a framework to create spaces that invite vulnerability and authenticity. College campuses are using restorative practices to respond to larger social justice issues such as sexual misconduct, abuses of power and privilege, and bias incidents (Karp, 2019). Using the principles of restorative justice, facilitators are able to craft community-building circles that ensure trust, active listening, respectful dialogue, and if necessary, allow for individual and communal healing. Restorative dialogues help to improve the overall campus climate and promote campus change, and GAPS can become key drivers for this process. At the Center for Restorative Justice at the USD, GAPS who obtain a certificate in Restorative Justice are invited to become practitioners and facilitate circle dialogues on campus and in the greater San Diego Community. When a campus community or its individual members experience harm, restorative justice can be used to guide students through difficult conversations using a Healing Centered Engagement (HCE) lens. For example, when campuses have experienced hate crimes or acts of intolerance, restorative circles have become healing spaces for participants to process impact. Any thoughtful restorative justice process should simultaneously address the needs and obligations of the key stakeholders and also consider the systemic reasons that allowed for the harm to take place (Karp, 2019). Similarly, restorative circles facilitate conversations around the greater sociopolitical climate and engage participants in addressing racial injustices, sexism, classism, and other emerging issues in a structured, guided, and intentional space. Restorative spaces can also provide the opportunity for participants to come up with restorative agreements and action plans, thus promoting student engagement and advocacy.

STUDENT ADVOCACY AND INVOLVEMENT

Fostering student advocacy is one of the best practices to grow and maintain graduate student engagement and presence in campus life. Advocacy empowers students and allows them to channel their individual and collective voice. Structures of advocacy are facilitated through involvement in graduate student organizations, GSG, and graduate student presence on key university committees. Increase student advocacy by inviting graduate students, as is appropriate, to sit on committees and offer feedback related to decisions that may affect them. Graduate student involvement, whether in local graduate student organizations or in nationally affiliated professional associations, holds many benefits for graduate students, including socialization to the academic profession (Gardner, 2005).

Graduate Student Organizations

The development of student organizations or clubs allow students to get involved and make connections in their time as students and beyond. Local student organizations can provide incoming students with instant connections to their peers, making them feel more involved and integrated into their institutional culture (Gardner & Barnes, 2007). These graduate student organizations may be field-related to help promote and recognize excellence in academics, research, and service to these professions. Membership in these student organizations includes vast benefits, including professional development, scholarships, awards, resources, leadership development, and recognition through regalia and other societal displays. As members, students have access to webinars, career resources, job sites, and research in their field. Graduate student organizations can also focus on identity to allow for spaces for students to create professional networks, find community, and have inclusive dialogue centered on their voice. These might include Latinx Graduate Student Association, Black Graduate Student Association, and LGBTQIA+ Graduate Student Association, to name a few. The benefits of GSG and organizations are vast, but should not serve as a proxy for institutional and structural support. Whenever possible, specialist staff who focus on the interests, challenges, and development of graduate students should be embedded into existing central resources (career services, health promotion and wellness, campus activities, cultural centers, etc.). Additionally, there should be intentionality in examining institutional data to help advocate for needed institutional and structural resources.

Graduate Fraternity and Sorority Chapters

Many GAPS were involved in fraternity and sorority life as undergrads. If a GAPS' fraternity or sorority chapter is at their current institution, there is a potential to get involved with them and connect with a new community of Greek Life members. GAPS involved in Greek Life also have the option to join Professional/Graduate chapters with the purpose of connecting graduates with one another. Another way for GAPS to stay involved with their fraternity or sorority is for them to join alumni chapters, which are informal groups whose goal it is to create and facilitate both networking and socializing events. Graduate and Alumni chapters of a fraternity or sorority are often designated by a city or region rather than a host institution.

Graduate Student Government

GSG makes up the centralized governance structure with electable leadership positions that seek to provide advocacy opportunities. These student-governed associations can serve to support the development of professional, scholastic, and social communities in different schools. Additionally, associations provide leadership opportunities for students, offer an organized way for them to provide feedback to faculty and staff, and facilitate an increase in awareness of and participation in professional associations, conferences, certifications, and workshops. Representation on faculty search committees or university task forces can easily contribute to students' socialization, as it allows students to learn about faculty and university governance as well as offering opportunities to network with other faculty and administrators on their campuses (Gardner & Barnes, 2007). GSGs have significant influence in their campus communities. GSG leadership have the unique opportunity to capture the GAPS experience and advocate on their behalf in the various spaces they occupy. GSG official statements, student protests supported by the GSG, and other efforts around activism have resulted in modifications to University policies, practices, and even culture. Like any shared governance mechanism, there is often tension between power-holders. Student-led governments view themselves as autonomous and university administrators view them as a mechanism for gaining feedback and consensus for initiatives. In practice, there is a strong case for oversight, but only to maintain sustainability, equity, and open communication, and avoid mission-drift.

UNIONIZATION AND ACTIVISM

Students across college campuses are encouraged to participate in a variety of civic engagement activities. GAPS involved in advocacy, union efforts, and protests often engage in equity and justice work and demonstrate a strong sense of community. Working toward social justice and change are foundational practices for creating global citizens and forming future change-makers—and an important part of higher education institutions realizing their missions.

National Organizations

National organizations provide another opportunity to engage GAPS across their academic field and connect them to a wider network outside the institution. Most professional degrees (JD, MBA, MD, PharmD, etc.) have a national association and offer a graduate student membership tier. Advisors should encourage students to join as a way to connect them to their chosen profession; departments may offer micro-grants to cover the membership and/or conference fees to facilitate professional development. Professional associations serve as socializing outlets for the students as they learn to seek out the cultures that reflect their own values and those to which they aspire in a future career (Gardner & Barnes, 2007). Across the campus, many graduate students may also have an opportunity to join a unionized labor movement. However, these organizations focus on GAPS engaged as teaching assistants and research assistants and may leave out thousands of students in master's degrees and other professional programs who are not engaged in unpaid or underpaid work on campus.

Graduate Student Unions

Graduate Student Unions are an additional space where GAPS can advocate for their rights and exercise representative democracy. The graduate student labor union movement campaigns for workplace protections for GAPS, such as health care, medical leave, insurance, and pay standards, but also provides an opportunity for scholar-activism. Emerging professionals in many fields (not solely in academia) gain experience in advocacy, policy-making, and collective bargaining through these activities. Consequences loom; however, the relationships between students and faculty and/or the department may become tense or fractured. All students are learners and all learners have to critically assess their choices considering the commitment and possible outcomes; support from professional staff will assist in this process. The opportunity to work with a wide range of students across an institution and to improve the work conditions of future graduate students is an attractive and honorable activity.

Traditionally, unionization has been more prevalent in public rather than private institutions. Until 2000, only graduate students at public universities were permitted to form unions under the rules of the National Labor Relations Board, the federal agency that governs unions in the United States (Whitford, 2014). A 2016 National Labor Relations Board ruling is likely to change that because it effectively "gave graduate students the right to collectively bargain in the private sector" (Patel, 2019, para. 1). Consequently, the tide has been turning, considering elite institutions that led the opposition to graduate student unions for years, including Brown, Columbia, and Harvard Universities, are collectively bargaining with their graduate student unions (Patel, 2019). While pay is one of the main driving forces for unions, there are other issues that make it to the bargaining table that are central to the GAPS experience. Union activists have long advocated for parental leave benefits, mental health services, and gender equality, but those issues are more crucial in graduate student contract bargaining than even a decade ago (Patel, 2019). The protections that GAPS are fighting for are part of a larger conversation about equity. However, there is also an opportunity to enact more immediate change through activism.

Protests and Activism

Many of the policies, programs, and protections that exist on college campuses were born from student activism and/or protests. Historically, student-led protests have been catalysts for great change. As detailed earlier, many of these surfaced from the graduate student unions, labor protests, and benefits disputes, while others have mirrored social justice problems happening in the greater society. This is not to say that activism on college campuses is limited to students; some have received significant support from faculty and administrators who have a personal connection to a national movement. In the early 1960s, the Civil Rights movements, the Chicano(a) Student Movement (CSM), and anti-war movements targeting U.S. involvement in Vietnam were critical in shaping this period of youth-led upheaval (Rhoads, 2016). These movements spilled over onto college campuses in this time frame and set the stage for future major movements.

More recently, #BlackLivesMatter and movements in support of Dreamers, named for their support for the Development, Relief, and Education for Alien Minors (DREAM) Act, and other immigration-related issues have found much support on college campuses (Rhoads, 2016). Occupy Wall Street, Gun Control, protections for the indigenous communities whose land campuses reside on, and the rights of the LGBTQIA+ community are issues that have also surfaced on college campuses. Although race and immigrant-related equity concerns have marked a good deal of student activism during the early part of the 21st century, violence against women and related Title IX debates have also been highly influential in generating student direct action, as exemplified by the Carry That Weight campaign (Rhoads, 2016). GAPS have long stood beside undergraduate students in support of these causes. GAPS have also played key roles in protests that have centered on finances, that is, the costs of tuition and of student housing. In some instances, GAPS have been able to capitalize on the momentum of existing movements to push for significant culture and climate change on their campuses. For example, supporting culturally based movements helped to pave the way for culturally informed resources to be established, such as identity-based centers and study spaces, and culturally responsive pedagogy training for faculty. Additionally, these opened the door for tenure-track faculty from underrepresented communities to be hired as well as the diversification of the curriculum to include multicultural and social justice education.

Student activism and protests on college campuses have taken on various forms. Graduate student leader crafted statements, peaceful protests, letters of support, walk-outs, teach-ins, strikes, and picket lines are a few examples of various ways students have voiced their concern and gained traction for a cause. During the global pandemic, graduate students' traditional forms of protest were hampered by

137

social distancing protocols and empty campuses as picket lines are not easily replicated on Zoom; however, COVID-19 could usher in a new era for graduate student
activism (Zahneis & Patel, 2020). Students were able to protest social justice and
inequity issues on their campuses by turning off their cameras and displaying an
image of support for a movement. Social media and the internet have expanded
the reach and the structure of contemporary activism as it has traditionally been
displayed. Social media giants, such as Facebook, Instagram, Snapchat, TikTok,
and the use of hashtags has propelled activist campaigns to a national and global
level. Opportunities for student advocacy are vast, and there are many channels.
Graduate students not already involved in this type of advocacy work should be
encouraged to find service opportunities that speak to them, fostering deeper connections to the institution, to local communities' needs, and to civic responsibility.

SERVICE-LEARNING AND COMMUNITY SERVICE

University service-learning used as a cocurricular instructional activity is often designed to promote awareness of social justice issues in the surrounding
community. Documented outcomes for undergraduate students from service-
learning are a sustained interest in serving in the community (Einfeld & Collins, 2008), growing awareness of the root causes of social problems (Mitchell,
2007), and reduced stereotypes as well as recognizing one's own privileges
(Jones & Abes, 2004). However, little research has examined graduate programs
utilizing service-learning or community engagement as a companion or parallel
learning space for exploring praxis (Eyler, 2009; Rutti et al., 2016). In graduate
education, the experiential component most often utilized is professional fieldwork. While the field component of teacher training has become standard, the
use of service-learning as a curricular companion is less often employed (Eyler,
2009). The fieldwork requirement provides professional training, supervised
work experience, and an opportunity to apply theoretical concepts in real-world
situations. Service-learning as part of the co-curriculum allows graduate students to connect with a wider network of cross-campus students and staff as well
as to engage with local community members.

Service-learning and volunteer projects are just as valuable to the development of graduate students as undergraduates. The focus on many campuses on
the development of "young minds" keeps cocurricular initiatives stuck in a model
that serves traditionally aged college students. But our campuses are becoming
more diverse, with the average age of college-goers rising each year, especially
for part-time and graduate students (Bustamante, 2020). Volunteer opportunities and service-learning curriculum can be related to an academic field and still
draw in students from other disciplines to increase socialization and institutional

connection. For example, dozens of law schools run community immigration clinics, utilizing law students to assist in assessing cases, gathering data and documents, and advising clients with various processes. Students who wish to volunteer or intern with the clinics are also welcomed in, connecting students from policy, social work, psychology, education, and health fields, just to name a few. The focus on a large community problem, such as homelessness, is another example of bringing students together from a wide array of fields (architecture, engineering, public health, occupational therapy, sociology, economics, etc.) to work on interdisciplinary approaches to the great social ills of our time. Student affairs is most often the home for service-learning and volunteer centers, and should partner with graduate student leaders and community organizers to offer opportunities that utilize graduate student expertise across academic disciplines.

Revisiting the theme of mentorship as a form of service, it is important to consider that engaging GAPS in opportunities to mentor undergraduates (or new graduate students) provides significant developmental growth for both partners. Graduate mentors made gains in leadership, help-seeking aptitudes, and their own teaching and communication skills (McConnell et al., 2019; Reddick et al., 2012). Using a social exchange framework to consider what mentors gain, Reddick et al. (2012) found the learning to be significant for GAPS, especially illuminating the "hidden curriculum" of what to ask, who to ask, and what were the unspoken expectations of graduate students. Other insights provided by graduate mentors were that they had to reflect on their own values and goals, developed as instructors, trainers, and coaches, and felt a sense of responsibility for diversifying their own academic fields and/or the pipeline of underrepresented students in advanced degree programs. Last, mentors reported they wanted to engage in this type of service work because others had invested time in mentoring them. If student affairs professionals are mission-centered on developing the whole student, then engaging GAPS in different types of service opportunities allows for civically minded growth and helps students find ways to apply their passions, research, and skills to improve both campus and community.

ASSESSMENT

Good practice in graduate student engagement involves ongoing data collection and analysis (Pontius & Harper, 2006). Students' voices, captured by ongoing assessment of the graduate student cocurricular experience, inform campus partners' decisions on how to better support the ever-evolving demographic of this graduate and professional student population, as further discussed in Chapter 9. Assessment efforts should focus on (1) the quality of the graduate student experience, (2) the effectiveness of services as they relate to graduate student success, and (3) the effectiveness of services in supporting each department's goals. These can be administered in several ways, including individual interviews and focus groups as well as questionnaires and surveys to determine the affective dispositions of current and former graduate students toward campus-wide programs and services (Pontius & Harper, 2006). Assessment administrators can consider, for example, the incorporation of focus groups or mid-semester check-ins to collect data at various points during the student life cycle.

The USD Office of Graduate Student Life, in collaboration with the Institute of Research and Planning, administers a Graduate and Law Student Experience Assessment every three years. This assessment is designed to understand the Graduate and Law Student experience both inside and outside the classroom and explore opportunities to improve their experience. The survey collected information about the following topics related to graduate and law students' experiences at USD: (1) academic experience, (2) Office of Graduate Student Life programming, (3) cocurricular events/activities, (4) academic/online resource usage, (5) finances, (6) employment status/volunteering, (7) workshop topics of interest, and (8) preferences for receiving information.

Data gained from surveys can be used to understand which programs, offices, and resources best support a large and growing population. It determines the level in which GAPS want to be engaged and the types of programs in which they want to engage. In looking at sense of belonging, 84% of students indicated that they felt valued and included by the faculty, 83% felt valued by peers, 75% by the administration and staff, and 73% by their department. Of those who felt valued by their home department, 95% indicated interest in connecting with peers in their program, 89% with recent alumni, 84% with students in other programs, and 62% with identity groups (gender, race, sexual orientation, etc.). These significant numbers illustrate that programs that connect current GAPS to their peers and alumni are seen as high value programs. Student engagement is viewed as an avenue for students to build community and thus become successful in their time as students, having made institutional connections with others. Additionally, students placed value on the following cocurricular events: 83% on alumni networking events, 81% research skills workshops, 73% identity-based spaces, and 53% on family events. This information provided the Office of Graduate Student Life an opportunity to partner with offices that could support different areas of engagement, such as Alumni Relations.

Assessment data also provides insight into student utilization of academic and student support resources. Assessment results in 2016 showed that in certain instances, 80% of students were not aware that many of these resources existed (such as writing support, library specialists, counseling, health and wellness, etc.). This data proved beneficial in meeting with campus partners to modify their marketing strategies, language, and programming and be intentional about participating in graduate student onboarding efforts. Disaggregating data for the different schools and offices that support graduate students has prompted changes in how they approach student engagement and campus activities. Key to the success of assessment efforts is its institutionalization, which increases the level of involvement of key stakeholders and student participation.

CASE STUDY 2

By Josh Cooper

Title: The "Beyond the Classroom" Assessment

Institution: William James College (WJC) is a private nonprofit college of psychology and behavioral sciences, rooted in experiential education. WJC educates close to 1,000 students in the fields of psychology, health and human services, and organizational leadership. Over 90% of the student body is working toward a Doctoral or Master's degree, and the campus is nonresidential. In alignment with the college's mission for experiential education, all students are required to have an internship requiring several days a week of full-time work. As a result, the student life team struggled to build community and develop student involvement.

Problem of Practice: Seeing steady declines in participation in graduate student life activities, the Dean of Students at WJC and his team in Student Life utilized a design thinking approach to develop the "Beyond the Classroom" survey to understand student life outside the institution. Design thinking in this context situates students as co-creators (Meinel & Leifer, 2012). Learning from them, more about their lives and needs, was critical to redesigning student engagement programs at WJC.

Josh Cooper, the Dean of Students, and his team in Student Life recognized the challenges and the changing dynamics associated with their student body and the structure of the academic programs. Each day, different programs and concentrations are active on campus. Coupled with internship requirements and the busy schedule of working adults in a nonresidential educational program, it has been difficult to cultivate consistent student engagement.

Evidence of the Problem: Dean Cooper and his team examined several years of student life assessments to try to learn more about why engagement was low. Event attendance records, program surveys, and student services omnibus surveys were compared to overall student body statistics.

141

Furthermore, his team reviewed the number of student groups from year to year along with their membership data, the number of events the groups sponsored each year, and their attendance. When measuring these numbers over time with the size of the student body, there was evidence to support an intentional intervention to improve engagement. Goals included improving program/event attendance, increasing the number of student volunteers and participants in student government and student groups, and increasing the overall student participation in the community.

Initiative: While it would be natural to turn to student development theory, Dean Cooper looked to other fields and alternative methods. The student life team used design thinking to engineer a solution. They could not build community and improve engagement if they did not look at the full graduate student experience. This meant looking at student life outside the college walls and then unpacking how that impacted the college culture. From there, Dean Cooper and his team developed the "Beyond the Classroom" survey to better understand the complexities of graduate student life. The survey focused on any life aspect that could impact being a graduate student: commute time, hours spent at part-time jobs, caregiving responsibilities, physical and mental health concerns, financial insecurity, and life events and/or responsibilities that students considered hurdles to their academic success.

The Dean of Students' office was transparent in their marketing, incorporating their hopeful learning outcomes, and saw that 50% of the student body completed the survey. The assessment helped to solidify and quantify information that had only ever been observational or anecdotal. The results were used over the next six months for brainstorming and to realign the student life strategic plan to the data provided by actual WJC students. This led to an entire redesign of student leader training, new pathways for accessing services and resources, and the development of an action plan to improve engagement. The lessons learned led to not just large programming changes but also many smaller changes that incrementally led to improved student engagement and community-building. Smaller changes were simple, such as shortening the lengths of programs as well as offering the same event multiple times during the week to increase accessibility. However, there were also larger philosophical changes to their approach.

The concept that most resonated with the student life team was drawn from the work of Simon Sinek (2009) on inspiring leaders—it doesn't matter what you do, it matters why you do it. There is always such a focus in student life on what we do for the community, what services are provided, and what events are being held, but not enough time spent on purpose. Often, graduate-level programming ends up being a continuation of undergraduate student life. Since the graduate students are so invested in their educational and professional path, the office spent time understanding their "why." One outcome from this is that now the office works to build cocurricular components into all programs and events, even if they are social in nature. As Dean Cooper states:

> Graduate students have additional responsibilities that sometimes make their availability to step away more difficult. If we can always aim to have a co-curricular aspect or component to our programs, even if they are intended to be a social event, it may increase student attendance and engagement.

The decision to frame everything, even social activities, in relation to how they enhance the academic experience immediately improved participation in community events.

Another focus area, connecting design thinking to the assessment data, was the restructuring of student partnerships. The "IKEA effect" concept explains how people can be subjectively biased toward and place higher value on products they partially create (Norton et al., 2012). The Dean's team involved students in the "building" of programs to engage student leaders and support their development. They adapted leadership training for student government and student organizations made involvement easier for students. Once invested in any project, the shared ownership increased participation. Students were now invested in bringing other students along to participate and experience their workshops and events. This co-creator approach not only improved the work of the students, but increased the number of student organizations, brought healthy growth to the student government, and increased student attendance at programs and events.

Implications for Policy and Practice: In the end, the team realized that to support their students, they had to frame all of what they learned and did within two ideas. First, if they were going to adapt to meet the needs of their graduate students and improve engagement, they would have to accept it would take experimentation and the ability to learn from failures. Second, as they interacted with students, it was necessary to promote reasonable expectations. This meant keeping an open dialogue, creating strong

143

partnerships with their students, and maintaining a high level of transparency. Graduate students lead complicated lives and to fully engage them in the college community, students benefit from open communication, a willingness by the student life team to innovate, partnerships between students and staff, and an institutional acceptance that they have complex identities as students, emerging professionals, caretakers and family members, and community members. Engaging them holistically as students while they are part of the college community will develop a bond with the institution that can be revisited in later years through alumni outreach.

Case Study 2 References

Meinel, C., & Leifer, L. (2012). Design thinking research. In *Design thinking research* (pp. 1–11). Springer.

Norton, M. I., Mochon, D., & Ariely, D. (2012). The IKEA effect: When labor leads to love. *Journal of Consumer Psychology, 22*(3), 453–460.

Sinek, S. (2009). *Start with why: How great leaders inspire everyone to take action.* Penguin.

ALUMNI ENGAGEMENT

Throughout this chapter, a variety of engagement strategies have been introduced and recommended, using the student life cycle as a progressive guide. Cultivating engagement that fosters belonging, community, connectivity, wellness, mentorship, advocacy, persistence, and resilience is the mission of graduate affairs professionals, all in the aim of students reaching their full potential. Even beyond enrollment, the student life cycle continues as graduates become engaged alumni. If the faculty, staff, and students (all possible institutional agents) have been successful in engaging GAPS, then the students will feel connected to the institution for years to come.

Alumni should be invited back to serve as coaches and mentors, even if they are still emerging professionals themselves. Near peer models are significant, especially for historically marginalized groups who benefit more from seeing others, with whom they identify, and have been able to overcome challenges in getting to and through graduate school and found employment on the other side. A recent study found that alumni with a heightened sense of belonging are more likely to give to their graduate school (Drezner & Pizmony-Levy, 2020). Particularly notable in this study was the value placed on engagement that goes beyond finances. While institutions might ultimately want or focus their attention on monetary donations, alumni engage with their graduate alma mater in a multitude of ways, including following news, helping students, attending events, or volunteering their time. Alumni newsletters and social media groups across a variety of platforms help with news-sharing and promoting opportunities for involvement. More established alumni should be invited to serve as coaches and sponsors to students, connecting them to a wider professional network, encouraging social capital-building, and reassuring students struggling with the ambiguity of being both a student and an emerging professional. Panels, guest speaker events, and more informal mixers, to introduce alumni to students and allow for discussion, opens the door for more authentic relationships to grow. Only after a sustained connection is built with an alumnus will any appeal for financial support be appropriate. Engaging alumni with a motive of fundraising should be cast aside and replaced with one of community-building and a spirit of collaboration (Osborn et al., 2015). The most important part to consider in engaging alumni is that they were a connected student while they were enrolled, so that they will remain an involved and caring alum, who will invest in the students coming up behind them. Fostering a *build as you grow* culture with current students should yield engaged alumni who will support institutional efforts.

CONCLUSION

Student affairs structures are in place at most campuses to engage students in organizations, student government and policy-making, professional exploration and development, wellness and health promotion, research, fellowships, community service, and more. The historical design of these activities presupposes that 18–22-year-old undergraduates need these supports and that GAPS can drive and design their own developmental activities. However, like many significant shifts in higher education, improvements are demanded by students. GAPS are uniquely positioned, as more experienced students and as emerging professionals, to speak with authority on the ways they would like to engage with others across the campus and beyond. Advising and student affairs experts can co-create new and highly engaging spaces to offer both holistic care and development opportunities to GAPS.

The number of Americans with advanced degrees has doubled since 2000 (U.S. Census, 2019), and as the number of students enrolled in professional programs increases, so must the services designed to support their needs and their successes. If we do not serve *all* of our students, then we do a disservice to all of them. Here, we have recommended a number of promising practices to more fully engage GAPS across the college life cycle. Offering a variety of pathways that integrate skill- and community-building is the best *full service* menu, allowing practitioners to be explicit about why these programs are recommended. Ideas being tested now include checklists, game boards, and badges designed to incentivize graduate students to get more involved in university life. The approach is up to the designer, but connecting students intentionally to wellness programs, leadership opportunities, social justice and activist networks, and other students outside of their academic silo will yield long-term benefits for their personal and professional growth. And that is good for both the students and the university, increasing the likelihood of civic and alumni engagement for years to come.

REFERENCES

American College Health Association. (2019). *American College Health Association-national college health assessment II: Graduate and professional student executive summary spring 2019.* American College Health Association. Retrieved from https://www.acha.org/documents/ncha/NCHA-II_SPRING_2019_GRADUATE_AND_PROFESSIONAL_REFERENCE_GROUP_DATA_REPORT.pdf

Bain, S., Fedynich, L., & Knight, M. (2011). The successful graduate student: A review of the factors for success. *Journal of Academic and Business Ethics, 3*, 1.

Bustamante, J. (2020). College enrollment & student demographic statistics. *Education Data.org.* Retrieved from https://educationdata.org/college-enrollment-statistics.

Council for the Advancement of Standards in Higher Education (CAS). (2019). *CAS professional standards for higher education* (10th ed.).

Chesler, M., Lewis, A., & Crowfoot, J. (2005). *Challenging racism in higher education: Promoting justice.* Rowman & Littlefield.

Crede, E., & Borrego, M. (2014). Understanding retention in US graduate programs by student nationality. *Studies in Higher Education, 39*(9), 1599–1616.

Curtin, N., Stewart, A. J., & Ostrove, J. M. (2013). Fostering academic self-concept: Advisor support and sense of belonging among international and domestic graduate students. *American Educational Research Journal, 50*(1), 108–137.

DeBowes, M. M. (2006). Intergroup dialogues: A promising practice for cross-cultural engagement. *The Vermont Connection, 27*(1), 1.

Di Pierro, M. (2012). Strategies for doctoral student retention: Taking the roads less traveled. *The Journal for Quality and Participation, 35*(3), 29–32.

Drezner, N. D., & Pizmony-Levy, O. (2020). I belong, therefore, I give? The impact of sense of belonging on graduate student alumni engagement. *Nonprofit and Voluntary Sector Quarterly.* https://doi.org/10.1177/0899764020977687

Einfeld, A., & Collins, D. (2008). The relationships between service-learning, social justice, multicultural competence, and civic engagement. *Journal of College Student Development, 49*, 95–109.

Elkins, D. J., Forrester, S. A., & Noël-Elkins, A. V. (2011). The contribution of campus recreational sports participation to perceived sense of campus community. *Recreational Sports Journal, 35*(1), 24–34.

Evans, T. M., Bira, L., Gastelum, J. B., Weiss, L. T., & Vanderford, N. L. (2018). Evidence for a mental health crisis in graduate education. *Nature Biotechnology, 36*(3), 282.

Eyler, J. (2009). The power of experiential education. *Liberal Education, 95*(4), 24–31.

Fakunmoju, S., Donahue, G. R., McCoy, S., & Mengel, A. S. (2016). Life satisfaction and perceived meaningfulness of learning experience among first-year traditional graduate social work students. *Journal of Education and Practice, 7*(6), 49–62.

Fredrickson, B. L. (2001). The role of positive emotions in positive psychology: The broaden-and-build theory of positive emotions. *American Psychologist, 56*(3), 218.

Gardner, S. K. (2005). *"If it were easy, everyone would have a Ph.D." Doctoral student success: Socialization and disciplinary perspectives* [Unpublished doctoral dissertation]. Washington State University, Pullman.

Gardner, S. K., & Barnes, B. J. (2007). Graduate student involvement: Socialization for the professional role. *Journal of College Student Development, 48*(4), 369–387.

Gansemer-Topf, A. M., Ross, L. E., & Johnson, R. M. (2006). Graduate and professional student development and student affairs. *New Directions for Student Services, 2006*(115), 19–30.

Gazza, E. A., & Hunker, D. F. (2014). Facilitating student retention in online graduate nursing education programs: A review of the literature. *Nurse Education Today, 34*(7), 1125–1129.

Giacomini, N. G., & Schrage, J. M. (2009). Building community in the current campus climate. In J. M. Schrage & N. G. Giacomini (Eds.), *Reframing campus conflict: Student conduct practice through a social justice lens.* Stylus Publishing, LLC.

Glover, K. (2019). Graduate student life brief. *National Association of Graduate-Professional Students.* Retrieved from http://nagps.org/newsite/wp-content/uploads/2019/03/Graduate-Student-Life-Brief-NAGPS-2019-1.pdf

Intergroup Relations. (n.d.). *Intergroup relations: A partnership between LSA and student life.* https://igr.umich.edu/

Kaplan, A. (2019). 2018 voluntary support of education. CASE. *Council for the Advancement and Support of Education.* Retrieved from https://www.case.org/resources/2018-voluntary-support-education

Karp, D. R. (2019). *The little book of restorative justice for colleges and universities: Repairing harm and rebuilding trust in response to student misconduct.* Simon and Schuster.

King, S. B. (2014). Graduate student perceptions of the use of online course tools to support engagement. *International Journal for the Scholarship of Teaching & Learning, 8*(1), 1–18.

Jimenez y West, I., Gokalp, G., Pena, E. V., Fischer, L., & Gupton, J. (2011). Exploring effective support practices for doctoral students' degree completion. *College Student Journal, 45*(2), 310–323.

Jones, S. R., & Abes, E. S. (2004). Enduring influences of service-learning on college students' identity development. *Journal of College Student Development, 45,* 149–166.

Lechuga, V. M. (2011). Faculty-graduate student mentoring relationships: Mentors' perceived roles and responsibilities. *Higher Education, 62*(6), 757–771.

Lunsford, L. G., Crisp, G., Dolan, E. L., & Wuetherick, B. (2017). Mentoring in higher education. *The SAGE Handbook of Mentoring, 20,* 316–334.

McConnell, K., Geesa, R. L., & Lowery, K. (2019). Self-reflective mentoring: Perspectives of peer mentors in an education doctoral program. *International Journal of Mentoring and Coaching in Education, 8*(2), 86–101.

Mitchell, T. D. (2007). Critical service-learning as social justice education: A case study of the Citizens Scholars program. *Equity & Excellence in Education, 40,* 101–112.

Nesheim, B. E., Guentzel, M. J., Kellogg, A. H., McDonald, W. M., Wells, C. A., & Whitt, E. J. (2007). Outcomes for students of student affairs-academic affairs partnership programs. *Journal of College Student Development, 48*(4), 435–454.

Okahana, H., & Zhou, E. (2016). Graduate enrollment and degrees: 2006 to 2016. *Council of Graduate Schools.* Retrieved from https://cgsnet.org/ckfinder/userfiles/files/CGS_GED16_Report_Final.pdf.

O'Meara, K., Griffin, K. A., Kuvaeva, A., Nyunt, G., & Robinson, T. N. (2017). Sense of belonging and its contributing factors in graduate education. *International Journal of Doctoral Studies, 12,* 251–279.

Osborn, D., Alkezweeny, J., & Kecskes, K. (2015). Beyond the university: An initiative for continuing engagement among alumni. *Metropolitan Universities*, *26*(3), 171–187.

Ostrove, J. M., Stewart, A. J., & Curtin, N. L. (2011). Social class and belonging: Implications for graduate students' career aspirations. *The Journal of Higher Education*, *82*(6), 748–774.

Patel, V. (2019, April 22). Grad students at private colleges were cleared to unionize 3 years ago. Here's what's changed. *Chronicle of Higher Education*. Retrieved from https://www.chronicle.com/article/grad-students-at-private-colleges-were-cleared-to-unionize-3-years-ago-heres-whats-changed/

Pontius, J. L., & Harper, S. R. (2006). Principles for good practice in graduate and professional student engagement. *New Directions for Student Services*, *2006*(115), 47–58.

Reddick, R., Griffin, K., Cherwitz, R., Cérda-Pražák, A., & Bunch, N. (2012). What you get when you give: How graduate students benefit from serving as mentors. *The Journal of Faculty Development*, *26*(1), 37–49.

Rhoads, R. (2016). Student activism, diversity, and the struggle for a just society. *Journal of Diversity in Higher Education*, *9*(3), 189–202. https://escholarship.org/uc/item/5q34p1t0

Rutti, R. M., LaBonte, J., Helms, M. M., Hervani, A. A., & Sarkarat, S. (2016). The service learning projects: stakeholder benefits and potential class topics. *Education+Training*, *58*(4), 422–438.

Schoem, D., Hurtado, S., Sevig, T., Chesler, M., & Sumida, S. H. (2001). Intergroup dialogue: Democracy at work in theory and practice. In D. Schoem & S. Hurtado (Eds.), *Intergroup dialogue: Deliberative democracy in school, college, community, and workplace* (pp. 1–21). University of Michigan Press.

Sheldon, K. M., & King, L. (2001). Why positive psychology is necessary. *American Psychologist*, *56*(3), 216.

Spalter-Roth, R., & Erskine, W. (2007, March). ASA research brief: Race and ethnicity in the sociology pipeline. *American Sociological Association Research and Development Department*. Retrieved from https://www.asanet.org/sites/default/files/files/pdf/ raceethsociologypipe.pdf.

Sue, D. W., Capodilupo, C. M., Torino, G. C., Bucceri, J. M., Holder, A., Nadal, K. L., & Esquilin, M. (2007). Racial microaggressions in everyday life: Implications for clinical practice. *American Psychologist*, *62*(4), 271–286.

U.S. Census. (2019). *Number of People with Masters and PhD degrees*. Retrieved from https://www.census.gov/library/stories/2019/02/number-of-people-with-masters-and-phd-degrees-double-since-2000.html

Walter, L., & Stouck, J. (2020). Writing the literature review: Graduate student experiences. *The Canadian Journal for the Scholarship of Teaching and Learning*, *11*(1), 1–17.

Whitford, H. (2014). The Role of graduate student unions in the higher education landscape. *New Directions for Higher Education*, *2014*(167), 17–29.

Woolston, C. (2019, November 14). PhD poll reveals fear and joy, contentment and anguish. *Nature*, *575*, 403–406.

Zahneis, M., & Patel, V. (2020, April 30). Covid-19 changes the calculus of grad-student activism. *Chronicle of Higher Education*. Retrieved from https://www.chronicle.com/article/covid-19-changes-the-calculus-of-grad-student-activism/

A Diversity, Equity, and Inclusion Approach to Graduate Student Access and Outcomes

Maria Dykema Erb, Kathy Wood, and Matt Newlin

Programs and initiatives to support undergraduates from diverse backgrounds have largely become the norm on college campuses. However, for students who pursue graduate or professional degree programs, this formalized institutional support is often limited or nonexistent. This happens for a multitude of reasons, ranging from insufficient budgets to limited staff capability, to lack of awareness of critical graduate student support systems. It is vital that colleges and universities respond to their diverse student populations by creating an inclusive scaffolding system that takes into consideration the needs and identities of diverse graduate student populations. By broadly defining diversity, graduate and professional schools are able to create more centralized campus-wide programs for graduate student retention and success. While certainly not an exhaustive list, some of the specific student populations addressed throughout this chapter and the case studies include Black, Indigenous, People of Color (BIPOC), first-generation, military-affiliated, low- and middle-income, lesbian, gay, bisexual, transgender, queer, questioning, intersex, asexual, and agender (LGBTQIA+), international, undocumented, and those with varying abilities.

It is important to note that in this chapter, the authors will use the phrases "graduate school" and "graduate students" to refer to any post-baccalaureate educational experiences (e.g., MA, PhD, JD, MD, MSW, etc.). The authors acknowledge the nuanced nature of each degree program or type of graduate/professional school, but have endeavored to speak to as broad an audience as possible in this chapter.

DOI: 10.4324/9781003121671-9

DIVERSITY, EQUITY, AND INCLUSION (DEI) CENTRALIZED EFFORTS

According to the Council of Graduate Schools Graduate Enrollment and Degrees report (Okahana et al., 2020), graduate student enrollment continues to become more diverse. In addition, diversity and inclusiveness is one of the top priorities for graduate deans according to the Council of Graduate Schools Pressing Issues Survey (Okahana, 2017). There have been several national grant programs such as the Alliances for Graduate Education and the Professoriate (AGEP) that have focused on providing support to underrepresented students of color in the science, technology, engineering, and mathematics (STEM) fields at research universities. Graduate student centers are becoming more common on campuses offering professional development and community-building opportunities, as well as affinity space for students of color, LGBTQIA+, and international students. Encouragingly, more student affairs professionals are being hired to focus on the recruitment and retention of graduate students from diverse backgrounds.

In Griffin et al.'s (2016) qualitative study, they surveyed 14 "institutional agents" or graduate diversity officers (GDOs) who were charged with improving retention of graduate students of color. Acknowledging Tinto's Theory of Individual Departure (1993) for undergraduates, they built upon Lovitts' (2001) doctoral student retention framework which included academic integration, social integration, and the development of cognitive maps within a student's department or program by identifying three strategies to support retention. They are: (1) individual support by GDOs outside the department or program; (2) building strong mentoring relationships with faculty; and (3) building communities beyond the department which had social, academic, and professional development components. These strategies are most successful when there is a supportive campus and departmental environment, institutional support, and adequate financial resources. The authors stated that while continued efforts for student recruitment were important in considering graduate student outcomes, the student retention experience was critical (Griffin et al., 2016). Given the common retention strategies that have been identified amongst institutions in this study, the importance of a centralized effort for the retention of diverse graduate students is imperative.

An example of an established, centralized effort is the Diversity and Student Success (DSS) program in The Graduate School at The University of North Carolina (UNC) at Chapel Hill. DSS was created to better retain students from diverse backgrounds; to see them through degree completion; and have a positive impact on their experience as graduate or professional students at UNC. Students who come from diverse backgrounds may not always seek out assistance when they

150

encounter barriers to continuing their graduate education. Those barriers might include: financial difficulties, challenges within their academic department, or personal issues/situations that may arise. Five of the six initiatives created were to address specific populations: Carolina Grad Student F1RSTS (first-generation in a graduate program), Global Grads (international), Initiative for Minority Excellence (BIPOC), Military-Affiliated Grad Students (active duty, veterans, National Guard, and Reservists), and Queer Graduate and Professional Students (LGBTQIA+). The sixth initiative, the Summer Undergraduate Pipeline, was created to provide diverse undergraduates a pathway to graduate education.

Central to the creation of each initiative has been the care and encouragement of the *whole* student: not just their academic success, but also their holistic development:

- All DSS initiatives offer a variety of academic, professional, and personal development workshops and social activities to meet various student needs/ interests and build community.
    - Community-building efforts such as weekly BIPOC writing group, monthly first-gen Friday socials, postgraduation career preparation workshops for international graduate students, finding a mentor/how to communicate with a mentor workshop series, meaning-making for graduate students workshop series, and so on.
    - Recognition of accomplishments like DSS Scholar Profiles in monthly newsletters and on social media, and end of the year graduation recognition ceremonies.
- Each initiative has an individual advisory board that consists of graduate student participants. These board members meet biannually to assist the DSS co-directors in shaping the initiatives and to advise on programming needs/interests.
- All participants in DSS initiatives have access to various funding opportunities that provide financial assistance from recruitment to retention to degree completion.
- The DSS co-directors provide one-on-one consultations for mentoring and assistance with navigating any challenges students may encounter throughout their degree programs.

Another important population to consider is students who are first in their families to attend college and/or first in their families to pursue education beyond a baccalaureate degree. First-generation students who pursue education beyond the baccalaureate level is still an under-researched topic, but the extant literature available is valuable to practitioners. Research has found first-generation students are more likely to be from underrepresented groups (Roksa et al., 2018) and that race and gender can exacerbate the challenges first-generation students face in graduate programs (Holley & Gardner, 2012). These challenges can include cultural expectations and familial obligations (Lester Leyva, 2011; Martinez, 2018; Willison & Gibson, 2011), as well as finding a community of peers and feeling a sense of belonging (Gardner, 2013; Martinez, 2018). Beneficial supports include formal mentoring programs (Piatt et al., 2019), summer institutes and/or bridge programs (Winkle-Wagner & McCoy, 2016), and research opportunities (Willison & Gibson, 2011).

For example, at the Brown School of Social Work at Washington University in St. Louis, the "I'm First" program was created to support first-generation master's-level students. As an elite, top-ranked school of social work in the country, the Brown School culture and policies are opaque to first-generation students who lack the cultural and social capital necessary to thrive in that environment. "I'm First" created resources and a community of support that included staff, faculty, alumni, and the dean of the school, herself a first-generation student. Programs and workshops were created to help first-gen students navigate the admissions process and scholarship interviews; learn important research skills and data analysis software (e.g., R, Stata, SPSS); and build a professional network to assist with securing practicum opportunities and employment. The initiative was anchored by encouraging Brown School community members to publicly identify as first-generation by posting "I'm First!" stickers on their office doors and including the identification as part of their syllabus.

COMMUNITY AND SENSE OF BELONGING

Students are more likely to thrive in graduate school if they understand—and can navigate—the norms and expectations of their new environment and if they feel they are genuinely accepted as part of the community. Strayhorn (2012) found that socialization and sense of belonging positively influence success (i.e., grade point average [GPA] and satisfaction) in graduate school. Socialization includes being introduced to the subtleties of a particular school or field as well as understanding professional norms and behaviors. This socialization leads to a sense of belonging as it "produces certain outcomes that move individuals from being perpetual 'outsiders' to valued 'insiders'" of the institution or field (Strayhorn, 2012, p. 98). The importance of connection was echoed by Pascale (2018), who asserted authentic friendships with both peers and faculty improve the sense of belonging for graduate students. This can include mentor/mentee relationships as well as genuine friendships that transcend simply shared academic interests.

An illustration within UNC's DSS program that echoes the value and importance of community and sense of belonging was the development of student-led empowerment groups. The BIPOC student advisory committee identified a desire to create affinity space that would allow students of varying identities to come together in a safe space, share lived experiences, and support one another throughout their academic journey. The following groups resulted:

- Asian Pacific Islander Desi American (APIDA) Grads
- Brotherhood of Success (BOS)
- La Familia
- Sisterhood of Empowerment in Academe (SEA)

These groups meet once a month for identity development workshops, conversations with faculty, and social gatherings to create a cohesive community and sense of belonging.

As diverse graduate and professional students feel more empowered and resilient, they are likely to be more productive in the completion of their degree, find joy in their work, and successfully graduate having had a more positive experience because of the support offered through centralized programming.

COLLABORATION AND PARTNERSHIPS

An additional gap that requires a creative and inclusive approach for diverse graduate students is traditional student services. At many colleges and universities, student services are available to any student enrolled at the university, including graduate students. However, the (incorrect) perception is these offices and resources are available only to undergraduate students. This misconception is not limited only to graduate students; often, administrators and faculty are equally unaware of which resources graduate-level students can utilize on campus. However, this is not the only challenge. Oftentimes, staff in student support offices that traditionally serve undergraduate students are not trained on how to best support graduate students, nor are they given the proper resources. As a result, graduate students who need additional support—most often first-generation, international, and BIPOC students—are left to struggle on their own.

In an effort to provide more student services for graduate students, practitioners should consider partnering with various departments, offices, and centers across campus to assist in delivering student programming in their area of expertise. Partnerships can build practitioners' capacity to serve their students as well as expand the scope of services being offered. Some partnerships might include graduate professional development programs, career services, counseling and psychological services, student wellness, identity centers (e.g., BIPOC, LGBTQIA+, military veterans), academic support/writing centers, disability services, student life/activities, and more.

Due to the sensitive nature and the importance of confidentiality, many professionals may avoid discussing the challenges encountered by graduate students from low-income families, working-class backgrounds, and/or those who may be struggling financially during their graduate program. These students may benefit from financial literacy and planning resources which student affairs professionals may not be comfortable developing on their own. At the Brown School of Social Work at Washington University in St. Louis, graduate students in the Master of Social Work and Master of Public Health programs were struggling with financial stressors that were disrupting their academic performance. Money-related worries such as budgeting student loan debt management were becoming frequent distractions from their coursework and professional preparation. The Director of Financial Aid at the Brown School began offering regular debt management and money management workshops for all students to attend. Quickly, though, the students shared other financial topics about which they felt unknowledgeable and unprepared.

To address students' needs and improve their financial wellness, the Director reached out to campus and community partners to develop an eight-part "Investing in Your Future" seminar series which was offered each year. Some of the topics and experts included:

- Negotiating Your Salary—Brown School Career Services
- Managing Money and Saving for the Future—The Federal Reserve Bank of St. Louis
- Building and Maintaining Credit—local credit rehabilitation nonprofit
- Investments and Retirement 101—Wells Fargo Advisors
- Tax Preparation and Filing—H&R Block

By reaching out to local organizations and businesses, the Brown School was able to provide education and resources that students had not received in the past. Community partnerships are often easy to develop through networking and cold call requests that make clear requests and provide expectations to the individual(s) being approached.

One of the most important partnerships for graduate programs is with student wellness and/or counseling and psychological services offices. Graduate students experience numerous stressors throughout their degree programs: intense research, financial difficulties, uncertainty about the job market, relationship and family pressures, etc. As the national mental health crisis amongst graduate students continues to reach peak levels, it is imperative for graduate programs and schools to respond proactively with appropriate resources that center around the wellness needs of students.

The Council of Graduate Schools has recognized these needs and recently formalized the call to action by establishing the *Supporting Mental Health and Wellness of Graduate Students* initiative to:

> create a foundation for evidence-based policies and resources to: (1) support graduate student mental health and well-being, (2) prevent psychological distress, (3) and address barriers to effective support and care. This initiative will give particular attention to the experiences of underrepresented racial and ethnic minorities pursuing graduate education.
>
> (Council of Graduate Schools, 2019)

At UNC at Chapel Hill, the majority of wellness programming efforts have been targeted toward the undergraduate student population. As such, the wellness needs of graduate students have received little attention and have largely gone unmet. DSS partnered with both the Office of Student Wellness and Counseling and Psychological Services to address specific needs of diverse graduate students. The primary purpose of doing so was to provide skill building and avoid mental health crises. Some of the workshop topics include:

*   Black joy and resilience
*   Communication skills
*   Healthy relationships
*   Laughter yoga
*   Navigating conflict
*   Mindfulness meditation
*   Stress and resilience

SUGGESTIONS FOR PRACTICE

*   **Identify the unique needs of your diverse graduate populations** and provide programming and a network of support for them. Remember that one-size-fits-all does not work for these specific graduate populations and intersectionality of identities must also be kept in mind. Ensure that students are always at the center of your decisions and regularly involve them through advisory boards in your planning for programming and feedback.
*   **Sustainable infrastructure and capacity building** are integral to serving graduate student populations. An objective, critical review

155

of practices can illuminate ways students may be disadvantaged while in graduate school. Practitioners should focus on ways to reduce redundant processes and policies that do not best serve their students' interests. Find ways to eliminate inequitable processes that can improve students' experience. This can also make administrators' work more efficient and effective, thereby facilitating better student relationships.

In addition, a centralized effort for the support of diverse graduate students will allow for a pooling of resources rather than individual departments and/or schools within an institution setting up their own programs. This gives students the opportunity to meet peers across a college or university and build community with those who share similar experiences. It can also create economies of scale to provide more financial and human resources to meet the needs of diverse graduate students. By ensuring adequate staffing, this will allow a team to provide the best support to their students and avoid compassion fatigue and burnout.

Engage campus partners (faculty, administrators, student affairs, etc.) to support your efforts. By doing so, the campus will become more attuned to the needs of diverse graduate students and will be more willing to provide programming and opportunities at the graduate education level.

- **Assessment** can be a daunting endeavor for practitioners with little or no experience with survey design, data collection, and data analysis. It can seem even more intimidating at large or research-intensive institutions where the Institutional Research office is already mired in requests from executive leadership, accreditation, and faculty projects. This should not inhibit regular, comprehensive analysis of student experiences, needs, and challenges.

  While online survey tools are abundant (e.g., Qualtrics, SurveyMonkey, Google Forms), some of the best qualitative data is gathered through focus groups and one-on-one interviews. Additionally, this method demonstrates to graduate and professional students that the school cares about and is invested in them as a person.

  When developing assessment tools for your programming, some outcomes to measure might include: (1) sense of belonging and community; (2) ability to face and navigate challenges; (3) successful navigation of the university; (4) preparation for postgraduate life; (5) development of sense of self; and (6) leadership development. See Chapter 9 for more in-depth assessment practices and examples.

- **Understanding current issues and challenges** facing diverse graduate students is imperative. Practitioners should be aware of what is happening on their own campus and what is happening nationally in respect to graduate students' experiences. Examples that can affect the nature of a welcoming campus climate include anti-racism protests and activism, LGBTQIA+ rights, immigration policies that affect international students' statuses, and so on. By being aware of these issues, proactive responses can be developed to support students instead of responding in reactionary mode.

- **Create a sense of belonging** with and for diverse graduate students at your college or university. By students feeling like they belong and have a reliable support system, they will be empowered and will thrive throughout their degree program. This, in turn, will lead to better retention rates and more engaged alumni postgraduation because of their positive experiences.

The above recommendations provide practitioners with a solid foundation from which to serve a diverse population of graduate students. However, every institution is a unique environment with its own opportunities and challenges. Starting or expanding current student support practices may be inhibited by institutional policies, staffing needs, or limited budgets. To this end, following are three case study examples of how institutions have provided new and innovative student success programming to their graduate students. Each case study provides practitioners with distinct approaches to addressing the needs of different populations of students. The first case study is on international and first-generation student initiatives at the University of Washington (UW), the next is on students with varying abilities at the University of Michigan (U-M), and the last is on undocumented students at Tulane University.

CASE STUDY 1

By Ziyan Bai, Jaye Sablan, and Bill Mahoney

Title: International and First-Generation Graduate Student Initiatives at the University of Washington

Institution: The University of Washington (UW) is a large public research university enrolling over 40,000 students in 2020. The UW Graduate School, Office of Graduate Student Affairs, holistically supports the graduate student experiences of over 15,000 graduate students on three campuses, across 300 graduate programs.

Problem of Practice: We developed the International and First-Generation Graduate Student Initiatives to fill service gaps pertaining to the community-building and professional development needs of these underserved student populations.

Evidence of the Problem: To assess the unmet needs of the international graduate student population, we hired a Higher Education Policy doctoral student to identify service gaps. She surveyed existing campus services, reviewed empirical student needs studies, and drafted a report of offerings from peer institutions. Numerous challenges were identified, including: difficulties in cross-cultural communication, lack of knowledge of the U.S. higher education system and workplace cultures, and insufficient sense of belonging (Amirali & Bakken, 2015; Hartshorne & Baucom, 2007; Nguyen, 2013).

To perform a needs assessment among first-generation graduate students, we hired a consultant (PhD in Education) to conduct semi-formal focus groups with first-generation graduate students across disciplines and to survey relevant offerings at peer institutions. Similar to above, our consultant reviewed literature on the experiences of first-generation graduate students—identifying the need to foster a sense of belonging, create community-building opportunities, and develop events and informational resources to holistically support successful graduate student experiences (Gardner, 2013; Portnoi & Kwong, 2011; Seay et al., 2008).

Initiative: The International Graduate Student Initiative consists of quarterly professional development workshops and semi-annual social events. Professional development events center on the theme of communication (e.g., skill development, networking with faculty, and career exploration), while community-building events focus on student celebrations and opportunities to hear from successful international graduate students and faculty.

The First-Generation Graduate Student Initiative encompasses quarterly community-building events aimed at enhancing students' sense of belonging (e.g., bridging family, intersecting identities, and graduate school; self and collective care practices; and managing imposter syndrome). Each event highlights a personal or professional development story from a first-generation graduate student, staff, or faculty member. We regularly incorporate screenings from a collaborator's *First In Our Families* project, a program that features first-generation graduate student digital stories.

For both initiatives, we established learning goals for each program and conducted summative evaluations for the majority of events. Evaluations assessed participants' acquired knowledge, competencies that still need development, and suggestions for future programming. Evaluation results typically highlight positive and constructive feedback: "graduate school is challenging, but manageable, with the tips I learned," "I have the option of getting mental health support when dealing with microaggressions," and "please contextualize workshop materials for both STEM and the Humanities fields in order to be inclusive."

Implications for Policy and Practice: Graduate student populations are diverse, and not all have the resources to navigate academic and professional domains. We hope this case study will offer ways for peers to address the unique community-building and professional development needs of international and first-gen graduate students.

Case Study 1 References

Amirali, S., & Bakken, J. P. (2015). Trends and challenges of recruiting and retaining international graduate students: An internal perspective. *Journal of Education Research, 9*(4), 425–433.

Gardner, S. K. (2013). The challenges of first-generation doctoral students. *New Directions for Higher Education, 163*, 43–54.

Hartshorne, R., & Baucom, J. (2007). Issues affecting cross-cultural adaptation of international graduate students. *Multicultural Learning and Teaching, 2*(2), 78–87.

Nguyen, H. M. (2013). Faculty advisors' experiences with international graduate students. *Journal of International Students, 3*(2), 102–116.

Portnoi, L. M., & Kwong, T. M. (2011). Enhancing the academic experiences of first-generation master's students. *Journal of Student Affairs Research and Practice, 48*(4), 411–427.

Seay, S. E., Lifton, D. E., Wuensch, K. L., Bradshaw, L. K., & McDowelle, J. O. (2008). First-generation graduate students and attrition risks. *The Journal of Continuing Higher Education, 56*(3), 11–25.

CASE STUDY 2

By Ethriam Brammer, Nitya Chandran, Dwight Richardson Kelly, Janet E. Malley, Abigail J. Stewart, Arthur Verhoogt, and M. Remi Yergeau

Title: Creating Accommodations for Graduate Students with Disabilities

Institution: University of Michigan

Problem of Practice: While there is significant research about accommodating undergraduate students with disabilities, there is almost no parallel research specifically on graduate students, despite their different educational experiences, opportunities, and requirements.

Evidence of the Problem: In the winter of 2020, all graduate students enrolled in the U-M Rackham Graduate School's various programs were surveyed ($N = 9,237$) as part of the Graduate Student with Disabilities Needs Assessment. The total sample of graduate students who responded to the survey during the four-week period in which it was available was 1,070 (a response rate of 12%).

The sample included broad representation across gender, race, ethnicity, and disability status. Respondents were also well distributed across graduate student statuses (i.e., master's, pre-candidate, and doctoral candidates) as well as Rackham's four disciplinary areas: the biological and medical sciences, physical sciences and engineering, social sciences, and the humanities and arts. Detailed information about the survey sample and methodology can be found in the Report from Committee on Graduate Student Experiences with Disability Accommodations (University of Michigan, 2020).

In addition, six focus groups were conducted over four weeks during the same winter 2020 term. There were a total of 20 participants with focus groups ranging in size between two and five participants, with most including three. Two of the focus groups took place in person and four over encrypted video conferencing technology due to the COVID-19 pandemic. All focus group interviews were recorded, professionally transcribed, and then cleaned and de-identified as needed.

Initiative: The findings of the study made clear the distinction between undergraduate and graduate students with disabilities and the difficulty graduate students experience when attempting to obtain and implement accommodations. It also shed light on the university's emphasis on undergraduate accommodations over the needs of graduate students, or, as Respondent 1 explained, "I've heard from many other graduate students that there's more challenges in getting them as a graduate student because I think a lot of SSD [Services for Students with Disabilities] is more streamlined for the undergraduate students."

The study also demonstrated how graduate students' complex and multiple roles, as both students and employees of the university, can significantly complicate a graduate student's ability to receive the necessary accommodations when an institution lacks a centralized unit to coordinate accommodations for students and employees—or, in the case of graduate students, students who are also simultaneously employees.

Respondent 2 explained the difficulty experienced by graduate students when faculty and leadership are unsure which office (e.g., Services for Students with Disabilities or the ADA Coordinator's Office) is responsible for providing graduate student accommodations:

> When trying to request those accommodations I was on an email chain with my advisor and someone from SSD, my coordinator from SSD, the [Graduate Student Affairs Officer and Senior Resolution Officer] from Rackham and my department chairs, and it's just like it was a months-long email exchange with everyone trying to basically shuffle me off to someone else and say that it's not their job to determine those accommodations. My department chair thought that it should be SSD's job and then SSD said it was outside their wheelhouse.

Respondent 3 echoed these frustrations, saying:

> I also have it in writing from my department that my department will not give grad students who are in student status any disability accommodations because we're not covered as employees. We can only ask when we're covered as employees.

When a university does not have centralized and coordinated services, this study demonstrates how graduate students are often caught in the middle—or simply fall through the cracks. Or, as Respondent 4 explains:

> I'm in a master's program and I taught the last three semesters and so it was interesting to navigate.... I've had mixed results with accommodations...SSD doesn't do it because it's not a student accommodation but the workplace. They didn't do it, it was just like I work with the professor to put some stuff in place.... GSI [Graduate Student Instructor] accommodations were just this weird limbo where there wasn't really a set protocol for it.

Implications for Policy and Practice: The authors of this report strongly recommend the centralization of the process of implementing policy with respect to students, faculty, and staff with disabilities. This includes providing information about available accommodations, assistance with obtaining those accommodations, and follow up as necessary to ensure that the accommodations are implemented. Without centralization of expertise and accountability, graduate students are likely to continue to undertake arduous and often fruitless efforts to obtain the necessary accommodations—or, in the worst-case scenario, graduate students may even depart from their programs due to the frustration caused by not having accurate information about how to obtain the accommodations they need to be successful.

Case Study 2 Reference

University of Michigan. (2020). *Report from Committee on Graduate Student Experiences with Disability Accommodations at the University of Michigan.* Retrieved from https://rackham. umich.edu/downloads/grad-student-disability-accommodation-experiences-umich.pdf

CASE STUDY 3

By Briana Mohan, Nicole Caridad Ralston, Linett Luna Tovar, and Vanessa Castañeda

Title: Supporting Undocumented Graduate Students

Institution: Tulane University (mid-sized, private, R1 institution)

Problem of Practice: Undocumented individuals in the Tulane University community have infrequently been acknowledged or supported by the institution. To address this situation, graduate students collaborated with other campus and community partners to advocate, educate, and organize successful initiatives, simultaneously transforming institutional relationships, practices, and culture.

Evidence of the Problem: Direct threats to non-U.S. citizens and people of color intensified after the 2016 presidential election, making the absence of meaningful, institutional support for undocumented members of the Tulane University community all the more apparent. There were no resources of any sort identified as being for undocumented students, staff, or faculty, or any public recognition that there were undocumented people in the university community. However, individuals were keenly aware of the intensifying pressures on themselves, their family members, friends, students, classmates, colleagues, and offices, especially within the university's international office.

Initiative: Shortly after the 2016 elections in the United States, a coalition of graduate students, staff, faculty, and undergraduates collaborated to support undocumented students by starting a group that would grow to become the Tulane Undocumented Student Support Committee (USSC). For over two years, this group pressured the university to put sustained resources toward this support and interrupted business-as-usual in institutional culture.

The leadership of the group was one of its most valuable dimensions and key to its success. Specifically, woman-identified graduate students and staff members from a range of ages, races, sexual orientations, histories with immigration and documentation, academic and professional training, and formative life experiences collaboratively led and sustained the group. Significantly, the committee was not created by any official university office or special initiative and its members were all true volunteers. The majority of participants were staff members and a core group of graduate students and individual faculty members also lent crucial perspectives and momentum; undergraduate students stepped in at various moments when campus-wide support was most important.

The actions of the committee were determined by its primary focus: to provide meaningful, sustained, and institutional support to undocumented members of the university community. One of the benefits that this approach afforded was the ability to confirm that there was undocumented graduate, professional, and undergraduate students, as well as formerly undocumented individuals and people who had undocumented family members; it was also possible to affirm that there were staff and faculty among these populations at Tulane.

For example, one early initiative was to have a dedicated university web page with resources for undocumented members of the community. The director of the Office of International Students and Scholars offered to utilize her ability to create public-facing web pages. Committee members contributed content, and tulane.edu/undocumented still leads with a 2017 letter of support for the continuation of Deferred Action for Childhood Arrivals (DACA) from the university president, a letter which USSC members drafted and pressured the administration to publish (Tulane Undocumented Student Support Committee & Fitts, 2017).

A much larger-scale effort and success was getting the university to hire an immigration lawyer to provide free legal consultations to any Tulane affiliate. The newly contracted lawyer became part of the Tulane University Legal Assistance Program, a long-running program in the Law School that already provided civil and criminal help to Tulane affiliates, primarily undergraduate students. Staff, faculty, and students continue to utilize this immigration-focused service every semester.

Implications for Policy and Practice: The graduate student leaders of the USSC proved to administrators that they are a powerful and important force in campus advocacy. The group provided a context for graduate students to build, grow, and sustain an initiative that was deeply important to them personally, politically, and intellectually. They also learned first-hand with and from staff and faculty about undocumented issues as well as how and why to push forward with important changes in the university. For higher education more generally, the example of the Tulane USSC demonstrates that graduate students can collaborate with other members of university communities to lead and transform institutions and people's lives for the better.

Case Study 3 Reference

Tulane Undocumented Student Support Committee & Fitts, M. (2017). Message on Tulane and DACA from President Fitts [Letter]. Tulane University. https://tulane.edu/undocumented

REFERENCES

Council of Graduate Schools. (2019). *Graduate student mental health and well-being.* Retrieved from https://cgsnet.org/graduate-student-mental-health-and-wellness

Gardner, S. (2013). The challenges of first-generation doctoral students. *New Directions for Higher Education, 163,* 43–54.

Griffin, K. A., Muniz, M., & Smith, E. J. (2016). Graduate diversity officers and efforts to retain students of color. *Journal of Student Affairs Research and Practice, 53*(1), 26–38. http://doi.org/10.1080/19496591.2016.1083437

Holley, K., & Gardner, S. (2012). Navigating the pipeline: How socio-cultural influences impact first-generation doctoral students. *Journal of Diversity in Higher Education, 5*(2), 112–121.

Lester Leyva, V. (2011). First-generation Latina graduate students: Balancing professional identity development with traditional family roles. *New Directions for Teaching and Learning, 127,* 21–31.

Lovitts, B. E. (2001). *Leaving the ivory tower: The causes and consequences of departure from doctoral study.* Rowman & Littlefield.

Martinez, A. (2018). Pathways to the professoriate: The experiences of first-generation Latino undergraduate students at Hispanic Serving Institutions applying to doctoral programs. *Education Sciences, 8*(32). https://doi.org/10.3390/educsci8010032

Okahana, H. (2017, April). Data sources: Highlights from the 2017 CGS pressing issues survey. *Council of Graduate Schools.* Retrieved from http://cgsnet.org/data-sources-highlights-2017-cgs-pressing-issues-survey-0

Okahana, H., Zhou, E., & Gao, J. (2020). *Graduate enrollment and degrees: 2009 to 2019*. Council of Graduate Schools.

Pascale, A. B. (2018). Co-existing lives: Understanding and facilitating graduate student sense of belonging. *Journal of Student Affairs Research and Practice, 55*(4), 399–411.

Piatt, E., Merolla, D., Pringle, E., & Serpe, R. (2019). The role of Science Identity Salience in graduate school enrollment for first-generation, low-income, underrepresented students. *The Journal of Negro Education, 88*(3), 269–280.

Roksa, J., Feldon, D., & Maher, M. (2018). First-generation students in pursuit of the PhD: Comparing socialization experiences and outcomes to continuing-generation peers. *The Journal of Higher Education, 89*(5), 728–752.

Strayhorn, T. (2012). *College students' sense of belonging: A key to educational success for all students.*: Routledge.

Tinto, V. (1993). *Leaving college: Rethinking causes and cures of student attrition* (2nd ed.). The University of Chicago Press.

Willison, S., & Gibson, E. (2011). Graduate school earning curves: McNair scholars' postbaccalaureate transitions. *Equity & Excellence in Education, 44*(2), 153–168.

Winkle-Wagner, R., & McCoy, D. (2016). Entering the (postgraduate) field: Underrepresented students' acquisition of cultural and social capital in graduate school preparation programs. *The Journal of Higher Education, 87*(2), 178–205.

Chapter 8

A Space and a Place for Graduate Education
Building Community and Belonging

Karen P. DePauw and Monika Gibson

While this book is a practical guide for Student Affairs practitioners serving graduate and professional school students and most likely will be perused by Divisions of Student Affairs and less so by Graduate Schools, it was our strong contention 20 years ago and is now our strong recommendation that Graduate Schools serve a critical role and fulfill a unique responsibility in serving graduate and professional students. Because of their leadership role in graduate education; their close connection to faculty, academic departments, and programs (the primary home for graduate students); and their constant interactions with graduate students from the point they apply to graduate school through admission, academic progress, funding programs, and professional development, Graduate Schools are best positioned to create inclusive, affirming interdisciplinary environments for graduate education—a space and place where graduate students may thrive. They can also be important partners to Student Affairs professionals to ensure that traditional Student Affairs services are properly tailored for, visible, and accessible to graduate students. As stated in earlier chapters, such Graduate School support, along with partnerships with Student Affairs professionals, must be intentional, preferably centralized in some form, and reflected in organizational structure. The lessons we have learned and stories we share can provide guidance and understanding of graduate student life; however, acquiring such expertise in Student Affairs does not diminish or replace the need for the leadership of the Graduate Dean, who may be best positioned to champion the cause, and the engagement of Graduate School personnel.

HISTORICAL CONTEXT OF GRADUATE EDUCATION

Graduate education in some form first appeared in the United States in the early 1600s when Harvard University issued the first Master's degree (Master of Arts)

DOI: 10.4324/9781003121671-10

shortly after its founding in 1636. The first PhDs in the United States were earned at Yale in 1861, initiating the growth of graduate education with emphasis upon doctoral education and the founding of the research university which provided undergraduate and graduate education and research in a single institution. In 1900, the Association of American Universities (AAU) was founded at a conference of the 14 PhD-granting universities over the concern for graduate education and consideration of "matters of common interest relating to graduate study" and providing "a greater uniformity of the conditions under which students may become candidates for higher degrees in different American universities…" (The Association of American Universities, 2020, para. 6).

Graduate education would continue its expansion of degree offerings and increasing numbers throughout the 20th and now into the 21st century. Graduate students, due to the nature of their studies and research, especially at research universities, were more the responsibility of the academic departments/colleges; Graduate Schools were focused on quality control and quality assurance and less on the lives of graduate students. Since the beginning of residential colleges and universities in the United States, Student Affairs professionals have existed almost entirely for undergraduate students and served historically as "in loco parentis." While the nomenclature and culture have changed with a more holistic student development focus, graduate and professional students were not typically considered within the portfolio and purview of Student Affairs personnel. Although this has changed recently and Student Affairs practitioners are now more interested and taking responsibility for working with graduate and professional students (this book being one example), universities still tend to prioritize undergraduate students and rightly so. A challenge in serving the graduate student population is in understanding that they are not simply *older undergraduates*, but that they have professional and personal lives often more complicated and multifaceted than the generally younger undergraduate population and that their relationship to the university is more than just that of a student. They are instructors, researchers, and administrators as well, with academic and professional aspirations and challenges of their own. The dilemmas and difficulties they face in graduate school are quite different from their undergraduate experience, and the skills and attitudes they developed during their undergraduate studies and often through many years in the workforce may not be sufficient or relevant for success in graduate school. Getting through many of the pitfalls of graduate school is often not a function of students' skills but of the institutional environment, including culture, policies and procedures, and support systems that enable or hinder successful progress. Graduate Schools can and must be important conduits that gather, organize, and sometimes help transform

167

institutional resources into programs, services, and procedures that are accessible to and appropriate for graduate students—and do this in concert with graduate students organizing themselves (see also Chapter 6).

By tradition or design, graduate education can be a uniquely isolating experience, which on the one hand suits hyper-focused study really well, but on the other hand has the unintentional consequence of creating stress and increasing the likelihood of depression, reducing or eliminating the social networks around students, and depriving students of important stimuli that could make their world richer and their academic success more likely. Relatedly, the primary focus of graduate education had been on degree attainment and research until recently, and Graduate School personnel were not necessarily invited to or tasked with providing student services beyond those primarily focused on admission and degree attainment.

This was the case in the early 2000s at Virginia Tech as well. A void left by Student Affairs ultimately would be filled by the Graduate School as a result of a confluence of several factors: the separation of Research and Graduate Studies into a research division and the Graduate School; the arrival of a new Graduate Dean empowered to lead significant change; the acknowledgement that a transformation in graduate education was necessary for a 21st-century university (Duderstadt, 2000); adoption of a thematic approach of building community for the graduate education population; and the perfect timing of an existing hotel and conference center becoming available for repurposing. But even all these elements together would not have amounted to anything new and different without strong institutional commitment at the highest level and a graduate dean who championed the cause and built the institutional structure to turn the concept of graduate community and graduate student services into functional reality.

Life and work in the 21st century require that graduate education (Graduate Schools) undertake transformation to provide meaningful education that is interdisciplinary, inclusive, and global. In 2003, the Virginia Tech Graduate School developed the Transformative Graduate Education (TGE) initiative around four pillars of graduate education: knowledge, scholarly inquiry, social responsibility, and leadership (DePauw, 2019). Information is also available on the Graduate School website (https://graduateschool.vt.edu/transformative-graduate-education-experience/tge-initiative.html). The TGE initiative was informed by key conditions of graduate study, including academic quality, time to fiddle with ideas, a baggy idea of truth, and a sense of community (Harper, 1980). Building community became a guiding principle and foundation for the development of the Graduate Life Center (GLC) and would guide the programs and opportunities offered by the Graduate School.

GRADUATE LIFE CENTER

Although many programs and opportunities designed for and focused on graduate students can be accomplished without a facility, the GLC was value-added and provided the physical space and place for graduate education: "When we built the GLC, we envisioned something larger, more complex and innovative. In fact, we built the space and place for an invigorating graduate community at Virginia Tech" (Virginia Tech, 2011). In our planning, we conceptualized the GLC through the following narrative:

> Transformative and inclusive graduate education can [be] become a reality at Virginia Tech. Having space and a place for graduate education is important and Donaldson-Brown provides the physical space and institutional place for 21st century graduate education. This facility, once renovated, will provide the space for the administrative functions of the Graduate School, Graduate Student Assembly, and other support services important to graduate students (childcare facilities, wellness, counseling, etc.). More importantly, it will also provide the place for and environment through which intellectual engagement and academic discourse will permeate the halls of academic institution (e.g., seminar rooms, library facilities, wireless technology, suites, coffee house, etc.). The renovated Donaldson-Brown will serve as a hub of energy and focus on graduate education. There will be no other place like this in the nation.
>
> (Virginia Tech, Program Statement, 2003)

> A new vision focuses and energizes a new tomorrow. What we are attempting to do has not been done at Tech before. We're not just developing new housing for graduate students. We're not just developing a student activity center (e.g., Squires). We're not just planning programs, scheduling events, and developing spaces for graduate students. We're not just moving the Graduate School and all of our programs/work/administration, etc. to a new location. We're doing all of these and more. We are envisioning something that is larger than the Donaldson Brown complex. We are building and invigorating a graduate community at Virginia Tech. This concept of "building graduate community" has been endorsed throughout the university and the Graduate School has assumed a leadership role.
>
> (Virginia Tech, Building Graduate Community, 2005)

In 2005, the GLC at Donaldson Brown on the Blacksburg campus of Virginia Tech was opened. The GLC brings graduate academics, administration, community, and residence life together in a unique way, providing the space and place for graduate education. The GLC is a partnership between the Division of Student Affairs and the Graduate School.

The shared management of the GLC (by the Graduate School, Student Engagement and Campus Life, and Housing and Residence Life) brought together unlikely partners who, under normal circumstances, would have had little to no interaction with one another and could comfortably function in their own realms with limited knowledge of the others' goals, priorities, and expertise. The GLC forced and enabled a collaboration or rather created a productive and constructive domain where collaboration was not only possible but absolutely necessary. Through these partnerships, greater insights were gained into one another's operations, motivations, and capabilities, and could harness different expertise and influence from each contributing unit to jointly improve to a greater degree the quality of life of graduate students.

Since its opening, the GLC has served as an incubator to build community and provide graduate students services not just in support of their academic pursuits, but also in their lives as individuals with dreams, aspirations, and a variety of challenges. In turn, graduate students have shaped the GLC, in its physical spaces as much as in its ideals and operation. In recognition of this work, the American College Personnel Association (ACPA) Commission for Graduate and Professional Student Affairs' Outstanding Innovative Program Award was awarded to the GLC in March 2011. The GLC had been acknowledged as a physical space and a place for belonging to build graduate community.

As we conceptualized graduate community, we intentionally set out to create an assortment of programs and services that respond to students' expressed or anticipated needs and also provide opportunities for involvement at a variety of levels. While any one of these can be launched on their own or abandoned as circumstances change, it is important to note that each contributes to particular and different aspects of community.

We had two overarching goals in building community:

- Provide centralized, or at least easy to find, assistance with academic, administrative, and life matters.
- Create a sense of belonging—a physical space as well as a conceptual place in which students can feel "at home," not alone with their issues and concerns, able to share their experiences, and receive direct and indirect support.

THE MAKING OF A COMMUNITY

Very early on, we identified a couple of important building blocks of community: some dependent on physical space, some not at all. Over time, we experimented with different programs and ideas, testing what worked and was worth keeping, tweaking promising attempts, and abandoning ones that fizzled out after a couple of years. Below are some examples.

Invite and Enable Students to Invest Themselves in the Community

Students will become part of a community if they continually receive from as well as contribute to it. Graduate Schools, because of their central and consistently present role in the life of graduate students, are in a good position to facilitate this by offering involvement opportunities at various levels, from low-level-low-impact to high-level-high-impact and everything in between. Graduate students can choose (and alter) their participation level according to their capacity, ability, and desire at any given time.

Low-level-low-impact events and opportunities are the easiest entry points to a community. Students may participate in only a small handful of these or become regular attendees as their comfort grows. Events and opportunities must be diverse in content and a target audience, inclusive, frequent, and repetitive, appealing to different interests and attributes so that students can recognize themselves in it. It is also important to note that sustained participation in low-impact opportunities over time can have as significant an impact as participation in high-impact opportunities, and awareness of opportunities without participation may still contribute to a sense of belonging. Content responsibility for any particular program or service should be housed in the unit (whether in the Graduate School, Student Affairs, or other area of campus) where subject matter expertise resides; however, Graduate Schools have an important coordinating role in ensuring that the compilation of all efforts is coherent, cohesive, and complementary across the spectrum:

— Regularly occurring social events sponsored and hosted by the Graduate School (e.g., weekly café, connect luncheons for various affinity groups, ice cream socials, shared craft projects, etc.) or by graduate student organizations (game nights, wine tastings, hikes, etc.) are easily accessible.
— Professional development programs offered by the Graduate School, by career development staff, or by other providers on campus, such as writing centers or organizers of experiential learning opportunities, as the two case studies in this chapter demonstrate, specifically addressing graduate student needs both for success in graduate school (e.g., writer's retreats, effective communication and presentation workshops, etc.) and after graduation (job search strategies, academic or industry career preparation, etc.) provide steady support year-round.

— Graduate Ambassador support for Graduate School-organized events a couple of times a year affords a sense of working for the common good with minimal time investment, yet building connection to the community.
— Original art and/or photography by graduate students is solicited twice a year to be displayed on the walls of the GLC. Students may participate with their own work and/or vote on the submissions as part of the contest. "Where are they now" posters of graduate alumni on the walls add layers of history.
— Students' participation on advisory boards and committees or in lunches with the dean provides opportunities to share perspective and influence policy or request programming and services; it also reinforces their investment in the community and improves their awareness of institutional context.
— A free lending library in the GLC reading room, where students can contribute or take books and games, connects students to a physical space.
— Health and wellness events and supplies in the GLC remind students of the importance of healthy habits and of our commitment to support not just their academic pursuits, but also a healthy work-life balance. Recreational sports, counseling, and health services departments of Student Affairs can be subject matter expert partners in these endeavors.
— The GLC bikes program provides a handful of bikes for free use around campus. This program predates by many years the now more prevalent bike share programs that popped up on many campuses.

Medium-level, medium-impact opportunities require greater and more sustained engagement from students but also offer higher rewards:

— Graduate students staff the GLC welcome center in wage positions, supervised by Student Engagement and Campus Life, the Student Affairs experts of operating a building this size. Through their paid work, they shape the operations and daily life of the building, also serving as first points of contact for visitors.
— GLC Fellows, a reimagined version of the traditional resident advisor roles jointly supervised by the Graduate School and Residence Life, provide programming not only for graduate student residents but also for the entire graduate community. They also develop a greater understanding of building operations.
— The Graduate Scholars Society was initiated by students, based on the belief that graduate students should not only be dedicated researchers but also engaged citizens. It brought together graduate students and faculty who committed to the exploration of contemporary issues in society through regularly occurring small group discussions of various intriguing and current topics.

172

— Diversity Scholars are graduate students who specialize in and advocate for the awareness, knowledge, and skills associated with diversity and inclusion in the Graduate School and greater community through dialogue, advocacy, and change. Students propose, design, and implement projects.

High-level, high-impact opportunities are most suitable for students who have or wish to develop leadership skills and who are willing to contribute a significant amount of time to the graduate community:

— The Graduate Student Assembly (GSA) offers a variety of leadership positions, from president to executive board members to chairs of various funding programs and professional development opportunities.
— The Graduate Honor System is a student-run organization that upholds and enforces academic integrity, working in close collaboration with faculty and the Graduate School.
— The Graduate Student Representative to the Board of Visitors works closely with the GSA as well as the Graduate School and Student Affairs to advocate for graduate students at the highest level of university governance.
— Leadership positions in other graduate student organizations, whether connected to discipline, affinity group, or special interests.

Establish Traditions

Traditions shape as well as ground community in the presence and the past, and they provide a sense of reassurance when faced with the unknowns of the future. They should be comforting, uplifting, and happening in a reliable and predictable way. For example:

— We offer a weekly "GLC Café" year-round, rain or shine, whenever the university is open. Because graduate education does not operate on the traditional undergraduate calendar, it is especially important to provide some services, such as this one, when the campus may feel empty but graduate students are very much present in their labs.
— We host and cohost large anchor events for graduate students during the year, such as the annual welcome (back) barbeque, luncheons during Thanksgiving and spring breaks, and a Graduate School picnic in March.
— Some events around orientation are repeated every semester, such as lunches with the dean, "Make yourself at home in Blacksburg," and a welcome week information fair.
— We publish a weekly listserv posting with topics of interest to graduate students curated by Graduate School staff. The content includes events and

activities tailored for or of specific interest to graduate students, research/ volunteer opportunities, on-campus job opportunities, and administrative announcements. The April Fool's Day special edition has achieved legendary status since its inception in 2008.

Preserve a Shared History and Memories

Graduate Schools, because of their central and coordinating role, are well positioned to gather, organize, preserve, and share historical records related to graduate education. This requires sustained effort, interest, and dedication, and thus should be an explicit institutional commitment reflected in a job description:

- We maintain a large footprint on various social media, including Facebook, Twitter, and Instagram, regularly sharing photos and stories.
- We connect with graduate alumni and involve them in professional development events for current students, reward their achievements with an annual award, and invite them back for a Graduate School homecoming where they may connect with current students.
- We regularly publish stories involving graduate student and alumni activities and achievements in Virginia Tech's daily news.

REFLECTIONS

The 15+ years of experience and programs have demonstrated the value of graduate centers for building graduate community and their significant impact on the lives of graduate students. They have also highlighted the significance of the Graduate School's role and the graduate dean's power to convene people and resources in support of graduate students. In order to mark this anniversary of the GLC, we chose to conduct an oral history project of the GLC with assistance of VT Stories. Through interviews with graduate alumni, current faculty, staff, and graduate students, we have confirmed the value and long-lasting impact of the GLC through a greater understanding of how community was built and sustained and why a physical space and place for belonging matters in the lives of graduate students. Given the value of the words spoken from the interviewees, we offer a few quotes followed by a summary of our reflections:

> The thing about the GLC is that when I go in there, as soon as I walk in through those doors, I instantly feel like home. It's very comforting, mentally...You go into a place and you feel like you are at peace inside, and that has shaped my experience. The GLC also has all these events there that helps

put graduate education into different perspectives. I notice very stark differences between my program and other programs and how other students are dealing with things, and sometimes this helps.

Loved the relationships that you build (while working in the GLC). I was seen as a multi-dimensional person with relationships to other humans. I met all my best friends there. All from different departments, found each other in the common areas. There aren't all that many common areas for graduate students.

A lot of universities think only about undergraduate students when they are designing student services. I see the Graduate Life Center as a physical space, as being a physical representation of Virginia Tech's promise to not forget about graduate students, and I think that plays out really well with the services and the things that go on at the Graduate School.

Building graduate community is the foundation of the GLC and a key component of the TGE initiative. The interviews revealed some valuable perspectives about how graduate students experience(d) community and a sense of belonging. Often, respondents indicated that they felt and enjoyed the community around them, although they may not have realized its significance until after they graduated and moved away and experienced its absence. The shared memories and stories are indeed a strong indicator of the long-lasting impact of the GLC.

The ever-changing members of the graduate community continue to provide valuable input that shapes GLC operations as well as many of the programs, events, and activities offered by the Graduate School. Since the inception of the GLC graduate student input was and is sought through surveys, student representation on committees, and regular feedback via the "with the Dean series" (lunch with the Dean, GuacTalk, Connect lunches, etc.). Student engagement with the life of the building continues to be an important element of their sense of belonging, but the graduate community is understood and experienced beyond the physical spaces of the GLC.

Throughout the first 15 years, many GLC traditions were established, which contributed to the sense of community as much or more than the physical spaces. Some traditions we designed intentionally, knowing the value they will add to graduate students' lives. Some have come about by accident, but became all the more important and appreciated, such as the April Fool's edition of the weekly listserv posting, which grew out of a prank-posting by graduate student residents of the GLC. These serendipitous developments cannot be designed or planned, but they can be anticipated and acted upon when they occur if our mindset is constantly focused on the pulse of the community.

In addition to confirming the value of community, we have also been re-inforced in our understanding that, as were the writers of the case studies in this chapter, services and opportunities, regardless of their provider, must be tailored for graduate students in content and delivery. We should also note such tailoring requires ongoing assessment of students' needs and the outcomes of our efforts, which is further addressed in Chapter 9.

CONCLUDING COMMENTS

In 2018, the National Academies of Science, Engineering, and Medicine (NASEM) issued a report and guidelines for the ideal graduate education. Among these guidelines are inclusive and equitable learning environment, mental well-ness, and work-life balance; communication skills; understanding different per-spectives and interdisciplinarity; and professional development opportunities:

> Importantly, this report also calls for a shift from the current system that focuses primarily on the needs of institutions of higher education and those of the research enterprise itself to one that is student centered, placing greater emphasis and focus on graduate students as individuals with diverse needs and challenges. An ideal, student-centered STEM graduate education system would include several attributes that are currently lacking in many academic institutions.

The report specifically highlights the importance of supportive peer communi-ties and suggests that graduate programs (and we would add Graduate Schools) assist students with "engaging in activities and experiences outside of the labo-ratory with fellow graduate students from within and outside of their depart-ments" in order to "both broaden their perspectives about other disciplines and career options and develop networks that can serve them well throughout grad-uate school and in their future careers" (NASEM, 2018, p. 84).

Although the report is focused on science, technology, engineering, and mathematics (STEM) graduate education, the concepts of the ideal graduate ed-ucation are applicable and pertinent to all graduate students and can be found embedded within the community of the GLC and the TGE initiative.

Our interviews with former graduate students revealed that the sense of com-munity they experienced while in graduate school at Virginia Tech often did not become obvious and truly significant until after they left and realized what was no longer around them. It is an interesting challenge to create a community that is so natural, so organic that students fold into it almost without noticing. How do you create spaces and places that facilitate that? How do you find the right balance of high- and low-touch activities and services and provide the ideal kinds of opportunities for students to create their own? How do you renew yourself year after year, abandoning favorite projects (like our Grad Olympics or the annual design contest "where crazy art meets fake science") that no longer seem to work for the newest generation of students and inventing brand-new ones that foster the desired engagement?

Each university, each campus, each Graduate School, or Student Affairs division has to find its own answer to these questions. Through our 15 years in the GLC, we have distilled our experiences to the following principles that guide us:

- Create a graduate culture and framework for student support, shared with and by academic programs and Student Affairs, within which graduate students can thrive.
- Maintain strong, formal and informal, daily connections with graduate students that help maintain conversations and put students at ease.
- Regularly affirm the support of the Graduate School, including the Graduate Dean, who can be the high-level champion for the cause.
- Work closely with academic departments and programs to promote a positive and supportive culture for graduate education.
- Employ graduate students (graduate assistants as well as wage) who are "boots on the ground," who bring new energy, enthusiasm, and inspiration year after year.
- Collaborate with other units across campus, including Student Affairs, to harness a wide array of expertise and resources in support of graduate students.
- Connect with other Graduate Schools and keep a repository of shared ideas.

A space dedicated in name and function to graduate students is an indirect but constant affirmation and reminder of institutional commitment to graduate students and an explicit foundation of a physical and virtual community and a backdrop for services and amenities supporting graduate education and graduate students. The GLC at Virginia Tech has served this purpose and exists as one example of "a space and place for graduate education" that can be implemented at other colleges and universities.

CASE STUDIES

The two case studies included in this chapter illustrate how programs and services traditionally available to undergraduate students can and should be intentionally redesigned or reinvented to address the distinctly different needs of graduate students. In each example, subject matter experts have identified a need and tailored their service or program specifically for graduate students, recognizing the potentially far-reaching positive impact their efforts will have on graduate students' success, both during and after their degree program. The University of California, Los Angeles (UCLA) Graduate Writing Center provides an example of how the writing consultants can serve as coaches and help graduate students navigate the critical and sometimes challenging component of graduate education—writing. The virtual Public Humanities Internship case study highlights the importance of a partnership between academic affairs and career support (Student Affairs) and offers an example in humanities and humanistic social sciences extending possibilities beyond the traditional science and engineering career development programs.

CASE STUDY 1

By Marilyn Gray

Title: The UCLA Graduate Writing Center as a Resource for Navigating Graduate School

Institution: University of California, Los Angeles (public, R1 Doctoral University)

Problem of Practice: Graduate students experience their graduate programs and access student services differently than undergraduate students. They are less likely to use general student support services, which are often seen as being for undergraduate students, even when graduate students are eligible to access these services. One reason for this perception is that student services are often designed with undergraduate students in mind and only adapted for graduate students in minor ways, if at all. Graduate students similarly view writing support offered through university writing centers as primarily for undergraduate students, especially when writing centers have predominantly undergraduate students working as peer tutors/consultants. The frequent undergraduate-centric approach of writing centers and the resulting perception is one of the compelling reasons for having a separate graduate writing center, or at least specific graduate student services within a larger writing center. Given that graduate student services are still underdeveloped in comparison to undergraduate student services, services that specifically target and are tailored for graduate students, when they exist, become an entry point for graduate students to use support services outside their own academic departments.

Initiative A—Support for Navigating Student Services: At the UCLA Graduate Writing Center, we first and foremost train graduate writing consultants to provide writing feedback to their peers. We review features of writing in different disciplines as well as the common genres of graduate school (seminar papers, theses, fellowship essays, conference presentations, journal articles, etc.). Additionally and importantly, we train our writing consultants on student services available to graduate students so that they can make referrals when appropriate. A graduate student may not be aware that a particular service exists or how to access the student service, but if a graduate peer provides tailored information on what is available and how to access the service, then this information sharing can extend the network of graduate students who know about and eventually use services. Graduate writing consultants who are trained to make recommendations about student services will likely share information not just with students in writing appointments, but also with graduate students in their home departments, student groups, or other peer networks. In this way, the Graduate Writing Center becomes an important source for disseminating information about student services.

Initiative B—Support for Navigating Graduate Education: Besides expanding the reach of student services in the graduate and professional student population, graduate writing centers are important sites of learning the expectations of graduate school, so many of which show up in written requirements. Graduate writing consultants are trained to look first at higher-order concerns (structure, argumentation) and then lower-order concerns related to style and mechanics. This developmental approach encourages writers to address and clarify big picture issues before working out technical and stylistic issues. As an important component of this approach, writing consultants frequently discuss features of the writing genre at hand, such as audience expectations and other conventions. When graduate students face a new writing task, they often do not know all of the expectations surrounding the new writing situation, so a conversation between the consultant and graduate student writer can help the writer map out what they know and what they still need to learn.

Writing consultants will never know all the expectations of the fields and genres that they see in writing appointments, but they can be trained to assess what the writer knows and what the writer still needs to understand better. In the event that the writer needs more information about the current writing genre, the writing consultant can pursue a number of strategies. The writing consultant can review the instructions for an assignment or fellowship or other document type when these instructions are available. The consultant can then compare these guidelines with the writer's text to see how well they are addressed. If explicit instructions are not available, the consultant can look at a model with the student to analyze features of the particular type of writing and help the student make choices about what features to apply to their own work. And finally, when the writing consultant cannot address all the writing questions, especially field-specific ones, they can be a sounding board and partner for brainstorming the questions to ask of faculty advisors or other authoritative sources of information (like program directors for grants).

In this way, the role of the writing consultant could additionally be described as one of graduate school coach. Because so much of the knowledge acquired and applied in graduate school impacts the writing stage, the writing consultant's role potentially encompasses not just expectations pertaining to writing, but also the research process surrounding the writing as well as the social and procedural aspects of complex writing projects. For example, when writers are working through processes of forming thesis committees or navigating other requirements, consultants can share their own experiences, as well as help students strategize questions to ask and ways to work with advisors and faculty effectively.

Implications for Policy and Practice: The graduate writing center has the potential to be a vital support of information for graduate students on how to navigate graduate school. Peer writing consultants can disseminate information and support other students in accessing additional student support services when appropriate. In the process of working with students on formal writing requirements or other important writing projects, the writing consultants can clarify expectations of graduate school and the conventions of particular types of writing, which contributes to the student's professional development in written communication. Writing consultants who are trained in these additional dimensions of support can play a vital role in helping their graduate student peers succeed in graduate school. The goal of maximizing graduate student support through writing support services should be an intentional part of program design and training for graduate student writing consultants as well as graduate support staff more generally.

CASE STUDY 2

By Kristen Galvin

Title: Virtual Public Humanities Internships (2020–), part of a larger initiative *Envision Humanities: A Graduate Student Toolkit for the 21st Century*

Institution: Center for the Humanities and the Public Sphere, University of Florida (public, R1 Doctoral University)

Problem of Practice: Due to the consensus of "getting a job" as *the* metric of collegiate success, professionalization via experiential learning has become normalized within undergraduate education and most commonly in the form of internships for academic credit. However, such opportunities have proved controversial in humanities graduate education at the doctoral level. Career exploration and preparation outside of traditional academic teaching is at times perceived as complicit with neoliberal university structures, with the prioritization of "professionalization" equated with the corporatization of higher education. Yet, this stance overlooks that humanities doctoral programs have always centered and depended upon the professionalization of their students—by way of low-paid, highly repetitive, teaching "apprenticeships" in the form of limited-term fellowships. Such a privileged perspective shields faculty and administrators from facing a core problem that negatively impacts the livelihood of graduate students, both during and after their degrees: academia's exploitive labor system, whereby 78% of its teaching workforce is nontenured, with prospects of attaining a tenure-track position at slim to none (American Association of University Professors, 2020).

Evidence of the Problem: Leonard Cassuto has been a leading voice in doctoral reform, publishing two books and writing the monthly column "The Graduate Adviser" in *The Chronicle of Higher Education*. In the summer of 2020, he voiced the importance of incorporating internships into doctoral education, advancing "as we plan what graduate education will look like in the post-pandemic era, we should think of internship programs as one of our most fundamental, necessary, and worthy investments." He highlights the excellence and innovation of the University of Iowa's "Humanities for the Public Good" internship program, funded in part by the Andrew W. Mellon Foundation. Whether in-person or virtual, the program places students at local nonprofit organizations and costs approximately $8,000 per intern ($5,000 stipend to the intern and $3,000 to the site partner), although his article does not report any overhead for additional program costs. As a model, a comparable university would need at least $72,000 to similarly fund nine interns, which may not be a realistic option given the anticipated budget cuts in the coming decade.

Initiative: As universities unexpectedly migrated online in 2020, as Assistant Director for Graduate Engagement at the University of Florida's Center for the Humanities and the Public Sphere, I rapidly transitioned our pilot summer public humanities internship program to a virtual format. The original in-person version was predicated upon programs at multiple institutions and simultaneously promoted career diversity, experiential learning, civic engagement, and public utility as critical to the sustainability of humanities graduate studies. Modestly funded, the new program was comprised of four, six-week internships, paid as standard graduate assistantships, whereby interns worked 20 hours per week on a dedicated project. This new internship structure has also recently been called a micro-internship (Wingard, 2019). In addition, a complementary career development workshop series allowing for deeper reflection and career exploration and a small stipend for an optional public-facing project were offered to the intern cohort.

Implications for Policy and Practice: As program manager, I witnessed the mutual benefits of placing PhD candidates from a Research I University at local nonprofit organizations across cultural, arts, educational, and environmental sectors. The program had multiple positive outcomes, from strengthening community relationships with local host organizations, to one intern receiving a subsequent $5,000 grant from the Florida Humanities Council for an ongoing public-facing project with the site partner. Although the program ran for only one cycle and on a small scale, part-time paid remote internships have proven effective in enhancing humanities graduate training while expanding career horizons and clarity. Yet, larger advantages emerge at this crossroads in graduate education. Importantly, these virtual experiential learning opportunities also:

1. provide crucial financial support when teaching assistantships become scarce, especially when students exceed their financial packages and near degree completion;

2. promote radical inclusivity for women, people of color, noncitizens, and those with certain disabilities by diminishing multiple barriers of entry or the "internship gap";
3. facilitate time management with a more flexible work schedule than traditional teaching assistantships, which students often claim to impinge upon their dissertation research and writing time;
4. demonstrate the potential for sustainability and scalability when considering a virtual move to larger regional, national, and/or international organizations that may have deeper resources to cost-share.

Career exploration and preparedness through the direct experience of internships cannot be underestimated nor relegated to student responsibility alone as an extracurricular activity. Because posted internships are often located in major cities, participation is subject to degrees of exclusion, whether in terms of affordability, access, race, and/or caregiving. Looking ahead to the future of doctoral education in the humanities and humanistic social sciences, establishing an equitable and inclusive virtual internship program can create incalculable professional opportunities and support for graduate students and aid their journey in attaining a satisfying and meaningful career. Doctoral programs cannot risk to collectively maintain the pre-pandemic status quo. They must implement more viable, inventive, adaptable, and customizable strategies to accommodate the actual needs and realizable futures of their students.

Case Study 2 References

American Association of University Professors. (2020). *The Annual Report on the Economic Status of the Profession, 2019–20*. Retrieved from https://www.aaup.org/sites/default/files/2019-20_ARES.pdf.

Cassuto, L. (2020). Doctoral training should include an internship. *The Chronicle of Higher Education.* Retrieved from https://www.chronicle.com/article/doctoral-training-should-include-an-internship.

Wingard, J. (2019). Why micro-internships will be the next big thing. *Forbes.* Retrieved from https://www.forbes.com/sites/jasonwingard/2019/03/06/why-micro-internships-will-be-the-next-big-thing/?sh=24eceb58700c.

REFERENCES

Association of American Universities. (2020, November 17). *A century of service to higher education 1900–2000*. Retrieved from https://www.aau.edu/association-american-universities-century-service-higher-education-1900-2000#:~:text=The%20Association%20of%20American%20Universities%3A%20A%20Century%20of,Funding%20and%20New%20Relationships%20with%20the%20Federal%20Government

DePauw, K. P. (2019). Evolving landscape of global higher education: Challenges and opportunities from a graduate education perspective. In A. Badran, E. Baydoun, & J. R. Hillman (Eds.), *Major challenges facing higher education in the Arab World: Quality assurance and relevance* (pp. 125–132). Springer.

Duderstadt, J. J. (2000). *A university for the 21st century*. University of Michigan Press.

Harper, W. (1980). Some conditions for graduate study, *Quest, 32*(2), 174–183. https://doi.org/10.1080/00336297.1980.10483709

National Academies of Sciences, Engineering, and Medicine (NASEM). (2018). *Graduate STEM education for the 21st century*. Retrieved from https://www.nap.edu/catalog/25038/graduate-stem-education-for-the-21st-century

Virginia Tech. (2003, June). *Program statement for renovation of Donaldson-Brown: Transformative and inclusive graduate education*. Unpublished internal document by Virginia Tech.

Virginia Tech. (2005, February). *Building graduate community: A concept paper for Donaldson Brown complex*. Unpublished internal document by Virginia Tech.

Virginia Tech. (2011, October). *Graduate life center: Academic affairs (graduate school) and student affairs partnership*. Unpublished internal document by Virginia Tech.

Chapter 9

Assessment

Using Data to Support Graduate Student Success and Program Effectiveness

Anne E. Lundquist and Christine Kelly

Assessment is an institutional imperative and should be used by every graduate program to not only assess what individual students are learning and have learned, but also to better understand how the program is meeting its stated goals in order to use that assessment for improvement and change. For example, graduate programs that:

> collect data sought by peer reviewers in the accreditation process not only demonstrate their assessment, evaluation and research expertise, they show themselves to be full partners in student learning, and as colleagues who can contribute a commodity that is essential to institutional endorsement.
>
> (Gordon et al., 2019, p. 13)

And whether they received formal academic preparation for assessment or not, it is important for those leading graduate programs to recognize that "assessment is no longer something that should only be done by those outside of organizations... [A]ll of us have responsibilities for asking evaluative questions, making decisions based on the answers, and taking action to implement the recommendations" (Russ-Eft & Preskill, 2009, p. 46). In other chapters in this book, examples of how student affairs professionals have incorporated assessment into their practice have been shared. In this chapter, the authors take a deeper dive into what assessment is, its role in institutional effectiveness at program, department, and university levels, and provide strategies for incorporating assessment into practice. The authors also provide examples of assessment in action, including how to develop and use logic models to design an evidence-based practice and how to use assessment data to strengthen arguments for more resources. Finally, in the

DOI: 10.4324/9781003121671-11

two case studies at the end of this chapter, examples are shared on how student affairs professionals have used assessment to evaluate programs and how the data gathered from other assessment projects on campus can provide information for assessing your own program.

The terms *research, assessment*, and *evaluation* can mean many things to many people and can cause confusion for those new to higher education assessment, particularly those conducting assessment as only a part of their role rather than their primary focus. Research is a form of inquiry with carefully defined procedures where the results of the study are interpreted in terms of what they contribute to the cumulative body of knowledge (Gall et al., 2007). The purpose of research is to develop new knowledge or theory and test concepts, and the primary audience is other researchers and practitioners in the field who can apply the research findings in their settings. The term *assessment* is often used more broadly to include the entire assessment process or cycle. It includes assessment of student learning as well as assessment of programs, operations, or services: "Assessment... is disciplined and systematic and uses many of the methodologies of traditional research" (Suskie, 2009, p. 14). While research and assessment often share many of the same methods, research guides theory, and assessment guides practice (Schuh & Upcraft, 2001). *Evaluation* is generally used in the context of evaluating a program or service and refers to the process of determining the value, merit, or worth of something. *Program evaluation* is the systematic collection of information used in order to make judgments to improve or further develop program effectiveness and make decisions about the future (Patton, 2008; Suskie, 2009; Upcraft & Schuh, 2001). The primary purpose of assessment and evaluation is for decision-making and organizational learning; the intention is for the use of assessment and evaluation to guide good practice for the stakeholders at a particular institution (Lundquist, n.d.).

Many practitioners get nervous when faced with assessing their programs and services, particularly if they are new to assessment or if assessment is not the primary focus of their role. They question whether they have the knowledge, skills, and abilities to conduct effective assessment. And while there are many skills and competencies that can be developed over time, assessment should not be frightening, and it is not rocket science. Assessment is about learning and inquiry. It can start with something as simple as wondering if what you are doing is accomplishing what you intended, and then formalizing your purpose and approach in context, finding specific ways to address your questions. Fortunately, there are also multiple professional development opportunities and organizations dedicated to helping higher education practitioners improve their assessment skills (see Table 9.1). This chapter will focus on the variety of ways that graduate programs can assess the student experience and overall program effectiveness.

TABLE 9.1 Assessment Organizations and Resources

Organization	Offerings	Website
AACU	Value rubrics	https://www.aacu.org/resources/assessment-and-value
ACPA	Assessment Institute	https://www.myacpa.org/events/saai
AAHLE	Assessment resources, listserv, and conference	https://www.aalhe.org/assessment-resources
Anthology	Assessment and data analytics technology as well as consultation, free thought leadership, and an Assessment Credential	anthology.com https://baselinesupport.campuslabs.com/hc/en-us/articles/115005509706-Assessment-Credential-Curriculum
Assessment Commons	Resources by categories with web links	http://assessmentcommons.org/view-all-resources/
Council for the Advancement of Standards (CAS)	Forty-eight functional standards and three cross-functional standards for higher education programs	https://www.cas.edu/standards
IUPUI	Assessment Institute	https://assessmentinstitute.iupui.edu/
NILOA	Assessment resources	https://www.learningoutcomesassessment.org/
Student Affairs Assessment Leaders (SAAL)	Webinars, blog posts, assessment examples, resource repository, and peer-reviewed online *Journal of Student Affairs Inquiry*	http://studentaffairsassessment.org/
USC Center for Urban Education	Equity Scorecard (metrics for assessing equity)	https://cue.usc.edu/tools/the-equity-scorecard/

DESIGNING AND CONDUCTING EFFECTIVE ASSESSMENT FOR GRADUATE AND PROFESSIONAL PROGRAMS

When it comes to designing and conducting effective assessment for graduate and professional programs, practitioners can be daunted by where to start. There are many types of assessment that are relevant for graduate and professional programs and many concepts and approaches that are useful.

The Assessment Cycle and Process

It is important to develop a framework to guide assessment for the program. Creating an assessment cycle can be one way to keep on track. While there are many models (e.g., Bresciani et al., 2004; Fulcher et al., 2014; Keeling et al., 2008; Suskie, 2009; Yousey-Elsener, 2013), the simple four-part cycle in Figure 9.1 is an easy way to organize assessment activities into stages.

Consider the purpose of the assessment and how it relates to other programs and institutional priorities. Many people like to move right to deciding what

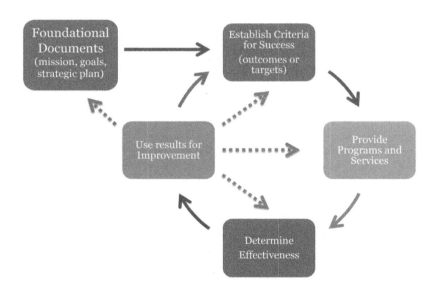

FIGURE 9.1 Example assessment cycle.

Source: Anthology. Baseline *Help Center,* https://baselinesupport.campuslabs.com/hc/en-us/articles/204304135-The-Assessment-Cycle.

type of data to collect and how to get the job done, but it is helpful to think the whole project through prior to starting.

Assessment can be organized into three broad categories: student learning; operational—administrative or service metrics that document how well the operations of the program are functioning; and program—the aggregate impact of a program, service, or intervention on a goal (Henning & Roberts, 2016). The following outline (adapted from Henning & Roberts, 2016; Schuh et al., 2016) serves as a starting place to develop an Assessment Plan:

1. Develop a purpose statement

   a. What are the issues at hand?
   b. Who is being assessed and why?
   c. Is the focus satisfaction, learning, program evaluation, benchmarking, other?

2. Engage stakeholders (for purpose, data collection, analysis, and use of results)
3. Determine methods

   a. Qualitative or quantitative?
   b. Formative or summative?

4. Determine what data to collect

   a. Examine existing data
   b. Determine methods and tools
      i. Surveys
      ii. Focus groups
      iii. Interviews
      iv. Document analysis
      v. Tracking and usage

5. Develop a time frame and plan for data collection, analysis
6. Share results
7. Use the results, and share how you used them

Bresciani et al. (2004) identified these questions that should be answered:

- What are we trying to do and why?
- What is my program supposed to accomplish?
- How well are we doing it?
- How do we know?
- How do we use the information to improve or celebrate successes?
- Do the improvements we make work? (p. 9)

You can also find a variety of publicly available templates online in the SAAL resource repository or the Anthology Assessment Credential.

Connecting Assessment to Institutional and Program Priorities

Assessment does not stand alone, or at least it should not. Effective assessment is tied directly to program and/or institutional goals and conducted with a clear purpose in mind. It can be helpful to link the assessment directly to the strategic plan for the program or to the institution's strategic plan in order to make it clear how the data collected will inform existing priorities and goals.

A logic model can be one way to organize this information. A logic model is:

> a framework and process for planning to bridge the gap between where you are and where you want to be. It provides a structure for clearly understanding the situation that drives the need for an initiative, the desired end state and how investments are linked to activities for targeted people in order to achieve the desired results.

(Millar et al., 2001, p. 73)

The logic model helps to build an evidence-based program and assists with:

* Shared language and vision for change
* Matching activities and outcomes
* Communication with stakeholders
* Enhanced accountability with an outcomes focus
* Resource allocation
* Identifying data needs and the framework for analysis

When designing a model for a unit, it helps to ask stakeholders for feedback. Also, realize that it will take time and constant revisions to create a model that works for your office. And even when you think you are done, you may need to revise again. Best practice in using logic models is that it will take approximately five years to measure outcomes and the impact of your work. The logic model can become the document you use to determine all programming, outreach, and marketing, resource allocation, and assessment projects for the office or program. It should be central to the ongoing strategic decision-making process, but also adaptive and flexible based on the results of continued assessment and evaluation, changes in demographics, shifting institutional or market priorities, etc.

At Claremont Graduate University (CGU), the Director of the Career Development Office (CDO) wrote a three-year strategic plan, which included the goal

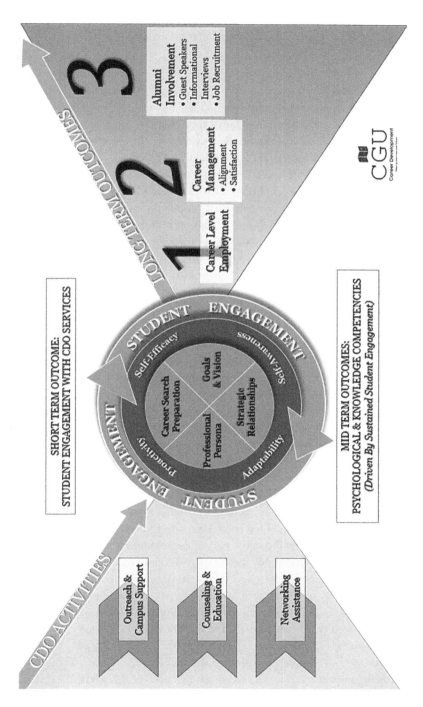

FIGURE 9.2 Claremont Graduate University career development logic model.

of running an evidence-based program. Fortunately, CGU has a highly regarded evaluation program and was able to leverage the knowledge base available to integrate assessment into the core practices. Figure 9.2 shows the most recent iteration of the model, developed over the course of three years. Earlier versions of the model were presented to campus stakeholders, including students and faculty, and at professional conferences to gain the feedback needed to improve the model. Earlier versions of the model failed to account for outreach and campus support and did not fully account for the psychological competencies required on the part of students for career success. The CDO now uses validated scales to assess these competencies in the entering student surveys, pre/post appointment surveys, program evaluation, and the exit survey. Thus, the CDO included the elements of the logic model in the evaluation and continues to evaluate the model to ensure an accurate picture is captured. Most recently, a team of students in the evaluation program at CGU reexamined the model and made suggestions for further refinement, demonstrating that creating and revising a model over time is a way to ensure it reflects the important work that needs to be done.

Organizing purposeful, systematic assessment linked to program and institutional goals and outcomes will be useful not only for internal program planning, but for accreditation purposes as well:

> Every accreditor has a list of standards that include criteria that aligns with student affairs work, such as addressing the institution's role in a diverse/ multicultural society, providing appropriate infrastructure and resources necessary to support learning and setting goals for student retention, persistence, and completion; and collecting and analyzing data to make improvements to help retention, persistence, and completion.
>
> (Gordon et al., 2019, p. 6)

An additional benefit to creating strategic plans and logic models is that the data can be used to advocate for more resources. While writing the strategic plan and developing the logic model for the CDO, the CGU Director realized the need to collect information about the career experience of incoming students to gain a deeper understanding of their career development needs. Starting in 2014 a survey was designed and given to all entering students to collect career preparedness data. By using the data from the first two years, a case was made for one of the goals of the strategic plan: adding more staff. Over time, the data consistently showed that between 60% and 65% of CGU's entering classes have less than three years of work experience and many lack clear career goals. The data was used to craft a request for additional staff, argued that the students were at risk of being unprepared to successfully launch post-CGU careers, and that a one-person office could not serve the needs of all the students in this high-risk group. Based on the report shared with senior administrators, two positions were added to the CDO. Gaining more resources for student affairs offices is always a challenge, as they are often not seen as mission critical, like elements of academic affairs. However, having evidence to support the need will aid in the success of the requests.

Postgraduation Outcomes

While it is vital to assess current efforts on behalf of graduate students, it is also important to consider the entire life cycle of a graduate student, from entering through to completion and beyond. While outcomes for undergraduate students have always been tracked and reported, until recently that was not the case for graduate students. Over the past ten years there has been an increased emphasis on graduate student outcomes, particularly for PhDs. In addition to the efforts led by the Council of Graduate Schools, the Graduate Career Consortium (an international organization of higher education professionals leading career and professional development for graduate students and postdocs) created the PhD Outcomes Task Force to explore ways to capture data on PhDs across the United States and Canada. In addition to discovering career outcomes, this data can also be used to inform current programming by providing information from alumni on their perceptions of what was missing from their educational journey.

There is ample evidence that student engagement leads to alumni satisfaction: "Listening to the feedback of current and former graduate students, and then acting upon that feedback, is crucial for the engagement and success of this population of students" (Hong-Novotney, 2018, p. ii). Involving alumni in programming for current students is a win-win for students and the university, and it is particularly important to engage new alumni. Since engaged students become engaged alumni and engaged alumni give back in ways that are essential to the university (such as time and money), alumni outcomes tracking is important for departmental program reviews and reaccreditation. Student Affairs offices in graduate programs play a vital role in building a strong alumni community. Further, we know that students tend to have a stronger alumni affiliation with their undergraduate institution than they do with their graduate institution, which makes ensuring graduate students keep in touch with the university where they earned their graduate degree a challenge and a campus-wide effort.

According to Hanover Research, alumni are the second largest source of funds in higher education, which is why alumni engagement programs often work so closely with Advancement and Development offices: "Alumni satisfaction with the student experience increases the likelihood of alumni volunteerism and philanthropy" (Barber, 2012, p 2). The overall experience a student has while enrolled plays a key role in whether or not students choose to give back to their institutions as alumni (Pumerantz, 2005). Student Affairs programs are central to this effort while students are enrolled and can pay dividends after a student graduates. A Gallup study found that a good experience at a career services department is correlated with students who find good jobs in their field after graduation and then give back to their institution. Graduates who found the career services office interactions very helpful are 2.6 times as likely to donate to their alma mater (Gallup-Purdue Index Report, 2016). Thus, creating ways for current students and alumni to interact is important to the fiscal health of the university.

Many universities are using alumni postgraduation outcomes data to evaluate program learning outcomes and competencies, and they are looking beyond simply the classroom experience. It is important for student affairs professionals to learn from alumni what resources they used and what experiences they had as a student that they attribute to their success after graduate school. Most universities use exit surveys to better understand the student experience, what resources they used, and any perceived barriers to their success. For example, at CGU, the Office of Institutional Effectiveness (OIE) sends out an exit survey which includes specific questions about students' use of and satisfaction with the CDO, the Center for Writing and Rhetoric, and the Preparing Future Faculty Program. Since this survey is completed by all exiting students, the information includes data from students who did not engage with these offices, thus helping student affairs offices to deepen their knowledge of the student experience by capturing data from students who do not use these offices. In order to increase student engagement, it is important to understand what perceptions or barriers may be impacting student use of an office or programs.

Using survey data to identify programming and service gaps can ensure you are meeting students' needs. For example, the University of Albany has a Graduate Student Assessment Survey that asks students to reflect on their overall experience with their graduate program. As student affairs professionals, we often plan programs based on what we perceive as students' needs, which can create blind spots if we are not also asking users. Even if you ask current students what they need, you may still be getting only part of the picture. Sometimes it takes looking back to understand what would have been helpful during your graduate program. Using data from alumni who have a few years of experience beyond their graduate program can deepen your knowledge of the impact of programs and the needs of those served. To collect additional data, many universities are using companies like EMSI and Burning Glass Technologies to locate their alumni. These companies provide information from alumni about their career paths and the skills they use from their graduate programs in their current careers. Some academic departments are using this information to evaluate the core competencies of their programs and to make modifications based on this new information. It can also be helpful to find out what overall alumni data is collected institutionally so learning outcomes can be reevaluated and used in program reviews.

Program Effectiveness and Program Review

Providing evidence of the success of programs is important to both internal stakeholders and external bodies. However, having meaningful data cannot be an afterthought. Building assessment into the DNA of everything is essential to provide powerful evidence and compelling stories about the contribution to the mission of the university. Program review can be one way to accomplish this. *Program review* is the systematic assessment of a program compared to a set of explicit or implicit standards as one method to improve the program (Weiss, 1997).

Program review is an opportunity for a program or department to step back and reflect on what is working and how they are fulfilling their mission. Referring back to the Logic Model or strategic plan for this can help guide the program review process: "Program review looks at the administration and effectiveness of the overall unit to assess strengths and identify areas for improvement" (Schuh et al., 2016, p. 112). A Program Review is a rigorous, systematic, objective, impartial, expert-based examination and an evaluation and self-evaluation process. Institutional requirements may dictate the elements of the program review process or programs may choose to select an existing framework for their review, like the Council for the Advancement of Standards (CAS). The main elements of program review include the basis for the comparison, collecting evidence to support judgments, assembling and training a team (internal and/or external) to review the evidence and rate the extent to which the determined standards are met, and a review of the ratings to identify areas of strength and places for improvement. In 2017, CAS released revised Graduate and Professional Student Programs and Services (GPSPS) standards to reflect important changes in the field. Ms. Pat Carretta, retired Assistant Vice President for University Life at George Mason University and chair for the GPSPS standards committee, notes: "the GPSPS standards recognize a variety of organizational and reporting models and emphasize the criticality of consultation, cooperation and coordination across student and academic affairs to ensure delivery of highest quality programs and services" (CAS, para. 4). In addition, she notes that:

at many institutions the focus on student and academic support services is primarily the undergraduate student. The CAS standards for GPSPS recognize the unique needs of graduate and professional students and provide a framework for developing and improving comprehensives services for this growing population.

(CAS, para. 5)

Consideration of program reviews should be an essential part of the process when proposing and designing new programming. A common problem we see in higher education is the proliferation of new programming to solve ongoing problems. The result is often ineffective programs that tend to repeat the mistakes of the past rather than solve the issue. This can happen due to a lack of knowledge or historical context for what has been tried in the past or from frustration with current programs that do not seem to be having the desired outcome in the desired time frame. Before proposing new programs, take time to see what the institution has done in the past to address the issue at hand. This may be a challenge if your predecessors did not keep good records of what they did and what the outcomes were. The lesson here is to always create legacy records of programs, including the research into past programs related to the topic, and records of program outcomes so there will be accurate records for the future.

As new programs are developed, evidence from prior programs should be used. Some programs just need revision rather than a total overhaul. You should also incorporate the program review process into the development stage. If you have clear goals, specific stated outcomes, and a plan for how to measure those outcomes, better programs with a stronger likelihood of success will be created. Further, this manages stakeholders' expectations, since the evaluation process should include milestone markers of when it is expected to realize your program's goals. We have seen programs ended before they had a chance to prove themselves due to unrealistic expectations and external pressures for results.

In Case Study 1, the author conducted an external evaluation of communication training programs at 13 Northeast American universities. She found that each of the programs had integrated the evaluation process into their program design and they used the data to make continuous improvements. Another theme she discovered was that the program planners all found the involvement of campus stakeholders was essential to their immediate success and to continuing the program into the future. And because they incorporated program review into their planning process, many were able to use the evidence to increase program funding and staff. The research project referenced in the case study also provided these institutions with an external program review that helped them benchmark their programs by comparing their process and results to similar institutions.

COLLABORATING WITH CAMPUS PARTNERS

It is tough to conduct assessment alone, especially with limited staff in small programs. Fortunately, as mentioned previously, there are organizations and conferences to assist with providing guidance and examples. Additionally, colleagues at consortium, regional, or similar institutional type campuses are often willing to share what they have developed.

It is equally important to collaborate internally with campus partners in order to conduct effective assessment. There are many offices that can help, so consider the campus organizational structure and context to identify which partners can be most effective. A few to consider are:

- Marketing and Communication: to help with sharing results, creating visually interesting reports, and to keep them informed about your program.
- Alumni, Advancement, and Development: to collaborate on ways to assess alumni and donors as well as share information and strategies.
- Admissions and Enrollment Management: to identify trends and share assessment results to use in the recruitment process.
- Career Services: to collaborate on postgraduation surveys and communications.
- Institutional Effectiveness or Planning: to collaborate or find out more about Program Review and how your program goals align with institutional strategic planning.
- Evaluation Center: collaborate on assessment design (and learn more about existing data collection).
- Teaching and Learning Center: professional development.

One of the most important offices to collaborate with before taking on a new assessment project is the Office of Institutional Research (IR). The professionals in that office are knowledgeable about methods and procedures, and can direct you to existing validated scales that might help answer assessment questions and point you to resources on proper data collection procedures. Also, you may be able to explore what data they have already collected that you can use to answer your question to see if it is even necessary for you to gather additional data.

Much of the current research in student affairs is undergraduate-focused. For instance, in Case Study 2, the authors conducted a literature review focused on the sense of belonging for those who identify as lesbian, gay, bisexual, transgender and queer (LGBTQ) graduate students of color; they found some research on undergraduates and very little focused on graduate students. Even research focused on retention and degree completion, which are serious issues in graduate education, tends to focus on undergraduates. And much of the existent student affairs research on graduate students tends to focus on students in professional programs, like Nursing or Business Administration, and not students in more traditional masters and doctoral programs, like English or Biochemistry. Thus, there are opportunities to add to the literature about the graduate student experience. In Case Study 2, the authors were able to use existing data to answer their questions. They found that campus climate surveys at their university already had items on "sense of belonging" that they could use. They note the advantages were that utilizing existing data allowed for comparison and benchmarking and that survey items were already tested and validated.

If new data is needed, ask IR about the procedures for data collection. What is the data collection policy? What are the rules for data management? What are the survey policies on campus? How do they manage survey timing? Some institutions have a master schedule of surveys so students do not get survey fatigue. You also need to know what questions they are already asking, so that additional surveys do not ask the same questions. Ask if there is additional training you may need on data collection and management. Most institutions have training on the responsible conduct of research that is required for data collection, especially if you will be using the data to create a publication, conference paper, or other written documents that will be shared outside your campus community.

CONCLUSION

Assessment does not have to be daunting; in fact, it can open opportunities for collaboration, new ways of thinking, identify program strengths to celebrate, and uncover challenges that need to be addressed. Creating an effective assessment strategy takes planning, but it is worth the time invested. Linking assessment to strategic program priorities and institutional goals will ensure that the time spent is efficient and effective and that the results will be used for improvement and change. Most people (outside of IR offices) did not enter higher education to conduct assessment: they entered the field in order to make a difference in the lives of students. Reframing our thinking about assessment to consider it a vital way for us to not only hold ourselves accountable for the resources entrusted to us, but also to make the greatest impact on student success, can help pursue assessment activities and planning with less trepidation—and even with delight. In essence, it is quite simple: what does our program do, how well are we doing it right now, and what could we do to improve what might be outdated or not working? And don't forget to celebrate the successes!

CASE STUDY 1

By Jovana Milosavljevic Ardeljan

Title: Broadly Based Graduate Student Support: Program Review from Graduate School Leaders' Perspectives

Institution: University of New Hampshire (public, R1)

Problem of Practice: Traditional graduate training helps students become experts at communicating within their fields. However, it often fails to provide broader skills for addressing more general audiences, which is crucial for diversifying graduate students' career paths and reaching different stakeholders (Coleman, 2018). The following study is one piece of a larger three-part study looking at the structure and role of communication support programs. It is a communication support program review within which programs' effectiveness was assessed. The need for administrative and faculty support, encouragement and guidance to enable students to develop broader skills set, is explored. The goal is to answer what faculty and administration can do to increase program effectiveness and to ensure that programs are well received and used by the students for whom they are created.

Evidence of the Problem: One purpose of education is to provide students with the knowledge and skills necessary for finding employment after they graduate. However, this is often not the case in graduate programs. The 2012 report *Pathways Through Graduate School and Into Careers* (Council of Graduate Schools and Educational Testing Service, 2012) notes the need to "examine the relationship between skills development and workforce needs" as a part of graduate education, calling for efforts "to understand and close gaps between graduate preparation and the skills needed in different employment sectors" (p. 6). Several studies have shown that graduate students who have limited communication skills that reach across these different careers need more support in developing literacies that will facilitate their transition from academia to the workforce (Cassuto, 2012; Denecke et al., 2017; Dunne et al., 1997; Ortega & Kent, 2018; Stewart, 2010). This study raises the following questions: What support programs exist? How is the support organized and who provides it? What student needs are addressed? Finally, what needs have not been addressed yet? These challenges provide the context and motivation for the study. It uses the perspective of graduate school administration as the initiators and sponsors of graduate student support programs.

Initiative: Using interviews with graduate school deans and other leaders from 13 universities in Northeast America, this study reviews the perceived role and outcomes of broadly based communication support programs and how the university can ensure that they are providing most effective support that addresses graduate students' needs. The participants were recruited by sending an invitation email to attendees of the 2018 Northeastern Association of Graduate Schools (NAGS) meeting. Out of the 20 respondents, 13 met the criteria—they were Graduate School Deans or designees from research institutions which have some type of communication support programs.

For this study, semi-structured qualitative interviews of graduate school deans and leaders were conducted. Interviews included five questions: (1) whose responsibility it is to provide support to graduate students to prepare them for the application of their graduate degrees in a workplace, (2) what structural changes have happened in existing support programs, (3) how the programs were funded, (4) how the programs were evaluated, (5) what the history of the programs was, and (6) what should a new dean keep in mind when starting a new communication support program.

Results: Three main themes surfaced from the interviews with the graduate school officials. When reviewing a program, it is suggested to consider the following:

1. Is the support institutionalized? Institutionalization refers to having an established office or center within an institution with the purpose of serving a particular need. The programs provide best outcomes if offered through institutionalized centers whose purpose is to create, organize, and deliver programming developed for graduate students and postdocs (as opposed to tag on support added to undergraduate-focused centers). It is important to evaluate how the support programs relate and correspond to the institution's characteristics, such as size, level of research activity, diverse graduate student needs, funding, and already existing support.
2. What is the role of the faculty and other stakeholders in providing the support? Faculty need to believe in support initiatives, endorse them,

and encourage students to utilize them. In order to increase student engagement, it is essential to establish a relationship with faculty who will encourage students to take part. Collaboration with faculty may lead to improved realization of faculty on how these support programs assist them in student development. Furthermore, involving other campus stakeholders such as career center, alumni office, library, writing center, and so on is critical in providing comprehensive support.

3. What are the potential programmatic challenges? These refer to starting (finding seed funding), maintaining (finding staff), and sustaining (securing long-term funding) support programs. Based on the interviews, best practice proved to be starting small, with one person or a few people who start providing support while collecting data and doing continuous evaluation. Those data are then used to make the case for expanding the programs.

Implications for Policy and Practice: The participants reported that their programs have been growing and developing over time due to the positive feedback from students and evidence that the support played an important role in (1) navigating graduate school and (2) career and professional development. The most successful examples of change over time are institutions which started with one-off events (often created ad hoc to meet a specific emergent need) and over time developed comprehensive professional development offices with full-time staff. This change was captured through both internal and external evaluation of the programs, which, based on the positive results, led to expansion. An example and detailed discussion on program growth can be found in Freeman (2016). Prior to starting any initiative regarding graduate student support programs, it is critical to do needs analysis and know well what already exists. The need assessment may include the following steps: (1) University-/Graduate School-level analysis of existing support; (2) Review of what other universities do and adjust it to your students and their needs; and (3) Use of one-off programs to test the waters. This review showed that most successful programs are the ones that are institutionalized because they can provide consistent, systematic, and continuous support. Involving faculty and other stakeholders proved to help with creation, delivery, and promotion of the programs. Therefore, it is recommended to develop a strong relationship with these groups and include them in every step of the process. Finally, it is critical to make the support focused on graduate students and not to put it as a tag on to undergraduate student resources.

Case Study 1 References

Cassuto, L. (2012). OK, let's teach graduate students differently. But how? *The Chronicle of Higher Education.* Retrieved from https://www.chronicle.com/article/OK-Lets-Teach-Graduate/130218

Coleman, M. S. (2018, June 4). *The three vs of graduate education.* Association of American Universities. Retrieved from https://www.aau.edu/newsroom/mary-sues-desk/three-vs-graduate-education

Council of Graduate Schools and Educational Testing Service. (2012). *Pathways through graduate school and into careers.* Council of Graduate Schools. Retrieved from http://www.pathwaysreport.org/rsc/pdf/19089_PathwaysRept_Links.pdf

Denecke, D., Feaster, K., & Stone, K. (2017). *Professional development: Shaping effective programs for STEM graduate students.* Council of Graduate Schools. Retrieved from https://cgsnet.org/ckfinder/userfiles/files/CGS_ProfDev_STEMGrads16_web.pdf

Dunne, E., Bennett, N., & Carré, C. (1997). Higher education: Core skills in a learning society. *Journal of Education Policy, 12*(6), 511. https://doi.org/10.1080/0268093970120606

Freeman, J. (2016). Designing and building a graduate communication program at the University of Toronto. In S. Simpson, N. Caplan, M. Cox, & T. Phillips (Eds.), *Supporting graduate student writers: Research, curriculum, and program design* (pp. 222–238). University of Michigan Press.

Ortega, T., & Kent, J. D. (2018). What is a PhD? Reverse-engineering our degree programs in the age of evidence-based change. *Change: The Magazine of Higher Learning, 50*(1), 30–36.

Stewart, D. (2010). Important if true: Graduate education will drive America's future prosperity. *Change,* (1), 36. https://doi.org/10.1080/00091380903449110

CASE STUDY 2

By Valerie A. Shepard, Raja Gopal Bhattar, and Aye Mon Htut-Rosales

Title: Understanding and Fostering Sense of Belonging for LGBTQ Graduate Students of Color

Institution: University of California, Los Angeles (public, R1)

Problem of Practice: While we know about barriers to the sense of belonging for graduate students who identify as LGBTQ and/or people of color, little knowledge exists that centers on an equity-minded analysis of data and strategies for enhancing belonging. While many campuses focus on data collection and assessment, little focus is given to analysis of data and thoughtful engagement with various campus partners in developing actionable strategies based on data. This project utilized intentional cross-campus collaboration as well as innovative data analysis and design to center traditionally marginalized populations and elevate their narratives.

Evidence of the Problem: This research agenda is crucially important, especially now; a literature review (e.g., Strayhorn, 2012, pp. 90–104; Strayhorn et al., 2015; Turkowitz & Felder, 2014) showed us there is not a lot of research available. Though graduate students are one-third of the University of California, Los Angeles (UCLA) campus, data on campus presents their experiences as monolithic, inherently erasing experiences of students with marginalized identities, especially those with multiple and intersectional identities such as LGBTQ graduate students of color. Recognizing these facets of identity and disaggregating data allowed us to understand important differences in how populations experience belonging on campus. Additionally, graduate students exist in virtually every UCLA department and represent the diversity of our student body. Yet, there lacked a cohesive collaboration to center data collection on graduate students and recognize the need for various forms of expertise to better understand who our graduate students are. Beyond sending emails to all graduate student listservs, our object is to build intentional relationships with graduate students in ethnic, gender, and identity centers and academic programs with higher representation of various identities to ensure our data is relevant and reflective of all graduate student experiences. Even the act of building collaborative relationships and tapping into trust networks increases trust and belonging for our students.

While higher education values assessment and data-driven interventions, often data collection methods disproportionately impact marginalized populations. Quantitative analyses normalize dominant experiences by setting them as baseline variables and compare other populations as they fare better or worse than the former group. For example, comparing how Black students do academically in relation to white students creates a deficiency framework and assumes that all students should be performing similar to white students. We want to pursue more equitable data analysis that does not normalize dominant group experiences. While our primary objectives were to enhance our own data collection and understanding of our students, our deeper passion is to enhance how this data can increase awareness of disparities in access and experience for students of various identities. We want to advocate for more nuanced data collection in other departments and development of policies that support graduate students with intersectional identities.

With this context, our project had four guiding goals: elevate experiences of LGBTQ graduate students of color; foster cross-campus collaboration for data collection and analysis; develop inclusive data analysis methods; and enhance campus-wide awareness, programs, and experiences for graduate students with consciousness of intersectional identities. Our hope is a cultural shift in awareness and support initiatives to foster better outcomes for LGBTQ graduate students of color and their various identities.

Initiative: Using available institutional data, we discussed the gaps in knowledge and asked: how do we best foster *sense of belonging* and a positive campus climate for LGBTQ graduate students of color through institution-level partnerships between and across our offices? Our collaboration was informed by our belief that supporting LGBTQ students, students who are people of color, and graduate students is the responsibility of the whole campus, not individual offices. The steps taken were:

1. Identified existing data

    - The division of Student Affairs, Graduate Division, and some academic entities are already a part of collaboration, therefore, making it easier to leverage buy-in
    - Students are a part of survey development as well as testing; rounds of revision are done to improve the quality of data
    - Utilize demographic data to allow for disaggregation

        - UCLA Student Affairs Information and Research Office (SAIRO) collects and reports on demographic data (gender, ethnicity, and sexual orientation data are used for this specific study)
        - Data on marginalized groups are examined in depth (by disaggregating data when possible)

    - Additional questions (gender identity, gender expression, and mentorship) were added to the survey as a result of the collaboration among the offices

- Abundance of data on student experiences, including open-ended qualitative data are now looked at in disaggregation

2. Established collaborative partnerships to enhance data analysis and interpretation, including SAIRO, LGBTQ Campus Resource Center, Graduate Student Resource Center, and respective practitioners to contribute their expertise and nuances. Student voices inform offices and the campus about experiences of marginalized groups by utilizing open-ended responses and rich qualitative data.

3. Utilized UCLA Student Affairs Graduate and Professional Student Survey (UCLA Student Affairs Information & Research Office, n.d.)
   - Survey developed by committee that includes broad representation from Student Affairs units and the UCLA Graduate Division, including graduate student representation
   - Survey instruments for 2010, 2014, 2017, and 2020 as well as reports, available at sairo.ucla.edu

Our analysis of institutional data centered on the question of whether any differences exist among experiences of sense of belonging among dominant and subordinate identities of graduate students.

Implications for Policy and Practice: We found differences in how graduate students of color, LGBTQ graduate students, and LGBTQ graduate students of color experience a sense of belonging. As scholar practitioners, our objective has been to translate this data into tangible actions to foster campus cultural transformation:

- Campus level:
  - This process brought our three offices to better understand how we support students, enhanced recruitment for interns who share multiple identities, and allowed us to be advocates for each other's offices in broader campus programs. Doing so made our work more cohesive and increased utilization of programs by graduate LGBTQ students of color.
  - Implementing consistent data collection questions across campus graduate programs. By developing these questions and providing such important data, we have been able to share this data with Graduate Division leadership and the UCLA Healthy Campus Initiative, bringing to light the importance of critical data collection and analysis strategies.

- Intentional advocacy with various departments about how to better foster sense of belonging for diverse graduate students in their programs.
- The LGBTQ Campus Resource Center developed internships specifically for graduate students to enhance LGBTQ graduate students of color campus communities.
- The GSRC further incorporated LGBTQ Campus Resource Center and other identity offices into annual orientation programs.
- SAIRO urged other departments to disaggregate available data to understand how to support graduate students.

- Beyond UCLA:

  - The survey items on gender identity, sexual orientation, and gender expression, developed as a result of this partnership, are now used on other surveys on campus and in the UCLA system to be more inclusive in data collection.
  - We presented this data and process at various national and regional conferences, and catalyzed a national conversation on equitable data collection and analysis for graduate students.

Guiding Questions: Based on our conversations with various campuses and at conferences, we developed some key questions to enhance practitioners' ability to better support LGBTQ graduate students of color:

- What is your current understanding of the experience of LGBTQ graduate and professional students of color on your campus?
- What data is available on your campus?
- What programming and resources are available?
- What innovative partnerships can help you ask questions that lead to actionable results?
- How can we advance an inclusive and critical research agenda, both on our campuses through assessment for program improvement in particular and for our field in general?

Beyond these questions, we have shared the UCLA Student Affairs Graduate and Professional Student Survey with colleagues on other campuses so that they can adapt a similar data collection and analysis approach to better understand their campus community.

Case Study 2 References

Strayhorn, T. L. (2012). *College students' sense of belonging: A key to educational success for all students*. Routledge.

Strayhorn, T. L., Johnson, R. M., Henderson, T. S., & Tillman-Kelly, D. L. (2015). *Beyond coming out: New insights about GLBQ college students of color*. Center for Higher Education Enterprise, The Ohio State University.

Turkowitz, A., & Felder, P. (2014). Graduate student learning and the lesbian, gay, and bisexual experience. In P. P. Felder & E.P. St. John (Eds.), *Supporting graduate students in the 21st century: Implications for policy and practice* (pp. 219–240). AMS Press.

UCLA Student Affairs Information & Research Office. (n.d.). *UCLA student affairs graduate and professional student survey (GPSS)* [Data set]. UCLA. Retrieved June 22, 2021, from https://sairo.ucla.edu/by-survey/grad-survey

REFERENCES

Anthology (Campus Labs). (n.d.). *Baseline help center*. Author. Retrieved from https://baselinesupport.campuslabs.com/hc/en-us/articles/204304135-The-Assessment-Cycle.

Barber, K. (2012). *A study of alumni engagement and satisfaction as related to alumni volunteerism and philanthropy* [Unpublished doctoral dissertation]. Valdosta State University. Retrieved from https://vtext.valdosta.edu/xmlui/bitstream/handle/10428/1221/barber-keith.pdf?sequence=1&isAllowed=y

Bresciani, M., Zelna, C., & Anderson, J. (2004). *Assessing student development and learning: A handbook for practitioners*. NASPA-Student Affairs Administrators in Higher Education.

Cassuto, L. (2012). OK, let's teach graduate students differently. But how? *The Chronicle of Higher Education*. Retrieved from https://www.chronicle.com/article/OK-Lets-Teach-Graduate/130218

Claremont Graduate University. (n.d.). *Career development logic model*. Author.

Council for the Advancement of Standards (CAS). (2017). *CAS releases revised standards for graduate and professional student programs and services*. Retrieved from https://www.cas.edu/blog_home.asp?display=76

Fulcher, K., Good, M., Coleman, C., & Smith, K. (2014). *A simple model for learning improvement: Weigh pig, feed pig, weigh pig* (Occasional paper No. 23). National Institute for Learning Outcomes Assessment.

Gall, M. D., Gall, J. P., & Borg, W. R. (2007). *Educational research: An introduction* (8th ed.). Pearson.

Gallup-Purdue Index Report. (2016). Great jobs. Great lives. The value of career services, inclusive experiences and mentorship for college graduates. *Gallup*. Retrieved from https://news.gallup.com/reports/199229/gallup-purdue-index-report-2016.aspx

Gordon, S. R., Shefman, P., Heinrich, B., & Gage, K. (2019). The role of student affairs in regional accreditation: Why and how to be included. *Journal of Student Affairs Inquiry, 5*(1), 1–25.

Henning, G. W., & Roberts, D. (2016). *Student affairs assessment: Theory to practice*. Stylus.

Hong-Novotney, A. W. (2018). *Listening to our graduate students' feedback: Graduate student exit and alumni surveys* [Unpublished master's thesis]. Humboldt State University. Retrieved from https://digitalcommons.humboldt.edu/cgi/viewcontent.cgi?article=1252&context=etd

Keeling, R., Wall, A., Underhile, R., & Dungy, G. (2008). *Assessment reconsidered: Institutional effectiveness for student success.* International Center for Student Success and Institutional Accountability.

Lundquist, A. E. (n.d.). Assessment, evaluation and research: Relationships and definitions in the field of student affairs. *Campus Labs.* Retrieved from https://baselinesupport.campuslabs.com/hc/en-us/articles/115005509706-Assessment-Credential-Curriculum

Millar, A., Simeone, R., & Carnevale, J. (2001). Logic models: A systems tool for performance management. *Evaluation and Program Planning, 24,* 73–81.

Patton, M. Q. (2008). *Utilization-focused evaluation* (4th ed.). Sage Publications.

Pumerantz, R. K. (2005). Alumni-in-training: A public roadmap for success. *International Journal of Educational Advancement, 5,* 289–300.

Russ-Eft, D., & Preskill, H. (2009). *Evaluation in organizations: A systematic approach to enhancing learning, performance, and change.* Basic Books.

Schuh, J. H., Biddix, J. P., Dean, L. A., & Kinzie, J. (2016). *Assessment in student affairs* (2nd ed.). Jossey-Bass.

Schuh, J. H., & Upcraft, M. L. (2001). *Assessment practice in student affairs: An application manual.* Jossey-Bass.

Suskie, L. (2009). *Assessing student learning: A common sense guide* (2nd ed.). Stylus.

Weiss, C. H. (1997). *Evaluation* (2nd ed.). Prentice Hall.

Yousey-Elsener, K. (2013). Assessment fundamentals: The ABS's of assessment. In D. M. Timm, J. D. Barham, K. McKinney, & A. R. Knerr (Eds.), *Assessment in practice: A companion guide to the ASK standards* (pp. 9–18). ACPA.

PART III

WHAT'S NEXT

Training Future Student Affairs Practitioners

Chapter 10

Curriculum Project

April L. Perry and Katherine Hall-Hertel

Elements of student affairs practice have existed since colleges were formed; however, many scholars agree that the professionalization of the field can be traced back to the first meeting of deans at the Conference of Deans and Advisors in State Universities in 1905 (Hevel, 2016). Prior to that, colleges relied on faculty to guide and discipline students. The concept of *in loco parentis* (in place of the parent) was the norm (Long, 2012), but by the mid-1800s, faculty had all but abdicated their role as disciplinarian. They embraced research, which left little time to manage undergraduate students. Colleges began to hire deans to manage their students' lives outside of the classroom. Those deans hired began the professionalism of the field. A particularly important milestone was the 1972 report from the American College Personnel Association, *Student Development in Tomorrow's Higher Education: A return to the academy* (Brown, 1972). The report argued that to be effective and credible, professionals working in student affairs needed training and education. Student Affairs professionals needed to collaborate with faculty to create a holistic learning experience for students. Theories of student development that focused on traditionally aged undergraduates were created in response (Long, 2012).

As the profession moved into the 21st century, calls to adapt theories to the increasing diversity of students in higher education grew louder. Research, theory, and professionalism propelled the field of student affairs, but much of that work focused on traditional undergraduates. The national associations that support the profession, American College Personnel Association (ACPA) and National Association of Student Personnel Administrators (NASPA), worked to offer broad support for professionals in various aspects of student affairs. Training student affairs professionals to work with graduate students, however, was not seen as a priority, as many assumed graduate students did not *need* developmental support. Even though graduate students comprise a significant portion of the enrollment in higher education, the profession of student affairs neglected

DOI: 10.4324/9781003121671-13

to identify and address the particular needs of graduate students until very recently. In this chapter, we present The What (context), So What (details of the initiative), and Now What (next steps) of the Curriculum Project developed by the Administrators in Graduate and Professional Student Services (AGAPSS) practitioners as a response to the lack of resources and training available to those who find themselves (intentionally or unintentionally) working with graduate and professional students.

THE WHAT? CONTEXT FOR THE AGAPSS CURRICULUM PROJECT

Similar to the way in which deans of students became professionalized over time, administrators in graduate education expanded their purview beyond the academic out of necessity (see Chapters 2 and 3). As noted in Chapter 1, a group of student affairs professionals gathered at a national conference in 1998 to share insights on working with this population of students. Out of that 1998 meeting came the first organized group for professionals working with graduate students: Graduate and Professional Student Services (GAPSS). This group met annually at the NASPA national annual conference to share challenges and solutions, while seeking new and better practices to serve graduate and professional students. Eventually the name was changed to AGAPSS to clarify that this was not a constituent group of graduate students, but one of student affairs professionals who worked primarily with post-baccalaureate students. Through these meetings, it became clear that there was no formal curriculum to guide this work. These professionals, some of whom were trained through traditional student affairs programs, worked to adapt and apply theories of development, student success, and well-being to graduate students.

A cursory review of commonly used texts in Student Affairs graduate programs illustrates this gap in the profession. As an example, one of the most commonly used texts in student affairs master's programs *Student Services: A handbook for the profession* (Schuh et al., 2016) includes only three paragraphs on GAPSS (p. 348) and an acknowledgement that more graduate programs are developing services for graduate students. The text recommends that more research on graduate students is needed (p. 650). Beyond that, graduate students are only discussed in their employee roles: for example, teaching assistants, graduate assistants, and resident assistants.

Because graduate and professional students are not addressed as a unique student population in most curricula, Gansemer-Topf et al. (2006) argue that more research is needed to understand graduate student development as a unique process. Even though existing adult development and student development theories can be useful in understanding graduate students, they note that it is important to assess students' individual development, since graduate students vary greatly in age and experience (Gansemer-Topf et al., 2006). Therefore, it is difficult for students (in higher education/student affairs programs) studying concepts and theories of holistic student development to effectively modify and apply these existing theories to graduate student development.

In reviewing some of the well-regarded student affairs/higher education programs in the country (e.g., Bowling Green University, Stanford, University of Maryland, College Park, UCLA), not one included a specific course on graduate or professional students as a student population. Even when programs talk about *all* students, they generally mean all *undergraduate* students. We argue that graduate students are unique and their needs are distinct from undergraduate students, because the educational experience is fundamentally different (see more in Chapter 3). Graduate and professional students are recruited into *programs* rather than institutions. Many graduate programs require that students work with a faculty advisor when they begin their program or certainly before they begin their own research. The focused, independent work required in graduate school differs from the broad survey approach of an undergraduate degree. This focus means that the educational experience is different too. Graduate students may be in competitive environments, seeking funding, publications, and other markers of success. These pressures may be exacerbated by higher levels of student debt. Graduate students comprise roughly 15% of enrollment in higher education, but hold nearly 40% of the student loan debt (Miller, 2020). Recent attention to graduate students' mental health (Di Pierro, 2017) illustrates the impact that this stress and isolation can have on graduate students. We argue that student affairs professionals should be trained to recognize these issues and provide services designed to support graduate student success. Based on this context, we believe the case for specialized curriculum focused on graduate student development is strong, and in 2019–2020, a group of AGAPSS practitioners made it a priority to begin to fill this void.

SO WHAT? DETAILS OF THE PILOT CURRICULUM PROJECT AND WHAT WAS LEARNED

As professionals working with graduate students, we are in a unique position to reflect on our own preparation for this work. We know that professionals can and should be better prepared, given that many come from academic disciplines outside of education. Likewise, AGAPSS exists to support professionals and to create greater awareness of the developmental needs of graduate students. As a consequence, practitioners and faculty need further training, professional support, and a common language with which to advocate for themselves and for their students at a campus-wide, regional, and national level. Thus far, no textbook on graduate and professional students exists. Recognizing the current gap in training and preparation, a group of AGAPSS practitioners, led by Dr. Katherine Hall-Hertel, had the idea to create *curriculum modules* that could be added as one-off sessions into preexisting higher education/student affairs graduate courses, offered as a full elective course, or used for on-the-job training. Volunteers identified topics based on their expertise and then created seven initial modules. The initial module topics included:

1. Graduate Student Mentoring vs. Advising
2. Graduate Student Career and Professional Skill Development
3. First-Generation Graduate Students in Traditional and Professional Schools
4. Graduate Communities and the Importance of Space
5. International Graduate Students in the United States
6. Graduate and Professional Student Funding
7. Mental Health and Wellness of Graduate Students

These modules included the module description, learning outcomes, lecture notes or activities, readings, discussion questions, and case studies. These were essentially created as *grab-and-go* class lectures/discussions that could be easily incorporated into a class. The plan was to pilot the modules, collect feedback from the faculty, and use that data to refine current modules and develop additional ones.

Once the initial seven modules were created, they were formatted into one document, and we solicited faculty who were teaching in higher education/student affairs graduate programs to participate in the pilot. We gained interest through faculty listservs and snowballing. Each faculty selected a module that would be relevant to one of their already-existing courses. The initial plan was to pilot the project in spring 2020 only, but due to COVID-19 complications, we extended the pilot to fall 2020 as well. Various modules were selected and implemented into nine classes in the pilot (five in spring 2020, and four in fall 2020). The modules were mostly implemented in master's programs, but one module was included in a doctoral class. Participating institutions were mostly located in the southeast U.S., but one pilot group was in the Pacific Northwest. These modules were implemented in classes across large research universities, regional comprehensive universities, and small private colleges. After implementing a module, faculty participants offered feedback through an online survey.

The faculty responses from the pilot were overwhelmingly positive. One faculty pilot participant said, "Thank you so much for creating these modules. This took a lot of work and will really be helpful for improving our grad programs. I enjoyed teaching and learning with my students!"

Faculty agreed with the identified gap in the existing curriculum, and that a repository for modules would not only be useful but something they would like to incorporate into their curriculum further:

> Overall, I think the repository would be great as graduate student services/ populations are much needed and we do not talk about it enough, in my opinion. Also, I think more students want to work in this type of area, and it's great to have the modules to help with this and help our students.
>
> (Faculty Pilot Participant)

Most of the faculty participants chose to implement their module into a capstone-like course, but they identified the strengths of these modules across the entire curriculum. As demonstrated in the quotes below, the strong aspects of the experience for many were identifying a gap and having the initial conversations that are often not included in the core curriculum:

> Our courses unpack the role of student affairs in higher education, and unfortunately we often forget to center graduate students in conversations about student affairs. My students were grateful for the opportunity to engage in a module solely dedicated to examining graduate student experiences and consider their needs in relation to student affairs work.
>
> (Faculty Pilot Participant)

> I believe that covering the information on graduate students was useful to my students. By the end of our session, they were asking really good questions about the topic and reconsidering assumptions.
>
> (Faculty Pilot Participant)

> Opening the students' eyes to this population as an entity of student affairs work was the highlight. Because they themselves are graduate (masters) students, they often do not think about the services/development/programming for this group.
>
> (Faculty Pilot Participant)

The faculty participants had some specific feedback for improving the current modules and moving forward with developing additional modules. These areas for improvement include streamlining the readings and activities, distinguishing content for masters vs. doctoral students, adding a few sections to the modules, and sharing ideas for additional module topics. The quotes below offer specific feedback on these items:

- Streamline readings and activities for each module so adoption is seamless:

  > There were a lot readings for one module, and our library did not have access to some of them. So, maybe divide the reading by most important/relevant and supplemental, and/or including links to the documents.
  >
  > (Faculty Pilot Participant)

  > Include a short description of each reading to help the instructor determine what would be most appropriate/beneficial to the students and to save faculty time from reading all of them ahead of time.
  >
  > (Faculty Pilot Participant)

  > Maybe create a one-page literature review, annotated bibliography, or fast facts that would be useful for each module.
  >
  > (Faculty Pilot Participant)

  > Include ideas for sample classes that each module may fit into (just to help faculty see the connection).
  >
  > (Faculty Pilot Participant)

  > The section called Class Discussion/Activity was not very clear. It could be better explained.
  >
  > (Faculty Pilot Participant)

- Specify tracks for masters vs. doctoral students:

  > Possible "tracks" for masters vs. doctoral. Or even the same module, but different discussion questions/case studies for a masters class vs doc class.
  >
  > (Faculty Pilot Participant)

  > Many of the readings/case study/activity were more relevant to faculty/practitioners working with doctoral students. My students (masters) had a hard time envisioning themselves working with doc students (as they themselves had not been there yet). More guided discussions/activities for masters vs doc classes might be a beneficial separation/addition.
  >
  > (Faculty Pilot Participant)

- Add sections around advocacy, action, and identity:

  > Maybe an advocacy piece should be built into all the modules.
  >
  > (Faculty Pilot Participant)

216

Refine the modules to include aspects of social class identity or anything on how social identity impacts graduate students.

(Faculty Pilot Participant)

- Ideas for additional modules:

I love all the modules already listed, but I do have a number of colleagues that work in professional schools or with specialized study like medical, dental, vet, and pharmacy. They have different needs across the spectrum from a student support lens. Maybe some more specialized modules covering students in those programs. Also, there is a lot of conversation about the dearth of jobs available for those grad students who want to work in/out of academics. I would love a module on what it means to work as faculty and what the options are to go alt-ac.

(Faculty Pilot Participant)

Integrating the modules into existing courses was difficult for some faculty due to time constraints and the global pandemic. A potential solution is to create a stand-alone course on serving graduate and professional students, even if it is offered as an elective course.

NOW WHAT? GOALS AND NEXT STEPS FOR THE FUTURE

The first and immediate next step in this project is to refine the current curriculum modules based on the feedback collected in the pilot. For this, we plan to update the author template to offer more clear parameters. Using the more detailed outline, we hope to identify more module topics and select qualified authors. We plan to do this by soliciting involvement from the contributors of this book, contacting the members of the AGAPSS Knowledge Community, and reaching out to other related groups, associations, and listservs for further contributions.

Next, we plan to build structural support for the content. This may be through a NASPA webpage, adding the content to ACPA's Faculty Resource Library, or creating our own stand-alone repository (similar to the syllabus clearinghouse). Additionally, we plan to promote the content for inclusion in existing curricula, which includes working directly with faculty networks in NASPA, ACPA, Council of Graduate Schools (CGS), and other related groups. Furthermore, as researchers and practitioners, we must continue to conduct research and disseminate findings, share successful strategies through publications and conference presentations, and commit to adding to this ongoing scholarly conversation.

In the future, longer-term action steps may include working with the Council for the Advancement of Standards in Higher Education (CAS, 2019) to potentially have a standard around graduate student knowledge and success added to the curriculum. Additionally, we want to make further and more direct connections to the ACPA/NASPA Professional Competencies for Student Affairs Professionals (ACPA & NASPA, 2015). Lastly, we may want to explore the creation of competencies specific for practitioners working with graduate and professional students, similar to how Campus Compact created specific competencies for Community Engagement Professionals (Dostilio, 2017).

> I think it would be useful to have a paragraph or two about why the module exists and how it can fit into the CAS standards for programs and/or the competencies.
>
> (Faculty Pilot Participant)

CONCLUSION

Through this chapter, we aimed to make a clear case that curriculum is needed and that the curriculum modules, in addition to this entire book, are useful tools. We have explained the context for the AGAPSS curriculum project, the details of the pilot, what was learned, and what we hope to achieve from here. The overall goal with the curriculum project was to take an initial step in filling an identified gap in training practitioners who work (or are hoping to work) with graduate and professional students. A secondary goal is to create awareness of graduate student affairs work as an intentional career path for practitioners. Although our work as graduate faculty, scholars, and practitioners continues, we believe the curriculum project is a significant contribution toward meeting these goals.

REFERENCES

ACPA College Student Educators International. (n.d.). *Syllabus clearinghouse.* Retrieved from https://www.myacpa.org/syllabus-clearinghouse-0

ACPA Commission for Professional Preparation and NASPA Faculty Council. (n.d.). *Faculty resource library.* Retrieved from https://www.livebinders.com/play/play?id=2193172

ACPA and NASPA. (2015). *Professional competency areas for student affairs practitioners.* College Student Educators International. Retrieved from https://www.naspa.org/images/uploads/main/ACPA_NASPA_Professional_Competencies_FINAL.pdf

Brown, R. (1972). *Student development in tomorrow's higher education: A return to the academy* (p. 16). American College Personnel and Guidance Association.

Council for the Advancement of Standards in Higher Education (CAS). (2019). *CAS professional standards for higher education* (10th ed.). Author.

Di Pierro, M. (2017). Mental health and the graduate student experience. *The Journal for Quality and Participation, 4*(1), 24–27 (Cincinnati: American Society for Quality).

Dostilio, L. D. (Ed.). (2017). *Community engagement professionals project: Establishing a preliminary competency model for second generation CEPs.* Campus Compact.

Gansemer-Topf, A. M., Ross, L. E., & Johnson, R. M. (2006). Graduate and professional student development and student affairs. *New Directions for Student Services, 2006*(115), 19–30.

Hevel, M. S. (2016). Toward a history of student affairs: A synthesis of research, 1996–2015. *Journal of College Student Development, 57*(7), 844–862. https://doi.org/10.1353/csd.2016.0082.

Long, D. (2012). The foundations of student affairs: A guide to the profession. In L. J. Hinchliffe & M. A. Wong (Eds.), Environments for student growth and development: Librarians and student affairs in collaboration (pp. 1–39). Association of College & Research Libraries.

Miller, B. (2020). Graduate school debt. *Center for American Progress.* Retrieved from https://www.americanprogress.org/issues/education-postsecondary/reports/2020/01/13/479220/graduate-school-debt/.

Schuh, J, Jones, S., & Torres, V. (2016). *Student services: A handbook for the profession* (6th ed.). Jossey-Bass.

Chapter 11

Conclusion
Toward Thriving

Valerie A. Shepard and April L. Perry

As a general introduction to student affairs practice for those who support graduate and professional students, we intend readers will use this book as a catalyst for further inquiry that will support their local practice. In this chapter, we discuss the framework we used to organize the book's structure to emphasize practical strategies for student affairs practice. Second, we reflect on several themes that emerged throughout the book: (1) considering a holistic approach to supporting graduate and professional student development; (2) assessment to understand and meet localized graduate and professional student needs; and (3) understanding how organizational structures of programs and schools either contribute to or hinder graduate and professional student success. Next, we discuss some limitations of *A Practitioner's Guide*. Finally, we expand on the guiding questions included in Chapter 1 as starting points for inquiry into existing programs and services for graduate and professional students, with a call to action for all those who support graduate and professional student thriving.

FRAMEWORK FOR *A PRACTITIONER'S GUIDE*

As discussed in Chapter 1, student affairs practitioners who primarily work with graduate and professional students have advocated for supporting the holistic needs of graduate students, albeit in an ad hoc manner. Chapter 1 gave context for why there is no agreed-upon common terminology that encompasses the large, incredibly diverse population that includes graduate and professional students. Over the past 20 years, especially since the Administrators in Graduate and Professional Student Services (AGAPSS) Knowledge Community has become more formalized, the need for additional training, professional development, and evidence-based theory and practice on which to base this work has become more and more clear. For example, the topic of the AGAPSS preconference session

DOI: 10.4324/9781003121671-14

at the National Association of Student Personnel Administrators (NASPA) annual meeting in 2018 was *Discrimination, not just an undergraduate issue: A special focus on discriminatory behavior experienced at the graduate and professional level.* The day-long preconference session focused on participants sharing critical information about how student affairs professionals' work to support graduate and professional students' holistic well-being was specifically connected to identifying "discrimination, bias and bullying that occurs in the following contexts: gender-based, sexual identity, race, ethnicity, nationality (including immigration status), disability, family status, and in the intersections among these contexts" (NASPA AGAPSS, 2018). The complexity of this topic was evident. Student affairs professionals who work with graduate and professional students need a clear understanding of how supporting graduate and professional student success is different than supporting undergraduate student success, and specific, actionable strategies to work in concert with all other stakeholders in the higher education community to create a learning environment that supports graduate and professional student thriving. The COVID-19 pandemic has only accelerated these trends; as the 2021 Council of Graduate Schools report on *Supporting graduate student mental health and well-being: Evidence-informed recommendations for the graduate community* has stated, the authors intend that the report will assist graduate deans to connect with partners who will "help [the reader] make a positive and lasting impact on the well-being of graduate students and on the health and inclusiveness of program environments" (p. 2).

What the Council of Graduate Schools report, publications such as the Council for the Advancement of Standards (CAS) *Standards for Graduate and Professional Student Programs and Services* (2019), and communities of practice such as AGAPSS all emphasize is the need for those who work to support graduate and professional student success to share information and work collaboratively to create an environment that supports graduate and professional student success. As editors of this book, we have modeled this collaborative structure, as we work in varied areas of the academy. Furthermore, every chapter is coauthored, and the centerpieces of Chapters 4–9 are the case studies which give practical strategies for working creatively across an artificial student affairs/academic affairs divide. Each of us from our unique perspectives have seen how working collaboratively can better inform training within student affairs higher education preparation programs as well as create knowledge and empower a community of student affairs practitioners and faculty who work to support graduate and professional student success.

We agree that, as Cassuto and Weisbuch have written, "the only option we rule out is inaction" (2021, p. 346), as they speak to an audience of program faculty, and suggest changes to graduate programs themselves to create a more student-centered learning environment. Felder and St. John (2014) presented research regarding inequality in graduate education, working "toward the goal of actualizing fairness and equal opportunity" (p. 244). In this book, we have presented concrete, evidence-based, theory-to-practice connections for those who work in student affairs roles to support these goals. In the following section, we reflect on themes that emerged throughout the book in these areas.

REFLECTION ON THEMES

One theme that emerged throughout this book is that, as the authors of Chapter 6 stated, "What is absent from the literature on strategies to support graduate students is a holistic and developmental approach that considers the student first, before the academic training" (p. 123). As members of AGAPSS were planning to write this book, faculty and practitioners who work in varied graduate and professional schools and across multiple functional areas stated that what would help them most in their day-to-day collaborations with faculty, administrators, and student affairs practitioners is a common understanding that graduate and professional students have needs that are different from and often more complex than those of undergraduate students. While Chapters 1 and 2 provide context for the state of the field, Chapter 3 provides a framework based in Maslow's hierarchy for this understanding, as the authors present how "post-baccalaureate student needs are diverse, complex, and interconnected" (p. 58).

The next step for serving those needs collaboratively is understanding them through careful inquiry. As the authors of Chapters 2 and 3 have illustrated, graduate and professional student populations are incredibly diverse. Collaborative assessment, addressed in detail in Chapter 9, is essential for understanding and meeting the needs of students in a local context. Chapter 4 demonstrates how onboarding students are an important part of engaging them and meeting their needs, and that reorientation can also be a critical component of this effort. While we also encourage readers to consult Tokuno (2008) for graduate orientation strategies, Chapter 4 connects graduate and professional student onboarding specifically to ongoing student engagement.

A related theme that emerged from Chapters 5–7 and reoccurred throughout the book is that holistic well-being and professional development for graduate and professional students are inextricably connected. Chapter 6 advocates for centering student voices as a practice for student engagement and for informing decision-making, and gives practical strategies for doing so from a student affairs lens. The authors also emphasize the importance of *nonclinical* forms of student engagement that support graduate and professional student thriving:

"This approach puts a focus on positive practices that reinforce self-care, allows for more peer connections outside the academic department, and provides a nonclinical setting for students to share their experiences across the university" (p. 126). Chapter 5 reiterates centering the student voice when discussing approaches to advising and mentoring, and the authors of Chapter 7 assert that "Central to the creation of each initiative has been the care and encouragement of the *whole* student: not just their academic success, but also their holistic development" (p. 151).

While centering student voices in decision-making is critical, an additional theme that all of the contributors addressed in different ways is that the organizational structures of programs and schools either contribute to or are barriers to graduate and professional student success. As the authors of Chapter 8 state:

> Getting through many of the pitfalls of graduate school is often not a function of students' skills but of the institutional environment, including culture, policies and procedures, and support systems that enable or hinder successful progress. Graduate schools can and must be important conduits that gather, organize, and sometimes help transform institutional resources into programs, services, and procedures that are accessible to and appropriate for graduate students – and do this in concert with graduate students organizing themselves.
>
> (pp. 167–168)

High-level champions, however, can create culture change that empower student voices and support a culture that encourages graduate and professional student thriving. The authors of Chapter 8 attribute their culture change in particular to "strong institutional commitment at the highest level, and a graduate dean who championed the cause and built the institutional structure to turn the concept of graduate community and graduate student services into functional reality" (p. 168). What does *functional reality* look like? That has been the goal of this book: distilling practical, actionable strategies to support student success. As the authors of Chapter 8 observe, their goals for building a community began from two principles:

- Provide centralized, or at least easy to find, assistance with academic, administrative, and life matters.
- Create a sense of belonging: a physical space as well as a conceptual place in which students can feel "at home," not alone with their issues and concerns, able to share their experiences, and receive direct and indirect support (p. 170).

Throughout this book, contributors highlight and discuss graduate and professional student sense of belonging in various ways—how it is different from undergraduate sense of belonging, how the institutional culture can contribute to it, how students' intersectional identities can impact their sense of belonging, and strategies for assessment to support graduate student community in ways that, as Chapter 7 illustrates, create an inclusive scaffolding system that supports student belonging and success.

DISCUSSION

As we reflect on these themes, we believe the contributors have made a case for having all stakeholders who support graduate and professional student success see graduate and professional students as students who have specific needs and complex intersectional identities. Our work is to create benchmarks for holistic well-being and outcomes, identify the promising practices that are available, make them relevant and inclusive, and develop partnerships where student affairs and academic affairs can overlap to support graduate and professional student success, in areas such as advising, mentoring, well-being, and career and professional development services. A critical starting point is understanding the unique needs of graduate and professional students in a local context, beginning with the time students transition into the university. It is not necessary to reinvent the wheel to do this; the CAS *Standards for Graduate and Professional Student Programs* (2019) and research available through entities such as those outlined in Chapters 2 and 9 can be the starting point for a stakeholder group in a local context. The groups need to include graduate students, student affairs professionals, and program faculty who can create benchmarks for student success and assess whether or not the campus culture facilitates graduate and professional student thriving. Working together and thinking creatively is crucial. For example, in Chapter 8, Case Study 2 discusses how Graduate Writing Center peer mentors, who could be thought of as academic support, also perform a critical student affairs role. Chapters 5–7 demonstrate how supporting student well-being and career and professional development overlap. All of the Case Studies provide examples of collaborative action to support the goal of meeting graduate and professional students' specific, diverse needs in a local context to support their success.

LIMITATIONS AND FUTURE DIRECTIONS

What was also clear to us as we were completing this book is the lack of research that is available, especially on historically marginalized student populations as well as on student development theory that applies specifically to graduate and professional students. Research on the structure of graduate and professional education and what works to support student success and what does not is also sparse. As we have seen, the recent Council of Graduate Schools report (2021) emphasized this lack of research as well. One limitation of our work here also pertains to graduate and professional student well-being. For example, while we discussed student well-being in a general way, we did not include specific discussions of substance use or eating disorders, both of which have been important topics of discussion in graduate and professional student affairs (Alger, 2019; Gardner, 2017). We also did not include extended discussions of how religious identity and student age impact graduate and professional student experience and sense of belonging. As a field, we can also continue to work to center and highlight graduate and professional student voices. Several contributors to this book were graduate students themselves at the time of writing. As Chapter 6 demonstrates, student affairs professionals should be mindful of balancing supporting students' advocacy efforts, professional development, and leadership development with making sure that the institutional structures are supporting them in their academic and professional pursuits. Further research is needed on promising practices to support these efforts from a student affairs lens. Chapter 3 refers to several articles written from the perspective of students; two further examples of books that include the perspectives of graduate and professional students are *The Chicana Motherwork Anthology* (Caballero et al., 2019) and *Graduate Education at Historically Black Colleges and Universities (HBCUs): A Student Perspective* (Palmer et al., 2016).

As we emerge from the COVID-19 pandemic, we see continued challenges and opportunities for collaboration, including increasingly working together across student affairs and academic affairs functional roles to support graduate student development and thriving, and building community in new, more accessible ways. The contributors to this volume have also highlighted some ways in which building community can happen in virtual spaces and outside of the university to support graduate student belonging. Student affairs professionals, however, need communities of practice themselves to support their work, as well as ongoing research on which they can base their practice to meet their students' localized needs.

CALL TO ACTION: TOWARD PROFESSIONALIZATION THAT SUPPORTS PROFESSIONALS AND GRADUATE AND PROFESSIONAL STUDENT THRIVING

Chapter 10 outlines the results of the pilot study of the Curriculum Project, an ongoing effort to create culture change within higher education preparation programs themselves and to see graduate and professional students as students. This effort is just the beginning, and we hope that additional research will be conducted to inform both curriculum and current student affairs practice. While Chapter 1 contains a set of guiding questions for inquiry, a starting point for a professional who is assessing the landscape of current programs offered at their institution, we present a call to action for culture change in a local context:

- Due to the complexity of graduate and professional student needs and intersectional identities, professional training in this specific area should be ongoing and required, if possible. NASPA AGAPSS is currently contributing to this effort through the Curriculum Project (see Chapter 10) and this book; there are also efforts and resources available through other communities of practice such as the Graduate Career Consortium. See the Appendix for an initial list.
  - A culture of evidence-based student affairs practice should be promoted at all levels.
  - All stakeholders should be familiar with relevant accrediting bodies as well as the CAS *Standards for Graduate and Professional Student Programs and Services* (2019).
- There should be a common understanding that the culture of the university supports graduate and professional student thriving, or creates barriers to it.
  - While there is not enough research available yet on intersectionality and graduate student development, what we do know is that graduate students have needs that can be met, especially if student affairs and academic affairs are working together.
  - All stakeholders should know the resources available and ensure the resources are tailored to students' unique needs.
  - Assessment is required to understand the local context. Consider well-being and career and professional development in tandem. Consider belonging. Center graduate and professional student voices in these efforts.
- There should be a coordinated effort to communicate to all stakeholders what is happening at relevant professional societies (i.e., research, benchmarking); get the information to the frontline professionals who can incorporate it into their programming, benchmarking, and practical strategies for student success and supporting graduate and professional student community.
- Professional community should be affirmed/supported for those in student affairs as a crucial stakeholder for graduate student success.
- We need further research on the history of, contexts of, and purposes for graduate and professional education—as well as research on graduate and professional student development—to understand contexts that contribute

to barriers to student success, to continue to work to remove those barriers, and to measure progress toward doing so.

We intend that this book, as a general introduction, promotes community building among all stakeholders in the higher education community who support graduate and professional student thriving. We hope that it catalyzes further research into this growing, crucial area of student affairs and promotes both graduate and professional student success as well as the well-being and professional development of all those who work to create a healthy learning environment for graduate and professional students.

REFERENCES

Alger, J. M. (2019). Graduate and professional students: Not done baking yet! Lessons learned from SUNY Downstate's graduate health professions students. *NASPA Knowledge Community Publication* [Annual Knowledge Community Conference Publication], 10–12. NASPA-Student Affairs Administrators in Higher Education. Retrieved from http://apps.naspa.org/files/2019-naspa-final.pdf

Caballero, C., Martínez-Vu, Y., Pérez-Torres, J., Téllez, M., & Vega, C. (Eds.) (2019). *The Chicana motherwork anthology.* University of Arizona Press.

Cassuto, L., & Weisbuch, R. (2021). *The New PhD: How to build a better graduate education.* Johns Hopkins University Press.

Council for the Advancement of Standards in Higher Education (CAS). (2019). Graduate and Professional Student Programs and Services. In *CAS professional standards for higher Education* (10th ed). Author.

Council of Graduate Schools. (2021). *Supporting graduate student mental health and well-being: Evidence-informed recommendations for the Graduate Community.* Executive summary. Retrieved from: https://cgsnet.org/graduate-student-mental-health-and-well-being-0

Felder, P. P., & St. John., E. P. (Eds.). (2014). *Supporting graduate students in the 21st century: Implications for policy and practice.* AMS Press.

Gardner, S. M. (2017). Inside the pressure cooker: Prescription drug abuse among graduate/professional students. *NASPA Knowledge Community Publication* [Annual Knowledge Community Conference Publication], 9–11. NASPA-Student Affairs Administrators in Higher Education. Retrieved from https://www.naspa.org/images/uploads/events/2017-naspa-final-updated.pdf

NASPA Administrators in Graduate and Professional Student Services (AGAPSS). (2018, January). *AGAPSS newsletter.* [membership newsletter]. Retrieved from https://conference2018.naspa.org/images/uploads/events/January_2018_Newsletter.pdf

Palmer, R. T., Walker, L. J., Goings, R. B., Troy, C., Gipson, C., & Commodore, F. (Eds.). (2016). *Graduate education at historically Black colleges and universities (HBCUs): A student perspective.* Routledge.

Tokuno, K. A. (Ed.). (2008). *Graduate students in transition: Assisting students through the first year.* National Resource Center for the First-Year Experience and Students in Transition.

Appendix

Selected Resources and Associations

Graduate Education and Graduate Student Affairs

By: Lisa C. O. Brandes, Yale University (retired)
lisaco.brandes@gmail.com (all reviews are my own)

BOOKS AND ARTICLES ON PURPOSE OF AND TRENDS IN GRADUATE EDUCATION

Listed in chronological order:

Smith, A. (1776). *An inquiry into the nature and causes of the wealth of nations.* W. Strahan and T. Cadell.

> *The laws of supply and demand, as they govern scholars and faculty: "That unprosperous race of men commonly called men of letters….have generally, therefore, been educated at the public expence, and their numbers are every-where so great as commonly to reduce the price of their labour to a very paultry recompence" (Book 1, Ch. X, Part II).*

Newman, J. H. (1852). *The idea of a university defined and illustrated.* https://www.newmanreader.org/works/idea/

> *Anglican, then Roman Catholic priest and theologian who argued for university learning for learning's sake, "knowledge its own end" rather than training for a profession, also discusses the role of Christian religion in higher education. Also separates the faculty member's skill of teaching vs. research, a dichotomy discussed and debated over the past two centuries.*

James, W. (1903, March). The PhD Octopus. *Harvard Monthly.* https://www.uky.edu/~eushe2/Pajares/octopus.html

> *The noted philosopher decries the increasing hold of "the PhD Octopus" on American academic life, overvaluing the "three magic letters" of PhD in making faculty appointments over any demonstration of teaching ability. Reasons cited are the relative youth and insecurity of graduate schools and the sham vanity marketing of a college's distinguished faculty.*

Strothmann, F. W. (1955). *The graduate school, today and tomorrow; reflections for the profession's consideration.* Committee of Fifteen. Retrieved from HathiTrust.

The committee emphasizes the division of research scholarship vs. teaching. Facing what they saw as a future undersupply of PhDs in all areas of society, this committee of 15 leading scholars suggested radically transforming the PhD to be no more than three years in residence and to form the scholar-teacher in the social sciences and humanities.

Ness, F. (Ed.). (1960). *A guide to graduate study: Programs leading to the Ph.D. degree* (2nd ed.). American Council of Education.

One of the earliest guides to graduate study and selecting PhD programs for prospective students. The publication of the guide in 1957 and a 2nd edition in 1960 was designed to encourage more students to apply to and attend graduate school. The 1960 Preface begins with the assertion of a shortage of PhDs: "The supply of college graduates who continue their formal academic preparation for careers in the learned professions is failing to meet the demands of industry, government, and higher education. Evidence of this fact is found on every hand … In the field of college teaching, even our most conservative statisticians are predicting shortages which, within a decade, may well attain critical proportions" (p. vii).

Berelson, B. (1960). *Graduate education in the United States.* McGraw-Hill.
Berelson, B. (1961, January). The criticisms of graduate education. *The Library Quarterly: Information, Community, Policy, 31,* 45–49.

This book and short article provide a comprehensive historical and systematic overview of U.S. graduate education, especially doctoral programs, with data, analyses, and recommendations. The author notes that longstanding criticisms of graduate education over the past 100 years are still relevant and discusses eight critical propositions. Despite such seemingly intractable issues, Berelson argues that US graduate schools hold "a critical position in the life of the mind of this country as the primary home of the American scholar," which has "brought American research and scholarship to a position of world leadership" (p. 58).

Caplow, T., & McGee, R. J. (1961). *The academic marketplace.* Routledge.

Sociological study of the academic labor market and conditions of hiring, employment, and promotions for faculty members. In the early 1960s faculty hiring boom times, the authors recommended moving from a personalized hiring model based on prestige and compatibility to a more open, regularized labor market valuing teaching ability and other skills.

Kerr, C. (1963). *The uses of the university.* Harvard University Press.

Former President of UC Berkeley; describes as "unfaculty" the graduate students, postdocs, researchers, and contingent faculty and staff who contribute to the research enterprise of full-time University faculty (pp. 65–67).

Katz, J., & Hartnett, R. T. (Eds.). (1976). *Scholars in the making: The development of graduate and professional students.* Ballinger.

Katz, J., & Hartnett, R. T. (1977, November-December). The education of graduate students. *The Journal of Higher Education*, *48*(6), 646–664. https://www.jstor.org/stable/1979010

Edited volume and article examine graduate education as a psychological, social, and emotional process; studies the graduate student and the interrelation of emotional and intellectual factors, with recommendations.

Smelser, N. J., & Content, R. (1980). *The changing academic market: General trends and a Berkeley case study.* University of California Press.

Labor market disequilibrium model of graduate education where, as in Caplow and McGee, prestige is valued more than demonstrated accomplishment. A look inside a Berkeley hiring committee as it tries to go beyond the still dominant informal word-of-mouth network to find more diverse candidates: "It is a striking instance of the 'cobweb effect,' in which the investment industry is always out of equilibrium with the industry it supplies" (p. 34); "By 1973, it was generally evident that the imbalances between supply and demand [for PhD academics] were extremely serious, and that, given long-term birth-rates and demographic trends, were likely to continue for several decades to come" (p. 36).

Bowen, W. G., & Sosa, J. A. (1989). *Prospects for faculty in the arts and sciences: A study of factors affecting demand and supply, 1987 to 2012.* Princeton University Press.

Predicted strong demand for future faculty in the 1990s and the 2000s, especially in the humanities. The widely cited study may have fostered increases in graduate school enrollments and rosy job expectations for PhDs. Their predictions did not foresee the future crises in academic labor markets, adjunctification, and state funding retrenchment.

Fiske, E. B. (1989, September 13). Shortages predicted in '90s in humanities. *The New York Times.*

Helped popularize the view that more PhDs would be needed for plentiful jobs in future, which turned out not to be true.

Atkinson, R. (1990, April 27). Supply and demand for scientists and engineers: A crisis in the making. *Science, 248*, 425–432. https://science.sciencemag.org/content/sci/248/4954/425.full.pdf

Similar to Bowen and Sosa, who are cited in the text, but focuses on STEM students, predicting a shortfall and calling for ramping up of production at all levels, especially PhD: "That shortfall could translate into an annual supply-demand gap of several thousand scientists and engineers at the Ph.D. level, with the shortage persisting well into the 21st century. Serious shortfalls are also projected for Ph.D.'s in the humanities and social sciences ... This projection suggests that the shortage of Ph.D.'s will become evident in about 6 years" (p. 429).

Boyer, E. (1990). *Scholarship reconsidered: Priorities of the professoriate.* Carnegie Foundation for the Advancement of Teaching. Jossey-Bass.

Landmark study arguing that the work of the professoriate has four distinct yet overlapping scholarly functions: the scholarship of discovery, the scholarship of integration, the scholarship of application, and the scholarship of teaching. Colleges and universities should value the "scholarship of teaching" as equal to traditional basic research, the scholarship of discovery. Chapter 6, "A New Generation of Scholars," discusses graduate education and graduate students, wherein Boyer strongly recommends specific pedagogical training for graduate teaching assistants (TAs). These arguments added to nascent U.S. TA training initiatives and Preparing Future Faculty (PFF) projects which followed, and later with faculty teaching initiatives and the growth of university teaching and learning centers.

Rosovsky, H. (1990). *The university: An owner's manual.* W. W. Norton and Co.

As a former Dean of the Faculty of Arts and Sciences at Harvard University, Rosovsky provides a general overview of university structure, function, and people for its "owners," namely faculty, administrators, students, funders, government agencies, general public, employers, and other stakeholders. Mentions graduate students and their concerns many times, including TA training, job prospects or lack thereof, professional training, differences from undergraduates, and diversity.

Pelikan, J. (1992). *The idea of the university: A reexamination.* Yale University Press.

The historian and former Yale Graduate School Dean enters the ongoing debate on the "crisis in higher education" with a contemporary reevaluation of Newman's (1852) views on the university, the supposed scholar vs. teacher divide, and prospects for reform on varied topics like social responsibility and lifelong learning.

Bowen, W. G., & Rudenstine, N. L. (1992). *In pursuit of the Ph.D.* Princeton University Press.

Research study using data from 1962 to 1986 sampled from ten elite universities, describing completion rates, time to degree (TTD), program scale, and career outcomes across six PhD disciplines; investigated funding sources, including teaching assistantships and fellowships as they relate to completion. Finds lengthy TTD of 13.4 years for English, History, and Political Science PhDs and 8.4 years for Math and Physics. Offers structural and administrative recommendations for improving overall organization, accountability, and functioning in graduate education at the department and school level.

McCloskey, D. N. (1993). In pursuit of the PhD: A review essay. *Economics of Education Review, 12*(4), 359–365. https://www.sciencedirect.com/science/article/pii/027277579390069S

Highly critical review of Bowen and Rudenstine, faulting them for sampling only a few elite institutions and for poor economic analyses of opportunity costs for graduate students. Disagrees with their recommendations for bureaucratic reorganization favoring elite institutions and certain fields, instead argues for wholesale overhaul of graduate education at all levels, programs, and institutions.

Graham, H. D., & Diamond, N. (1997). *The rise of American research universities: Elites and challengers in the postwar era.* Johns Hopkins University Press.

Extensive history of research universities as measured by faculty research productivity instead of reputation. While graduate students and graduate education are central to research production, this lengthy history spends only 4–5 pages on grad students, mainly noting oversupply of PhDs and program overexpansion at less elite levels.

Anderson, M. S. (1998). The experience of being in graduate school: An exploration. *New Directions for Higher Education, 101.* Jossey-Bass.

One of the earliest New Directions for Higher Education volumes on graduate education, from the student's perspective rather than school or national viewpoint; contrasts graduate student issues against well-studied undergraduate higher education landscape.

Lovitts, B. E., & Nelson, C. (2000, November-December). The hidden crisis in graduate education: Attrition from Ph.D. programs. *Academe, 86*(6), 44–50. https://eric.ed.gov/?id=EJ618323
Lovitts, B. E. (2001). *Leaving the ivory tower: The causes and consequences of departure from doctoral study.* Rowman & Littlefield.

Article and book on comparative cross-institutional research on attrition and persistence in U.S. doctoral study which is as high as 50% in some programs; notes fundamental attribution error or correspondence bias in reasons why grad students are said to leave: faculty and graduate programs attribute attrition or non-completion to the student, especially weak academic work; students, however, identify a host of factors impeding their completion, including poor mentoring, financial and familial stress, and lack of social connections, which can be ameliorated through program change and student support.

Weidman, J. C., Twale, D. J., & Stein, E. L. (2001). Socialization of graduate and professional students in higher education: A perilous passage? *ASHE-ERIC Higher Education Report, 28*(3). https://doi.org/10.1002/1536-0709(2001)28:3<1::AID-AEHE2803>3.0.CO;2-M

Drawing on adult socialization, role acquisition, and career development theories, focuses on the socialization process for the discipline and faculty profession as necessary to success as graduate students and later as researchers; affirms the importance of social connections among students and faculty in an academic department or discipline. The narrow disciplinary socialization focus may limit students with multiple roles and identities and privileges the faculty research profession as the main career goal.

Nettles, M. T., & Millett, C. M. (2006). *Three magic letters: Getting to PhD.* Johns Hopkins University Press.

Data analysis of survey of over 9,000 graduate students from top 21 PhD-granting institutions; found factors like adequate institutional funding and engaged and accessible faculty mentors were critical to student degree progress, with significant variations by demographic groups.

Maki, P. L., & Borkowski, N. A. (Eds.) (2006). *The assessment of doctoral education: Emerging criteria and new models for improving outcomes.* Stylus.

Advances and outlines new methods for assessing the effectiveness and success of doctoral programs; includes chapter by C. M. Golde, L. Jones, A. Conklin Bueschel, and G. E. Walker on the Carnegie Initiative on the Doctorate (see this appendix, p. 241).

Hyun, J. K., Quinn, B. C., Madon, T., & Lustig, S. (2006, May-June). Graduate student mental health: Needs assessment and utilization of counseling services (EJ743920). *Journal of College Student Development, 47*(3) 247–266. ERIC. https://eric.ed.gov/?id=EJ743920

One of the earliest surveys and data analyses of graduate student mental health, finding that over half of respondents reported having an emotional or stress-related problem in the past year. Recommendations include prioritizing mental health awareness and education, rethinking the pedagogy of grad education by emphasizing mentoring, and building linkages for grad student social and administrative support to fight isolation. Part of the widely cited UC system student mental health studies and reports which resulted in new services.

International Journal of Doctoral Studies (IJDS). (2006-). https://www.informingscience.org/Journals/IJDS/Overview

Annual edited volume beginning in 2006 with diverse and international authors and subjects: "The International Journal of Doctoral Studies (IJDS) is an international journal that publishes scholarly articles on issues in doctoral studies using the Informing Science framework. The journal publishes conceptual, theoretical and empirical papers." (https://www.informingscience.org/Journals/IJDS/Overview)

Benton, T. H. (2009, January 30). Graduate school in the humanities: Just don't go. *The Chronicle of Higher Education.* http://www.chronicle.com/article/Graduate-School-in-the/44846

Post-2008 financial crisis piece on ongoing humanities crises in availability of jobs in academia: "The reality is that less than half of all doctorate holders—after nearly a decade of preparation, on average—will ever find tenure-track positions."

Deresiewicz, W. (2011, May 23). Faulty towers: The crisis in higher education. *The Nation.* https://www.thenation.com/article/faulty-towers-crisis-higher-education/

Focus on collapsing academic job market in relation to larger U.S. economy: "The exploitation of contingent labor, a shrinking middle class, administrative elephantiasis: the turmoil in academia is a microcosm of American society as a whole."

Palmer, R. T., Hilton, A. A., & Fountaine, T. P. (Eds.) (2012). *Black graduate education at Historically Black Colleges and Universities: Trends, experiences, and outcomes.* Information Age Publishing.

Examines "the historical nature of graduate education at HBCUs and the programs' impact on society" (p. 3). Addresses student experience, engagement, socialization, outcomes, persistence, and alumni giving.

Bérubé, M. (2013). *2013 Presidential address* [address delivered at the 2013 Modern Language Association annual convention in Boston]. https://www.mla.org/Convention/Convention-History/MLA-Presidential-Addresses/2011-15-Presidential-Addresses/2013-Presidential-Address

As the president of the Modern Language Association, Bérubé declared there was a crisis in the humanities, especially in graduate programs, with attrition, long time to degree, poor faculty job prospects for graduates, the majority of faculty positions now being nontenure track, and the rise of alt-ac jobs.

Cassuto, L. (2013, July 1). Ph.D. attrition: How much is too much? *The Chronicle of Higher Education.* http://www.chronicle.com/article/PhD-Attrition-How-Much-Is/140045/

Discusses the issue of 50% or more doctoral attrition or non-completion citing Lovitts (2001); argues that faculty and PhD programs need to review the varied reasons for attrition and try to limit later-year attrition, especially in humanities: "Not all graduate students will stay the doctoral course, but more of them should—and when half do not, it's our fault."

Turley, N. (2013, October 7). Mental health issues among graduate students. Gradhacker [blog], *Inside Higher Education.* https://www.insidehighered.com/blogs/gradhacker/mental-health-issues-among-graduate-students

Notes high levels of anxiety, stress, and mental health issues among grad students; argues that graduate departments need to openly acknowledge the issues, provide training on mental health issues to academic advisors, and offer mindfulness and yoga practice to students.

Weissman, J. (2014, March 26). Loan-ageddon!: Graduate students are the new face of student debt. But is it a crisis? *Slate.* http://www.slate.com/articles/business/moneybox/2014/03/graduate_school_debt_is_it_a_crisis.html

Describes recent student loan and debt crisis as mainly driven by huge increases in debt among G&Ps, who make up 15% of students but now take out one-third of all debt. Argues that grad students with future high incomes or in income-based repayment programs may be less likely to default, and that federal policy fuels G&P debt growth.

Mason, M. A., Wolfinger, N. H., & Goulden, M. (2013). *Do babies matter? Gender and family in the ivory tower.* Rutgers University Press.
Mason, M. A. (2013, August 5). The baby penalty. *The Chronicle of Higher Education.* https://www.chronicle.com/article/the-baby-penalty/

Mason, while Dean of Graduate Education at UC Berkeley, led the first major study of U.S. academic life and family formation, for men and women, with data from graduate school through retirement; demonstrates that academic progress and parenthood are interrelated, with family formation negatively impacting women scholars, but not men in the U.S., limiting women's ability to pursue academic and research careers and creating a leaky pipeline. Mason regularly advocated for major academic and social policy changes to enhance gender equality, reduce discrimination, and enable parenting in universities and research settings. Many U.S. doctoral institutions, the NSF, and the NIH began programs for improved PhD student parental support, paid time off, and family funding, most likely as a result of Mason's research and advocacy.

American Bar Association Task Force on the Future of Legal Education (2014, January). *Report and recommendations: American Bar Association task force on the future of legal education.* https://www.americanbar.org/content/dam/aba/administrative/professional_responsibility/report_and_recommendations_of_aba_task_force.authcheckdam.pdf

After major law school disruptions with graduates' dismal legal job placements and plummeting admissions, the Task Force made recommendations to improve law schools and especially student services: "The Task Force concludes that the accreditation system would better serve the public interest by enabling more heterogeneity in law schools and by encouraging more attention to services, outcomes, and value delivered to law students" (p. 2).

Cassuto, L. (2015). *The graduate school mess: What caused it and how we can fix it.* Harvard University Press.

Addressed to faculty and administrators of doctoral programs; focus on limited preparation for certain faculty jobs now in short supply. Calls for changes, including prioritizing career diversity and putting student needs first: "The question shouldn't be how many Ph.Ds. we produce but whether they're happy or unhappy. When we teach Ph.Ds. to be satisfied only with professors' jobs, we are, quite simply, teaching them to be unhappy" (p. 237).

Bureau of Labor Statistics. (2015, May). STEM crisis or STEM surplus? Yes and yes. *Monthly Labor Review.* https://www.bls.gov/opub/mlr/2015/article/stem-crisis-or-stem-surplus-yes-and-yes.htm

States that "The academic sector is generally oversupplied, while the government sector and private industry have shortages in specific areas."

Horn, M. (2016, March 17). Disruption looms for law schools. *Forbes.* https://www.forbes.com/sites/michaelhorn/2016/03/17/disruption-looms-for-law-schools/#4d535e1f3a3c

Describes 15-year low in law school enrollments, with jobs crisis for graduates and large and growing debt burdens, $140,000 on average: "Law schools represent the canary in the coal mine for the rest of higher education, as they face perhaps the clearest and most imminent threat."

McKenna, L. (2016, April 21). The ever-tightening job market for Ph.Ds. Why do so many people continue to pursue doctorates? *The Atlantic*. https://www.theatlantic.com/education/archive/2016/04/bad-job-market-phds/479205/

Reviews well-known data from NSF on lengthy time to degree, poor academic job markets, and rising student debt, then wonders why it hasn't hindered recent growth in graduate admissions, noting law school admissions plummeted when legal job markets tanked earlier in the decade: "Is it because academia is a cult that makes otherwise sane people believe that there is no life outside of the university? Are graduate programs failing to inform their students about the realities of the job market? There are no answers to those questions in the charts and graphs from the NSF."

Patterson, T. (2016, July). Why do so many graduate students quit? Universities themselves may be contributing to burnout. *The Atlantic*. https://www.theatlantic.com/education/archive/2016/07/why-do-so-many-graduate-students-quit/490094/

Individual examples from students and faculty to discuss how institutions themselves may be causing attrition. Broad overview of issues includes mental health, poor mentoring, isolation, academic politics, and lack of firm career options. Provides some suggestions like multiple mentoring models.

Posselt, J. R. (2016). *Inside graduate admissions: Merit, diversity, and faculty gatekeeping*. Harvard University Press.

Study of doctoral admissions committees that recommends holistic review in graduate admissions to challenge implicit biases, increase transparency, and lead to more equitable outcomes.

Bartram, E. (2018). *The sublimated grief of the left behind*. [Essay]. Retrieved from http://erinbartram.com/uncategorized/the-sublimated-grief-of-the-left-behind/

A visiting assistant professor's widely read and discussed quit lit essay on finally giving up on an academic career; blames a broken system, asks not to see those "left behind" as failures, and not for pity but collective grieving: "I just wonder what would happen if we, as a community, stopped saying 'he's gone to a better place,' bringing a casserole, and moving on. What would happen if we acknowledged the losses our discipline suffers every year? What would happen if we actually grieved for those losses?"

Shreve, G. (2018, April 4.) Quit lit then and now. *Inside Higher Education*. Retrieved from https://www.insidehighered.com/views/2018/04/04/comparison-quit-lit-1970s-and-today-opinion

Overview of academic quit lit of the 1970s and 2010s, where PhD share their stories of leaving academia; Shreve finds more recent essays focus on expressions of feeling and emotion and more collective grief; while valuable, author wonders if shared grief is enough to create the change needed to fix the problem.

Cassuto, L., & Weisbuch, R. (2021). *The new PhD: How to build a better graduate education.* Johns Hopkins University Press.

> *Describes failed prior reforms in graduate education; argues that PhD programs need to prepare graduates for a wide range of careers, especially those outside the university; looks at the growth of more student-centered, career diverse graduate education practices for "a more humane and socially dynamic PhD experience" (inside cover, front matter). Chapter 1 includes a chronological list of graduate education reform efforts.*

LITERATURE ON GRADUATE AND PROFESSIONAL STUDENT AFFAIRS AND STUDENT SERVICES

Listed in chronological order:

Barr, M. J., & Others (Eds.). (1993). *The handbook of student affairs administration.* Jossey-Bass.

> *Comprehensive edited handbooks survey the field with chapters on operational and managerial issues for many functional student affairs areas; used as a textbook in higher education graduate preparation program courses. This 1993 edition, the first edition, focuses implicitly on undergraduates as students. This handbook does not explicitly mention G&P students or services, and only discusses doctoral study in student affairs in the chapter on "Advancing professionally through graduate education." Later editions of the handbook, like McClellan and Stringer (2016), the 4th edition, reflect a growing awareness within NASPA and among practitioners of a diverse range of students, their identities, and their issues, including G&P students.*

Pruitt-Logan, A. S., & Isaac, P. D. (Eds.) (1995, Winter). Student services for the changing graduate student population. *New Directions for Student Services, 42.* Jossey-Bass.

> *First major monograph to describe basic G&P student services: advising, counseling, housing, career needs; opening chapter describes the daily life of a graduate student for those unfamiliar with its challenges; for administrators and faculty and some practitioners, with chapter authors mainly from faculty and the Council of Graduate Schools.*

American College Personnel Association (ACPA), & National Association of Student Personnel Administrators (NASPA). (2004). *Learning reconsidered: A campus-wide focus on the student experience.* NASPA/ACPA. https://www.naspa.org/book/learning-reconsidered-a-campus-wide-focus-on-the-student-experience

> *Joint monograph on student learning lists G&P students as a group needing special attention and services, perhaps for the first time in a national student affairs association publication.*

Guentzel, M. J., & Nesheim, B. E. (Eds.) (2006, Fall). Supporting graduate & professional students: The role of student affairs. *New Directions in Student Services.* Jossey-Bass.

The second New Directions in Student Services G&P volume with chapters on general services, balance, student development, professional programs, career services, and graduate student centers, for practitioners and SA divisions.

Tokuno, K. A. (Ed). (2008). *Graduate students in transition: Assisting students through the first year.* National Resource Center for the First-Year Experience and Students in Transition. University of South Carolina.

First and only multi-chapter guide to graduate student orientation and transitions.

Brandes, L., & O'Dair, K. (2009, Spring). Broadening the reach of student affairs: Graduate and professional student services. *Leadership Exchange.* National Association of Student Personnel Administrators (NASPA). 24–27.

Article calls leaders' attention to the G&P experience, issues of building community, hot topics, and sample programs for student affairs; for SSAOs/VPSA, student affairs divisions, and grad school deans.

Mastroieni, A. (2014). Fundraising from doctoral alumni: Going beyond the bachelor's. In N. Drezner (Ed.), *Expanding the donor base in higher education: Engaging non-traditional donors* (pp. 87–101). Routledge.

Based on her doctoral research, Mastroieni's chapter is one of the few examinations of graduate student alumni as potential donors, countering the widespread belief that alumni will only donate to their undergraduate alma mater. Argues for targeted fundraising approach for doctoral alumni with specific appeals, training for fundraisers, improved communications and activities, and expectations of alumni engagement and stewardship.

Felder, P. P., & St. John, E. P. (Eds.) (2014). *Supporting graduate students in the 21st century: Implications for policy and practice.* AMS press.

Edited volume on diversity, equity, and inclusion using critical race theory and related lenses; chapter topics include funding, supporting African American, Latinx, and LGBTQ students, graduate student centers, mentorship, and socialization.

Jones, S. R., & Lightsey, P. (Eds.). (2021). *Transforming service: Reflections of student services personnel in theological education.* Association of Theological Schools (ATS).

A handbook for new and seasoned student services personnel in theological schools.

SELECTED REPORTS, PROJECTS, AND CONFERENCE PROCEEDINGS ON GRADUATE EDUCATION

Listed in chronological order:

National Science Foundation. (NSF). (1957-present). *Survey of Earned Doctorates.* https://www.nsf.gov/statistics/srvydoctorates/

Annual report and analysis of doctoral degree recipient trends, including demographics and diversity, career plans, numbers of degrees, analyses, and more.

Preparing Future Faculty (PFF) Program. (1993-present). https://preparing-faculty.org/

An initial partnership between the Council of Graduate Schools and the American Association of Colleges and Universities to prepare PhDs for varied kinds of existing faculty jobs, not only for jobs at research universities. Initial programs from 1993 to 2003 had grant funding; now PFF is a model with no funding.

Institute of Medicine, National Academy of Sciences, and National Academy of Engineering. (1995). *Reshaping the graduate education of scientists and engineers.* The National Academies Press. https://doi.org/10.17226/4935.

One of the first U.S. National reports on the STEM graduate education system and on students themselves: "Recommendations are aimed at creating a new PhD that would retain the existing strengths of the current system while substantially increasing the information available, the potential versatility of students, and the career options afforded to them by their PhD education" (front matter).

Millar, T. S., Mason, S. A., Gunter, R. L., & Millar, S. B. (1998, June 29–30). *Synthesis of the Science, Mathematics, Engineering, and Technology Graduate Education Forum* (ED472039). [Workshop Report]. National Institute for Science Education, University of Madison, Wisconsin Graduate School, National Science Foundation. ERIC. http://files.eric.ed.gov/fulltext/ED472039.pdf

C. Golde organized the two-day workshop; L. Brandes and many others presented innovations in teacher training, career services, diversity, and graduate student life.

Nyquist, J., & Others. (1999–2000). *Re-envisioning the PhD Project* [Conference and Promising Practices Report]. University of Washington. https://depts.washington.edu/envision/about/project_background.html

A $515,000 project funded by The Pew Charitable Trusts posed the challenging question: "How can we re-envision the Ph.D. to meet the needs of the society of the 21st Century?"

Report showcases a range of services and initiatives, including Teaching Assistant training, graduate career services, and graduate student life.

Woodrow Wilson National Fellowship Foundation [Renamed Institute for Citizens & Scholars, 2020]. (2005, September 1). *The responsive Ph.D.: Innovations in U.S. doctoral education.* https://woodrow.org/news/publications/responsive-phd/

Report on a five-year project working with 20 major U.S. public and private research universities; findings and recommendations for improvements in the PhD, emphasizing interdisciplinarity, preparation for a range of careers, enhanced recruitment/retention of doctoral students of color, and connections to societal goals. Innovations Report offers a wide range of promising practices and innovations from 20 participating schools.

Golde, C., & Dore, T. M. (2001, January). *At cross purposes: What the experiences of today's doctoral students reveal about doctoral education.* [Report.] The Pew Charitable Trusts. http://www.phd-survey.org

The survey and report show that what PhD students say they want during their graduate education and as career outcomes are at cross-purposes with the faculty expectations for student careers; argues for more student-centered and career-diverse models in graduate education, emphasizing the radical student centeredness of the 1995 COSEPUP and the 1998 NSF Workshop, which Golde organized.

Walker, G., Golde, C., Jones, L., & Conklin Bueschel, A. (Senior Staff). Carnegie Initiative on the Doctorate (CID). (2003–2008). http://archive.carnegiefoundation.org/professional_graduate_education/cid.html

This project examined PhDs as stewards of their academic disciplines; two publications resulted (2006, 2008, see below): "The Carnegie Initiative on the Doctorate (CID) was a five year action and research project that worked with doctoral-granting departments committed to restructuring their programs to better prepare graduates. Six disciplines were included: chemistry, education, English, history, mathematics and neuroscience."

Golde, C. M., & Walker, G. E. (2006). *Envisioning the future of doctoral education: Preparing stewards of the discipline—Carnegie essays on the doctorate.* Jossey-Bass.

Dimsdale, J., & Young, M., Co-Chairs, and University of California Student Mental Health Committee. (2006, September). [Final report]. *Report of the University of California student mental health committee.* University of California Office of the President. https://www.ucop.edu/student-mental-health-resources/about/smh-rpt---fullrpt-only.pdf.

University of California (UC) system-wide report noted high levels of student stress, depression and suicide ideation; resulted in fee and spending increases for new programs targeted at mental health and wellness; in particular, found that for graduate students, "43–45% reported mental/stress problems or needing help, but only 25–31% sought mental health services."

Walker, G. E., Golde, C. M., Jones, L., Conklin Bueschel, A., & Hutchings, P. (2008). *The formation of scholars: Rethinking doctoral education for the twenty-first century.* Jossey-Bass.

Delisle, J. (2014, March). *The graduate student debt review: The state of graduate student borrowing.* [Policy Brief: New America Education Policy Program.] New America. https://static.newamerica.org/attachments/750-the-graduate-student-debt-review/GradStudentDebtReview-Delisle-Final.pdf

Shows growth of debt across various master's and professional degrees and suggests that federal policy and institutional actions made degrees more expensive over the past decade: "…debt for graduate students in a range of master's and professional degree programs accounts for some of the most dramatic increases in student borrowing between 2004 and

2012. Moreover, this trend is not limited to what many already know are high-cost credentials, like those in medicine and law" (p. 1).

Hoo, K. A., & Windchief, S. (Eds.) (2019, Fall). Indigenous communities and
access to graduate degrees in STEM. *New Directions for Higher Education, 2019*
(187). https://doi.org/10.1002/he.20331

*Details the activities of the Pacific Northwest Circle of Success: Mentoring Opportunities
in STEM (PNW-COSMOS) Alliance: "Although this volume focuses on AI/AN graduate
students in STEM fields, it is meant to provide critical context that may be applied to other
minority students in similar or different institutional settings," emphasizing applicability
for faculty and administrators "who are interested in not only diversifying their student
bodies but also in students' persistence to degree completion success" (p. 5).*

SELECTED DISCIPLINARY ASSOCIATIONS AND GROUPS

Listed in alphabetical order:

Associations for many academic fields and types of G&P schools. All groups generally offer national and/or regional conferences or meetings, websites, news,
publications, and webinars. Many general associations have formal or informal
networking groups to encourage sharing among practitioners who serve G&P
students; if not, new G&P networks might be created by interested practitioners.

American Association of Colleges of Nursing (AACN) https://www.aacnnurs
ing.org/

*No specific AACN student affairs network; Organizational Leadership Network (OLN)
for associate & assistant deans may be relevant.*

American Association of Colleges of Pharmacy (AACP), Student Services SIG
https://www.aacp.org/ *Student services personnel SIG and resources for admissions and student affairs staff online*: https://www.aacp.org/resource/student-affairs-personnel

American Dental Education Association (ADEA), Section for Student Affairs
and Financial Aid https://www.adea.org/about_adea/SectionsSIGs/ADEA_
Sections.aspx

Association of American Medical Colleges (AAMC) https://www.aamc.org/

- AAMC Group on Student Affairs (GSA) https://www.aamc.org/-
  professional-development/affinity-groups/gsa *for admissions, student affairs,
  diversity, financial assistance, and records*
- AAMC GREAT Group (Group on Research, Education and Training)
  https://www.aamc.org/professional-development/affinity-groups/great *for
  faculty and administrators of biomedical PhD, MD-PhD, and postdoctoral programs.*

Association of Professional Schools of International Affairs (APSIA) https://apsia.org/

Association of Schools and Programs of Public Health (ASPPH) https://www.aspph.org/

Association of Theological Schools (ATS) of the United States and Canada http://ats.org
  Student Personnel Administrators Network (SPAN), *published first ever handbook*, Transforming Service: Reflections of Student Services Personnel in Theological Education, *March 2021.* https://www.ats.edu/resources/administrators/student-personnel-administrators

Business Schools:

- Association to Advance Collegiate Schools of Business (AACSB) https://www.aacsb.edu/—*global network of business schools; focused mainly on deans and accreditation.*
- Graduate Management Admissions Council (GMAC) https://www.gmac.com/professional-development-and-careers/pd-opportunities—*business school group with events and networking for professionals to discuss and share student affairs issues.*
- Graduate Business Student Services Association (GBSSA) http://gbssa.org

Canadian Association for Graduate Studies (CAGS)/Association Canadienne pour les études supérieures (ACES) https://cags.ca/ *Canadian Graduate School Association.*

Council of Graduate Schools (CGS-US) www.cgsnet.org
  Association for Master's and Ph.D.-granting Deans and programs in the U.S., with national and regional meetings, initiatives; focuses on academic affairs, admissions, and some professional development issues; Projects, Practices, Reports, and some grants. Examples: Investigating Challenges to Matriculation and Completion for Underrepresented STEM Graduate Students during the COVID-19 pandemic (in progress, partnership with Council for Opportunity in Education (COE) and the Council of Historically Black Graduate Schools (CHBGS), funded by the National Science Foundation's Rapid Response Research (RAPID) program: https://cgsnet.org/investigating-challenges-matriculation-and-completion-underrepresented-stem-graduate-students-during). The CGS' PhD Completion Project provided seed funds for programs like mentoring, dissertation workshops, and support groups, http://www.phdcompletion.org/; 2020–2021 project with JED foundation on Graduate Student Mental Health and Well-Being (report 2021), https://cgsnet.org/graduate-student-mental-health-and-well-being-0

Council of Historically Black Graduate Schools (CHBGS) http://www.chbgs.org

From their website: "assists member organizations in increasing enrollment, retention, and graduation of African-American students in graduate programs and to prepare them to become future faculty and leaders" (http://www.chbgs.org).

Law Schools:

- American Association of Law Schools (AALS), Section on Student Services, https://www.aals.org/sections/list/student-services/
- National Association of Law Student Affairs Professionals (NALSAP), https://www.nalsap.org

National Associations of Schools of Art and Design (NASAD) https://nasad.arts-accredit.org/

Mainly concerned with accreditation, admissions, and standards; no formal SA network apparent, but informal networks may exist.

National Associations of Schools of Music (NASM) https://nasm.arts-accredit.org/

Mainly concerned with accreditation and standards; no SA network apparent.

National Association of Schools of Theater (NAST) https://nast.arts-accredit.org/

Mainly concerned with accreditation and standards; no SA network apparent.

National Institutes of Health https://www.training.nih.gov/programs

Training grants, funding, policies, and programs for post-baccalaureate, doctoral, and postdoctoral trainees and program administrators. See also Enhancing the Diversity of the NIH-Funded Workforce, also known as the Diversity Program Consortium: https://www.nigms.nih.gov/training/dpc

National Science Foundation, Division of Graduate Education (DGE) https://www.nsf.gov/div/index.jsp?div=DGE

Fellowships and funding, policies, diversity, and initiatives for graduate students and programs and for faculty and administrators.

G&P FUNCTIONAL GROUPS & CONFERENCES

Listed in alphabetical order:

Administrators in Graduate & Professional Student Services (AGAPSS), a Knowledge Community (KC) of NASPA: Student Affairs Administrators in Higher Education. https://www.naspa.org/constituent-groups/kcs/administrators-in-graduate-and-professional-student-services

Network for graduate and professional school administrators and student affairs professionals serving graduate students; meetings, conferences, webinars, website, networking,

newsletters, and sharing of promising practices for graduate student services and support. You can elect to join this KC within your NASPA member profile.

Commission for Graduate and Professional School Affairs of American College Personnel Association (ACPA), a Student Affairs professional association. http://www.myacpa.org/comm/graduate/

Like AGAPSS in NASPA, an ACPA network for graduate and professional school administrators and student affairs professionals serving graduate students; meetings, conferences, web information, networking, and sharing of promising practices for grad student services and support. Occasionally collaborates with AGAPSS on projects. Some G&P professionals are active in both AGAPSS and CGPSA.

Consortium on Graduate Communication https://www.gradconsortium.org/

From their website: "An international association whose members provide professional development in written, oral, and multimodal communication to students before and during their (post-)graduate academic and professional programs."

Graduate Career Consortium (GCC) https://gradcareerconsortium.org/

An international voice for graduate-level career and professional development leaders; multiple resources, committees, tools, and ongoing projects, including GCC member institutions' graduate career outcomes database (https://doi.org/10.17605/OSF.IO/28DN6); Carpe Careers (https://www.insidehighered.com/career-advice/carpe-careers), a member-generated weekly career advice column in Inside Higher Education; *and* ImaginePhD *(https://www.imaginephd. com), a career exploration and planning tool for graduate students and postdoctoral scholars studying humanities and social sciences fields, which was developed and launched by GCC members.*

Graduate Student Success and Wellness Conference (2018-present).

Conference organized by Virginia Tech with UNC Charlotte and Appalachian State annually in May/June.

https://graduateschool.vt.edu/calendar-and-events/conferences.html

https://graduateschool.uncc.edu/news/success-and-wellness-conference-set-may-6-7

NAGAP, The Association for Graduate Enrollment Management https://nagap.org/

Organization for graduate enrollment management professionals, research reports, and some grants.

PROFESSIONAL ASSOCIATIONS WITH G&P SECTIONS

Listed in alphabetical order:

ACUHO-I, The Association of College and University Housing Officers. https://www.acuho-i.org/

Has online communities for members; may be a family or grad-prof housing group.

ACUI, Advancing Campus Community https://www.acui.org/

Representing campus centers or student union facilities and related student activities programs; 22 Communities, none currently focused on graduate student centers or grad life programming.

International Writing Center Association (IWCA) https://writingcenters.org/

Includes members who direct Graduate Writing Centers/Labs and who hire and train Graduate Writing Tutors. Also publishes the Writing Center Journal https://writingcenters. org/writing-center-journal/

NACADA: The Global Community for Academic Advising https://nacada.ksu. edu/

For academic advisors, with specialty group for graduate and professional student advisors.

National Association for Campus Activities (NACA) https://www.naca. org/Pages/default.aspx

For campus student life activities and staff and connections with entertainment and vendors. Has online member communities, but only members can see list of communities.

NAFSA: Association of International Educators http://nafsa.org

Has Member Interest Groups (MIGs) and Knowledge Communities (KCs), but none specifically focused on G&P students or services.

National Association of Graduate and Professional Students (NAGPS) http:// nagps.org/

Student-run advocacy and networking organization. Many campus G&P student governments are members.

National Orientation Directors Association (NODA), for Orientation, Transition and Retention (OTR) Professionals https://www.nodaweb.org/

Mainly focused on serving first-year undergraduates, but welcomes presentations and research on G&P orientation and transitions. Twelve NODA networks: the "Graduate Student Network" is for members who are graduate students in higher education/student affairs preparation programs; currently no network for those staff serving graduate students in transition.

National Postdoctoral Association https://www.nationalpostdoc.org/

For postdoctoral scholars and staff who serve them; at many universities, postdoctoral scholars and G&P services, like career services or teacher training, may be comingled. From their website: "At the individual, organizational, and national levels, we facilitate enhanced professional growth, raise awareness, and collaborate with stakeholders in the postdoctoral community."

National Resource Center for the First Year Experience and Students in Transition (NRCFYE) https://sc.edu/about/offices_and_divisions/national_resource_center/index.php

Like NODA, focused mainly on first year undergraduate college students, but did publish guide to graduate student orientation (Tokuno, 2008); listservs includes a Grad-List for graduate orientation/transitions: not very active, but G&P SA professionals could use and activate it.

The Leadership Alliance, https://theleadershipalliance.org/

From their website: "National consortium of major U.S. higher education institutions, and private industry promoting cultural diversity and developing underrepresented students as leaders in academia, the public, and the private sector."

GRADUATE INSTRUCTIONAL PROGRAM CLASSIFICATIONS:

Indiana University Center for Postsecondary Research. (n.d.). [1970-present.] The Carnegie Classification of Institutions of Higher Education. Author. https://carnegieclassifications.iu.edu/

For classifying higher education institutions based on types of students educated, degree programs, and research; most G&P students are enrolled at masters and doctoral universities, including new classification of doctoral/professional practice.

STANDARDS FOR GRADUATE AND PROFESSIONAL STUDENT PROGRAMS AND SERVICES:

Council for the Advancement of Standards in Higher Education. (2019). *Standards for graduate and professional student programs and services [Revised 2017]*. CAS professional standards for higher education (10th ed.). Author. www.cas.edu

First G&P student programs standard was created as Standard #24 in the 2009 edition through collaboration with AGAPSS authors; could be reviewed and revised in the coming years.

Contributors

EDITORS:

Valerie A. Shepard, PhD

Dr. Valerie A. Shepard (pronouns: she/her/hers) is a Senior Writer at UCLA Recreation. She has been a Student Affairs practitioner for over ten years and has held regional and national leadership positions in the NASPA Administrators in Graduate and Professional Student Services (AGAPSS) Knowledge Community. Prior to her current role, she was the Assistant Director of the UCLA Graduate Student Resource Center. She also worked on the development of ImaginePhD (a collaborative project of the Graduate Career Consortium: https://www.imaginephd.com/creators). She has a PhD in English Literature from UCLA.

April L. Perry, PhD

Dr. April L. Perry (pronouns: she/her/hers) is an Associate Professor in the MEd Higher Education Student Affairs program at Western Carolina University. Her research is primarily on student identity development, career development, student transitions, and institutional initiatives for student success. As a practitioner, April has worked in graduate school administration, student leadership programs, parent and family programs, fundraising and marketing, and academic tutoring services. She lives by the motto that the only thing better than watching someone grow is helping them grow. In 2016, April received the WCU award for Excellence in Graduate Student Mentoring, and in 2017 was named AGAPSS' Outstanding Professional. For more information about April, visit aprilperry.weebly.com

CASE STUDY AND CHAPTER AUTHORS (IN ALPHABETICAL ORDER):

Kayleigh Anderson-Natale, PhD

Dr. Anderson-Natale is currently the Director of Postdoc and Professional Development at the University of California, Irvine, where she coordinates professional development programs, and works individually with graduate students and postdocs to develop and realize their career goals. As a doctoral student at the University of California, Riverside (UCR), she focused her dissertation on gender gaps in the way STEM graduate students are funded, promoting graduate education. Between 2016 and 2018, she worked as the first Diversity and Inclusion Academic Liaison, through which she focused on improving the climate at UCR for graduate students.

Ziyan Bai, PhD

Ziyan Bai recently received her PhD in the field of Higher Education Leadership and Policy Studies. With over six years of research and professional experience in student affairs, she created and led the International Graduate Student Initiative, coordinating professional development workshops, community-building events, and student leadership opportunities. Additionally, she has disseminated her work through educational research and professional conference presentations, articles, and a book chapter. Ziyan strives to create more equitable educational experiences for students from underserved communities at the institutional level.

Trista Beard, EdD

Trista Beard is the Director of University of Southern California's Topping Scholars/Fellows Program which supports low-income and first-generation students with funding, community, and capital-building resources. Her research covers first-generation student success, social capital building, the impact of mentorship, and critical incidents in the journey to degree completion. She strategically designs programs to connect graduate students as a community of scholars and builds networks to empower them.

Raja Gopal Bhattar, PhD

Dr. Raja Gopal Bhattar (pronouns: they/them/theirs) is a nationally recognized higher education leader, advocate, consultant, and author. Previously, Dr. Bhattar has held leadership positions at UCLA, American River College, University of Chicago, University of Redlands, University of Vermont, Champlain College, and Semester at Sea (University of Virginia). Raja's work straddles qualitative and quantitative approaches to intersectional identity development and the experiences of LGBTQ people, immigrants, first-generation students, international students, and people of color in higher education. They have authored numerous articles and book chapters and presents regularly at national and regional conferences.

Ethriam Brammer, PhD

Ethriam Cash Brammer is a Chicano writer and scholar of P'urhépecha descent. He currently serves as an Assistant Dean for the Rackham Graduate School at the University of Michigan, where he is also the Diversity, Equity, and Inclusion (DEI) Implementation Lead. Dr. Brammer has translated many historically significant works of U.S. Latinx literature, including *The Adventures of Don Chipote: Or, When Parrots Breast Feed* by Daniel Venegas (Arte Público Press, 2000) and *Under The Texas Sun* by Conrado Espinoza (Arte Público Press, 2007).

Lisa C. O. Brandes

Lisa Brandes has been a champion for graduate student life and services over her 25-year career. After earning her PhD at Yale, then teaching undergraduates elsewhere, Lisa became the first Director of the McDougal Graduate Student Center at Yale. As the Graduate School's Assistant Dean for Student Affairs, she also ran Orientation and Commencement, advised graduate organizations, and coordinated campus services. She retired from Yale in May 2021. An active author, presenter, and consultant, she is a past NASPA AGAPSS KC National and Regional Chair, worked on the first CAS G&PS standards (2009), and has written several G&P services articles.

Tammy Briant Spratling, JD

Tammy Briant Spratling is Chief Executive Officer of Community Tampa Bay, an anti-discrimination nonprofit that empowers people to engage in cross-cultural interactions. She teaches Law and Student Affairs in the University of South Florida's master's program in College Student Affairs and Civil Rights Law at The Florida State University College of Law. Tammy previously served as Assistant Dean of Student Affairs at Stetson University College of Law.

Nicole Caridad Ralston, PhD

Dr. Nicole Caridad Ralston, Director of Education and Programming at Beloved Community, develops and facilitates content on diversity, equity, and inclusion. She is also an award-winning higher education professional and teaches "Diversity in Higher Education" as an adjunct professor at The University of New Orleans.

Vanessa Castañeda

Vanessa Castañeda, a first-generation college student and child of formerly undocumented Mexican parents, founded the Tulane Undocumented Student Support Committee (USSC) in 2016. She is also a PhD Candidate in Latin American Studies at Tulane University and a 2018 Fulbright Research Fellow for Brazil.

Nitya Chandran, PhD, MPP

Nitya Chandran is a Research and Evaluation Specialist in the ADVANCE Program at the University of Michigan. Prior to her current position, she was a postdoctoral fellow at ADVANCE and also completed the DEI Professional Certificate Program at Rackham Graduate School in the University of Michigan. Currently, at ADVANCE, she continues to be engaged in and support the research and evaluation aspects of various programs focused on campus climate, diversity, equity, and inclusion and faculty development. Nitya received her doctorate in Cellular and Clinical Neurobiology from Wayne State University, Detroit, Michigan, and most recently completed a Master's in Public Policy from the Gerald R. Ford School of Public Policy at the University of Michigan.

Angie Cook, MEd, MS

Angie Cook is the Associate Director of Graduate Retention Services in the University of Cincinnati's College of Nursing. She oversees academic advising, assessment, orientation, and other retention initiatives for the college's 2,000 graduate students. Angie has also worked as a frontline academic advisor and program manager for graduate students in business administration and information systems. Prior to supporting graduate student success, Angie worked in residence life, crisis management and student mental health, and academic advising for first-year, transfer, and adult student populations. Angie holds a master's degree in Student Affairs in Higher Education from Miami University.

Josh Cooper, MEd, JD

Josh Cooper is the Dean of Students at William James College. He has worked with graduate students for over 15 years. Prior to his current role, Josh worked at Harvard University School of Engineering and Applied Sciences and Boston University School of Law. Most recently, he was the 2020 recipient of the NASPA Region I Institutional Leadership Award. Josh earned his BA from Hamilton College, an MEd with a specialization in Higher Education Administration from Boston University School of Education, and received his JD from Suffolk University Law School.

Karen P. DePauw, PhD

In her 19 years at Virginia Tech, Dr. DePauw's (pronouns: she/her) major accomplishments include building a strong, diverse, and inclusive graduate community; establishing the national award-winning innovative Graduate Life Center (GLC); and implementing the signature academic initiative known as Transformative Graduate Education (TGE), including the global perspectives and preparing the future professoriate programs. She has served in leadership positions for the Virginia Council of Graduate School (VCGS), Council of Southern Graduate Schools (CSGS), Board of Directors of the Council of Graduate Schools (CGS), and Chair of the GRE Board. She was the recipient of the inaugural Debra W. Steward Award for Outstanding Leadership from the Council of Graduate Schools.

Katy DeRosier

Katy DeRosier is the Program Development Director for the Graduate School at the University of Washington. She cultivates large-scale, innovative initiatives that enhance the educational experience for students. By carefully orchestrating collaborations across the UW system, she ensures that project content, along with the tone and style, is both inclusive of, and encourages inclusion by, a complex ecosystem of users composed of students, staff, and faculty. Recent projects include the award-winning U501 "flipped" orientation for graduate and professional students. This model, along with the U501 Toolkit—a virtual roadmap—guides other institutions through the process of creating their own online orientation.

Stephanie K. Eberle, MEd

Stephanie K. Eberle (pronouns: they/them/their) is Executive Director and Assistant Dean of BioSci Careers at Stanford University, where they support the holistic needs of STEM MS/MD/PhD students and postdoctoral trainees. They were adjunct faculty at the University of San Francisco and Stanford's Graduate School of Education, serving interdisciplinary students. Stephanie regularly writes for *Inside Higher Ed*, is an internationally known presenter, and cowrote a counseling textbook chapter. They are Chair of the Board for the National Postdoctoral Association (NPA) and Co-chair of the National Association for Colleges and Employers' (NACE) Diversity/Womxn in STEM committee. Stephanie holds an MEd in counseling from Ohio University.

Maria Dykema Erb, MEd

Maria Dykema Erb is the inaugural director of the Boston University Newbury Center, which fosters the success of first-generation undergraduate, graduate, and professional students. Maria holds an MEd from The University of Vermont and has 29 years of higher education experience. Maria previously served as the Co-director of Diversity and Student Success in The Graduate School at The University of North Carolina at Chapel Hill. In this role, she established and developed an award-winning recruitment and retention program for graduate students from diverse backgrounds, including first-generation in a graduate program, Black Indigenous, People of Color (BIPOC), international, LGBTQIA+, and military-affiliated.

Emma Flores-Scott, PhD

As Director of Recruitment, Engagement, and Partnerships at Rackham Graduate School at the University of Michigan, Emma Flores-Scott works to expand access to graduate education and to support a diverse and interdisciplinary graduate student community. Emma earned her PhD in Educational Leadership and Organizational Policy with an emphasis in Higher Education from the University of Washington.

Kristen Galvin, PhD

Dr. Kristen Galvin is an Assistant Professor of Art History and Director of the Art History Program at the University of Colorado, Colorado Springs. She previously held the position of Assistant Director for Graduate Engagement in the Center for the Humanities and Public Sphere at the University of Florida, where she created and managed a suite of programs titled Envision Humanities: A Graduate Student Toolkit for the 21st Century. As an interdisciplinary scholar, she has published articles and book chapters on contemporary American visual culture, while also advocating for the public humanities, doctoral reform, and fair labor practices in higher education.

Monika Gibson

Monika Gibson found her way to graduate student services at Virginia Tech after working with international students at universities in Hungary and the United States for ten years. She has extensive experience in developing and implementing policies and programs, advising graduate students and student organizations, planning and executing events, and working across academic and student affairs boundaries. She played a key role in the establishment of the Graduate Life Center at Donaldson Brown in 2005. Monika earned a bachelor's degree in hotel and restaurant management in Hungary and a master's degree in educational leadership and policy studies at Virginia Tech.

Marilyn Gray, PhD

Marilyn Gray (pronouns: she/her/hers) is the founding Director of UCLA's Graduate Writing Center and leads a staff of graduate writing consultants from UCLA's diverse academic and professional programs. She facilitates writing workshops on a wide range of topics and is currently exploring ways to incorporate mindfulness into the Graduate Writing Center's programming.

Katherine Hall-Hertel, EdD

Katherine Hall-Hertel has worked in graduate education since 1994, serving as an assistant dean at Georgetown Law and then a graduate associate dean at UNC Charlotte. In both roles, Katherine developed programs, services, and policies to support graduate and professional student success. Professionally, she cochaired the AGAPSS Knowledge Community through NASPA and initiated the curriculum project. She has presented and served as a keynote at numerous conferences. Dr. Hall-Hertel earned her EdD in Higher Education Administration from The George Washington University and currently serves as associate graduate faculty and associate dean at UNC Charlotte.

Jamie Heck, PhD

Jamie is the Director of Academic Affairs in the College of Nursing at the University of Cincinnati. She has 19 years of higher education experience, including 11 years within the College of Nursing at the University of Cincinnati. Jamie earned her PhD in Higher Education Administration at Kent State University in 2013.

Matthew W. Imboden

Matt Imboden currently serves as Chief Student Services Officer for the School of Business at Wake Forest University, where he leads a dynamic team that purposefully integrates academic and student affairs functions in support of student success and professional preparation. Active for many years in AACRAO, ACPA, NASPA, and SACSA organizations in a variety of leadership roles, Matt currently serves as Chair of NASPA's Administrators in Graduate and Professional Student Services Knowledge Community. Matt is a doctoral candidate in Higher Education at the University of North Carolina at Greensboro.

Hillary Jenks, PhD

Dr. Hillary Jenks is the Director of GradSuccess, a suite of academic, social, and professional development programs for graduate/professional students and postdocs, in the Graduate Division at the University of California, Riverside. She received her PhD in American Studies & Ethnicity from the University of Southern California in 2008.

Christine Kelly, PhD

Christine Kelly, Director of Career Development at Claremont Graduate University, works to integrate career and professional development into the fabric of graduate education. She earned her PhD in communication at Purdue University and has 30 years' experience in higher education. She was a communication professor for 17 years before transitioning into graduate career development. In 2008, she became an active member of the Graduate Career Consortium (GCC) and is Past-President. She has written numerous articles on career and professional development topics and helped establish the Carpe Careers column in *Inside Higher Ed*, of which she is a contributing author.

Marlaina Kloepfer, EdD

Dr. Marlaina Kloepfer is a graduate education professional who has served the Philadelphia Region through positions in enrollment management, teaching, and advising. Marlaina completed her doctoral degree in Higher Education Leadership at Widener University in Chester, Pennsylvania. As a practitioner-scholar, her research focuses on the socialization and identity development specific to the graduate student experience.

Dawn Loyola, EdD

Dr. Dawn Loyola has two decades of graduate student advising experience and is currently the Director of Graduate Student Advising for the University of California, Riverside College of Natural & Agricultural Sciences. She earned her EdD in Higher Education Leadership at Maryville University, Saint Louis, in May 2020 under the supervision of Dr. Robin Grebing, researching STEM department climate and graduate student success. She previously completed her MA in Transpersonal Psychology from ITP/Sofia University in Palo Alto, California. Dawn is an active member of NACADA on the Steering Committee of the Advising Graduate & Professional Students Community.

Linett Luna Tovar

Linett Luna Tovar is an undocumented writer/performer and educator. She has been active in the fight for higher education access and affordability, both as a student and as a mentor. She is a co-founder of the Immigrant Youth Empowerment Forum and Scholarship Fund and currently serves as an enrollment coach to adult learners and immigrant students at Delgado Community College.

Anne E. Lundquist, PhD

Anne E. Lundquist is Associate Vice President for Campus Strategy at Anthology. She is the former Director of Strategic Planning and Assessment in the

Division of Student Affairs at Western Michigan University and dean of students/ senior student affairs officer at four liberal arts colleges. She has published and presented widely on assessment, strategic planning, higher education law, intercultural competence, and enterprise risk management. Her current research, writing, and presenting focus on the intersection of equity, assessment, and student success and mindful and embodied awareness practices for and with educators. Anne earned her PhD in Educational Leadership at Western Michigan University.

Bill Mahoney, PhD

Dr. Bill Mahoney, Associate Dean for Graduate Student and Postdoctoral Affairs, has over ten years of experience mentoring and advising graduate students in the School of Medicine, where he is Associate Professor of Laboratory Medicine & Pathology and Director of the Molecular Medicine and Mechanisms of Disease (M3D) PhD program. His office provides programming, connections, and support for graduate students and postdoctoral fellows, with particular investments in first-gen and international graduate students, general wellness, and career and professional development.

Heather N. Maietta, EdD

Dr. Heather N. Maietta is an Associate Professor in the Doctorate of Higher Education Leadership Program at Regis College. An award-winning educator, author, speaker, coach, and consultant, Dr. Maietta has helped college career and academic advising centers innovate their service delivery by fully integrating career advising into the larger campus ecosystem. Dr. Maietta's current research agenda investigates first-generation doctoral students as they matriculate through their degrees and into the workforce; the career needs of transfer students, specifically students who are forced transfer because of college closure; and workforce readiness of adult learners. Her full bio can be found at heathernmaietta.com.

Janet E. Malley, PhD

Janet E. Malley recently stepped down as director of research and evaluation for the University of Michigan ADVANCE Program where she was responsible for evaluation of all program initiatives, internal research studies, and climate assessments undertaken by the program. Prior to that, she was associate director of UM's Institute for Research on Women and Gender. She received her PhD in psychology from Boston University and completed a postdoctoral fellowship at the University of Michigan's Institute for Survey Research. She has significant expertise and experience with quantitative and qualitative data analysis of institutional data.

Jennifer R. McCauley, PhD

Dr. Jennifer McCauley is the Educational Program Manager for the Institute of Advanced Computational Science at Stony Brook University in Stony Brook, New York. She earned a Bachelor's Degree in psychology from Manhattan College (Riverdale, New York), a Master's Degree in Career Development from the College of New Rochelle (New Rochelle, New York), and a PhD in Industrial and Organizational Psychology from Capella University (Minneapolis, Minnesota). Her unique educational training and interests have led to several successful initiatives throughout her tenure in higher education for well over a decade.

George S. McClellan, PhD

George S. McClellan, Associate Professor of Higher Education at the University of Mississippi and cofounder of NASPA's graduate and professional student services knowledge community, served students for 35 years in student affairs professional positions. Recipient of the Annuit Coeptis Senior Scholar Award from ACPA and the Pillar of the Profession Award and the George D. Kuh Award for Outstanding Contribution to Literature/Research Award from NASPA, McClellan is (co-) author or (coeditor) of numerous books, chapters, monographs, and articles on student affairs and higher education. He earned a PhD in Higher Education from the University of Arizona and masters and bachelors degrees from Northwestern University.

Brandon S. McLeod

Brandon is the Assistant Director of International Programs at the University of Mississippi. He has more than ten years of experience in higher education as an instructor, advisor, and administrator. He has masters degrees in TESOL and English and is in the dissertation phase of his PhD in Higher Education with a graduate minor in Applied Statistics. He is a NAFSA Association of International Educators Trainer Corps Member and Ambassador. His doctoral research focuses on e-learning readiness among international students. His research interests include international and comparative higher education, instructional technology and e-learning, and widening participation.

Jovana Milosavljevic Ardeljan, PhD

Jovana Milosavljevic Ardeljan is a scholar from Serbia who came to the U.S. in 2014 to pursue a master's degree in linguistics and stayed for her PhD in Education specializing in Higher Education Leadership and Policy Studies. Currently she is a postdoctoral fellow in the Graduate School of the University of New Hampshire. She has over 5 years of experience presenting and publishing research on communication skill development for graduate students and postdocs that supports career diversified pathways. Her research is informed by her professional role in the Graduate School where she develops and delivers graduate student professional development programs focused on the importance of effective written and oral communication to translate advanced research into meaningful real-world applications.

Briana Mohan

Briana Mohan has been working in higher education for over 20 years and is a career advisor in the Office of Graduate and Postdoctoral Students at Tulane University. She also currently serves as Secretary of the Graduate Career Consortium, an international professional organization comprising members at research universities and medical schools serving graduate students and postdoctoral scholars.

Aye Mon Htut-Rosales

Aye Htut-Rosales is an experienced leader in Institutional Research and Assessment specializing in strategic planning, program evaluation, data collection and analysis, survey management, and higher education research. Aye is currently an Associate Director of Institutional Research and Effectiveness at Harvey Mudd College. Prior to that, Aye worked at UCLA for ten years including her role in Student Affairs where she conducted research and gave numerous presentations on equity, diversity, and inclusion. Aye received her master's degree from UC Irvine in Demographic and Social Analysis.

Jessica C. Moronez, PhD

Dr. Jessica C. Moronez teaches in the School of Social Sciences and Arts at College of the Desert in Palm Desert, CA. She received her PhD in Sociology from the University of California, Riverside, in 2020. She served as the Diversity and Inclusion Liaison (DIAL) from 2018 to 2020. During her time as the DIAL, she worked closely with multiple campus partners to advocate for graduate students in the areas of diversity/inclusion and sexual violence/sexual harassment.

Matt Newlin, EdD

Matt Newlin is a higher education practitioner and consultant with 15 years of experience in postsecondary education. He most recently worked at College Advising Corps as Director of Rural Initiatives. Prior to that role, he supported graduate students at the Brown School of Social Work at Washington University.

He holds a doctorate in Higher Education Leadership from Maryville University. His research and professional interests focus on first-generation, low-income, and rural students in higher education.

Dwight Richardson Kelly, MSW

Dwight Richardson Kelly recently earned a master's degree in clinical social work from the University of Michigan. As an undergraduate, he concentrated in disability studies and led disabled student groups at Sarah Lawrence College and Oxford University. His professional roles in disability services, education, and social work have included supporting many graduate students with disabilities. Dwight is a proud dyslexic.

Jaye Sablan, MA

Jaye Sablan (Native CHamoru, genderqueer, and first-gen), MA, is Assistant Director of Graduate Student Affairs at the University of Washington and leads the First-Gen Graduate Student Initiative. She has worked in the field of graduate student affairs for over six years and collaborates with university partners to develop wellness, intellectual, and professional development resources and programming to support the success of Masters and PhD students. Jaye is the coeditor of *Amplified Voices, Intersecting Identities: First-Gen PhDs Navigating Institutional Power*—two volumes published by Brill | Sense in 2020.

Mariann Sanchez

Mariann Sanchez is the Assistant Director for Graduate Student Life in the Division of Student Affairs at the University of San Diego. She advises the Graduate Student Government and Graduate Student Organizations and collaborates with campus partners to create and sustain spaces for student growth, engagement, advocacy, and community building.

Abigail J. Stewart

Abigail Stewart is Sandra Schwartz Tangri Distinguished University Professor of Psychology and Gender and Women's Studies at the University of Michigan. She has a PhD in Psychology and Social Relations from Harvard University, an MSc in Social Psychology from London School of Economics, and a BA from Wesleyan University. Her research interests include political activism, personality development and change in the context of experience and social history, and institutional change in higher education. She is coauthor with Virginia Valian of *An Inclusive Academy* (MIT Press, 2018).

Sarah Valdovinos, MEd

Sarah Valdovinos is the Principal Research Analyst in the Office of the Vice Chancellor for Health Affairs at UC Irvine. At the time of writing, she served as Assistant Director of the UCLA Graduate Student Resource Center. Her work focused on graduate student-specific services including orientation and retention programs, and community engagement. She also previously served as the Manager of Postdoctoral and Graduate Student Professional Development in the UCLA Graduate Division focusing on campus-wide professional development initiatives and managing UCLA's NSF-funded project, the Alliances for Graduate Education and the Professoriate (AGEP). Sarah earned her MEd in Student Affairs from UCLA in 2012.

Arthur Verhoogt, PhD

Arthur Verhoogt currently serves as associate dean of academic programs and initiatives (Humanities and the Arts) in the Rackham Graduate School of the University of Michigan. In this capacity, he serves as the liaison to Rackham's Graduate Student Mental Health Task Force and currently coordinates Rackham's efforts in partnership with other campus units to meet the most pressing, immediate needs of graduate students who need accommodations. Arthur is also a Arthur F. Thurnau Professor of Papyrology and Greek in the Department of Classical Studies.

Kathy Wood, BSPH

Kathy Wood is the director of Diversity and Student Success in The Graduate School at the University of North Carolina, where she has built an award-winning program for diverse graduate scholars. She has created a recruitment and retention program for graduate students with varying identities: first-generation in a graduate program, Black/Indigenous/People of Color (BIPOC), international, LGBTQIA+, and military-affiliated. Kathy has 18 years of DEI experience in higher education and holds a BSPH, with a focus on Community Diagnosis from UNC, Chapel Hill.

M. Remi Yergeau

M. Remi Yergeau is Associate Professor of Digital Studies and English and Associate Director of the Digital Studies Institute at the University of Michigan. Their research and teaching interests include disability studies, digital rhetoric, pedagogy, and the neurodiversity movement. They earned their PhD in English/Rhetoric, Composition, and Literacy from The Ohio State University.

Index

Note: **Bold** page numbers refer to tables and *italic* page numbers refer to figures. All topics regarding students in this index refer to graduate and professional students unless otherwise indicated.

Made in the USA
Monee, IL
06 June 2022